T0367000

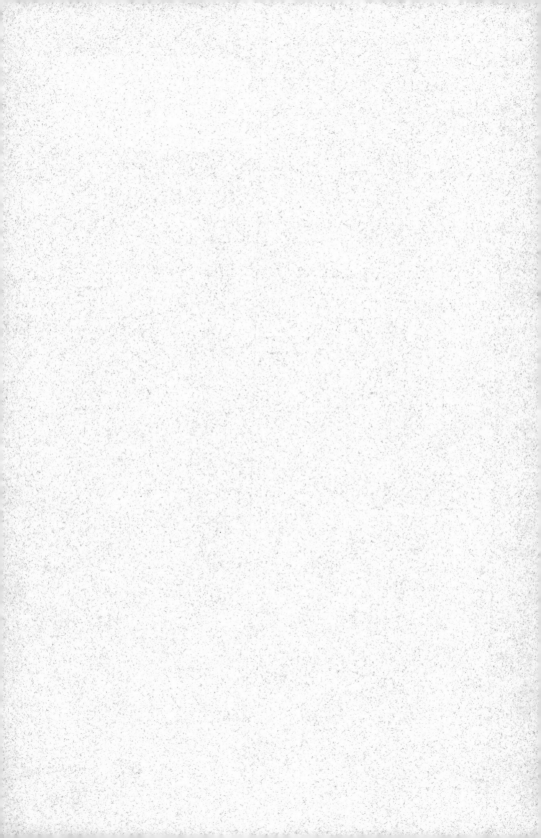

2 CORINTHIANS

PREACHING THE WORD
Edited by R. Kent Hughes

Genesis | R. Kent Hughes
Exodus | Philip Graham Ryken
Leviticus | Kenneth A. Mathews
Numbers | Iain M. Duguid
Deuteronomy | Ajith Fernando
Joshua | David Jackman
Judges and Ruth | Barry G. Webb
1 Samuel | John Woodhouse
2 Samuel | John Woodhouse
1 Kings | John Woodhouse
Job | Christopher Ash
Psalms, vol. 1 | James Johnston
Proverbs | Ray Ortlund
Ecclesiastes | Philip Graham Ryken
Song of Solomon | Douglas Sean O'Donnell
Isaiah | Ray Ortlund
Jeremiah and Lamentations | R. Kent Hughes
Daniel | Rodney D. Stortz
Matthew | Douglas Sean O'Donnell
Mark | R. Kent Hughes
Luke | R. Kent Hughes
John | R. Kent Hughes
Acts | R. Kent Hughes
Romans | R. Kent Hughes
1 Corinthians | Stephen T. Um
2 Corinthians | R. Kent Hughes
Galatians | Todd Wilson
Ephesians | R. Kent Hughes
Philippians, Colossians, and Philemon | R. Kent Hughes
1–2 Thessalonians | James H. Grant Jr.
1–2 Timothy and Titus | R. Kent Hughes and Bryan Chapell
Hebrews | R. Kent Hughes
James | R. Kent Hughes
1–2 Peter and Jude | David R. Helm
1–3 John | David L. Allen
Revelation | James M. Hamilton Jr.
The Sermon on the Mount | R. Kent Hughes

PREACHING *the* WORD

2 CORINTHIANS

POWER *in* WEAKNESS

R. KENT HUGHES

WHEATON, ILLINOIS

2 Corinthians

Published by Crossway
1300 Crescent Street
Wheaton, Illinois 60187

Cover design: John McGrath, Simplicated Studio

Cover image: Adam Greene, illustrator

First printing 2006

Reprinted with new cover 2012

Printed in China

All emphases in Scripture quotations have been added by the author.

ISBN-13: 978-1-4335-3549-9
ISBN-10: 1-4335-3549-1
PDF ISBN: 978-1-4335-1321-3
Mobipocket ISBN: 978-1-4335-1322-0
ePub ISBN: 978-1-4335-1875-1

Library of Congress Cataloging-in-Publication Data

Hughes, R. Kent.
2 Corinthians : power in weakness / R. Kent Hughes.
p. cm.—(Preaching the word)
Includes bibliographical references and indexes.
ISBN-13: 978-1-58134-763-0
ISBN-10: 1-58134-763-4 (hc : alk. paper)
1. Bible. N.T. Corinthians, 2nd—Commentaries. I. Title: Second Corinthians. II. Title. III. Series.
BS2675.53.H84
227'.307—dc22 2005023918

Crossway is a publishing ministry of Good News Publishers.

RRD 32 31 30 29 28 27 26 25 24
18 17 16 15 14 13 12 11 10 9 8 7

For
my pastor son
William Carey Hughes:
Live the paradox

But [the Lord] said to me,
"My grace is sufficient for you,
for my power is made perfect in weakness."
Therefore I will boast all the more gladly
of my weaknesses, so that the
power of Christ may rest upon me."

2 CORINTHIANS 12:9–10

Contents

Acknowledgments

Once again, I must thank my administrative assistant, Mrs. Pauline Epps, for her patience and expertise in preparing the manuscript for publication. Special thanks, too, go to Herb Carlburg, who not only prints the sermon transcripts but checks out every detail.

Any pastor knows that it takes both a pastor and a congregation to have a sermon and that engaged listeners help make the sermon. So, thanks to College Church in Wheaton for helping make the messages, such as they are, a little better.

And, as always, I'm so grateful for my wife, Barbara, who has freed me to spend the hours necessary for this work, and who is my best listener!

A Word to Those Who Preach the Word

There are times when I am preaching that I have especially sensed the pleasure of God. I usually become aware of it through the unnatural silence. The ever-present coughing ceases, and the pews stop creaking, bringing an almost physical quiet to the sanctuary—through which my words sail like arrows. I experience a heightened eloquence, so that the cadence and volume of my voice intensify the truth I am preaching.

There is nothing quite like it—the Holy Spirit filling one's sails, the sense of his pleasure, and the awareness that something is happening among one's hearers. This experience is, of course, not unique, for thousands of preachers have similar experiences, even greater ones.

What has happened when this takes place? How do we account for this sense of his smile? The answer for me has come from the ancient rhetorical categories of *logos*, *ethos*, and *pathos*.

The first reason for his smile is the *logos*—in terms of preaching, God's Word. This means that as we stand before God's people to proclaim his Word, we have done our homework. We have exegeted the passage, mined the significance of its words in their context, and applied sound hermeneutical principles in interpreting the text so that we understand what its words meant to its hearers. And it means that we have labored long until we can express in a sentence what the theme of the text is—so that our outline springs from the text. Then our preparation will be such that as we preach, we will not be preaching our own thoughts about God's Word, but God's actual Word, his *logos*. This is fundamental to pleasing him in preaching.

The second element in knowing God's smile in preaching is *ethos*—what you are as a person. There is a danger endemic to preaching, which is having your hands and heart cauterized by holy things. Phillips Brooks illustrated it by the analogy of a train conductor who comes to believe that he has been to the places he announces because of his long and loud heralding of them. And that is why Brooks insisted that preaching must be "the bringing of truth through personality." Though we can never *perfectly* embody the truth we preach, we must be subject to it, long for it, and make it as much a part of our ethos as possible. As the Puritan William Ames said, "Next to the Scriptures, nothing makes a sermon more to pierce, than when it comes out of the inward affection of the heart without any affectation." When a preacher's *ethos* backs up his *logos*, there will be the pleasure of God.

Last, there is *pathos*—personal passion and conviction. David Hume, the Scottish philosopher and skeptic, was once challenged as he was seen going to hear George Whitefield preach: "I thought you do not believe in the gospel." Hume replied, "I don't, but *he* does." Just so! When a preacher believes what he preaches, there will be passion. And this belief and requisite passion will know the smile of God.

The pleasure of God is a matter of *logos* (the Word), *ethos* (what you are), and *pathos* (your passion). As you *preach the Word* may you experience his smile—the Holy Spirit in your sails!

R. Kent Hughes
Wheaton, Illinois

1

Exalted Identities

2 CORINTHIANS 1:1, 2

AMERICANS WITH A SENSE OF THEIR OWN HISTORY should have no difficulty relating to the biblical city of Corinth because in many ways it parallels the bustling cities of the American West around the turn of the century—cities like Chicago, Denver, and San Francisco.

Classical Corinth had been destroyed in 146 B.C. by the Romans and had remained uninhabited for a hundred years, until 44 B.C. when Julius Caesar rebuilt it. So when Paul visited Corinth in A.D. 49–50, it was just over eighty years old with a population of some 80,000. Yet, during its short history Corinth had become the third most important city of the Roman Empire, behind Alexandria and Rome itself.[1] Situated on the isthmus of Greece, it was variously called the "master of harbors," "the crossroads of Greece," and "a passage for all mankind."[2] Corinth embodied an economic miracle and was the envy of the lesser cities of the Empire.

As with the cities of America's so-called "Western Expansion," the population of Corinth was largely immigrant and opportunist, filled with those seeking a better life. Corinth became the popular answer to Rome's overpopulation—and especially its freedmen (those who had formerly been slaves), who became Corinth's largest segment. Neo-Corinth also became a favorite venue for ex-Roman soldiers seeking a better life for their families. Corinth also attracted ethnic diversity from far and wide. Acts 18 reports of a substantial Jewish community that exercised self-governance (cf. vv. 8, 17).

In A.D. 50 Corinth was a young Roman city with shallow roots. Traditions were few, and thus society was relatively open. There was no city in the Empire more conducive to advancement.[3]

Because there was no landed aristocracy in Corinth, wealth became the sole factor for respect and ascendancy. New Testament scholar Scott Hafemann summarizes:

> Corinth was a free-wheeling "boom town," filled with materialism, pride, and the self-confidence that comes with having made it in a new place and with a new social identity. The "pull-yourself-up-by-your-own-bootstraps" mentality that would become so characteristic of the American frontier filled the air.[4]

The parallels with modern Western life continue. Corinth was a sports and entertainment culture. Caesar had reinstituted the Isthmian games in Corinth (which were second only to the Olympics). The city's theater held up to 18,000 and the concert hall some 3,000. Travel, tourism, sex, and religious pluralism were woven together in Corinth's new culture. Significantly, while Nero never visited Athens and Sparta, he spent considerable time in Corinth, enjoying the adulation of its voluptuous populace.[5] The similarities to modern Western culture are so striking that a California pastor, Ray Stedman, used to call Paul's Corinthian letters "First and Second Californians"!

Second Californians or not, we all must understand that the self-made-man ethos, the "I-did-it-my-way" pride and individualism, the *nouveau-riche* worship of health and wealth, the religious pluralism of Corinth—these together presented a formidable challenge to Paul's style, method, and message of presenting the simple gospel. The composite culture of Corinth does truly invite our calling this letter "Second Californians" or "Second Texans" or "Second Minnesotans" or "Second City."

Paul's relationship with the Corinthian church became stormy, to say the least. It began well enough when Paul, with the help of the godly couple Aquila and Priscilla and his faithful disciples Timothy and Silas, established the church in Corinth during a one-and-a-half-year visit (cf. Acts 18:1–17). There in Corinth, despite an outcry from his Jewish countrymen, Paul stood tall and preached the cross, leaving behind a remarkable church.

After Paul left Corinth, he traveled to Ephesus and from there to Jerusalem and then back to Ephesus, where he wrote 1 Corinthians—about three years after his initial founding visit. At the time of his writing that epistle, he planned to visit Corinth again to gather up a collection for the poor in Jerusalem. But in the interim he sent Timothy to visit the Corinthian believers (cf. 1 Corinthians 16:1–11). What Timothy encountered was an incipient, growing apostasy, likely the work of Paul's enemies who had recently come from Jerusalem. In a flash Paul decided to pay the Corinthians a visit, briefly tend to matters, and be on his way.

But what a shock awaited Paul—his infamous, "painful visit" (cf. 2 Corinthians 2:1)—seismic misery. The apostle's authority, even his apostleship, was called into question. If Paul was for real, why was there so much suffering in his life? they asked. Also, why was his ministry so lackluster when compared with the ministry of others? Why was his preaching so dull? And why did he change his travel plans if God was actually directing his life? Moreover, what lay behind his refusal to accept payment for his services, as most preachers did? Was he *really* collecting money for the poor? Why didn't Paul have letters of recommendation like the others? Why didn't he regale them with stories about God's power in his ministry? Was it because there were none? Tragically, this attack on Paul's ministry and person had led many of his Corinthian converts to reject him and his preaching for "a different gospel" (cf. 11:4).

Paul left Corinth wounded and devastated. In his own words, "I made up my mind not to make another painful visit to you" (2:1). Still stung, back in Ephesus, Paul sent Titus to Corinth with a new and "severe" letter (2:5). It was a letter of great emotion. "For I wrote to you," says Paul, "out of much affliction and anguish of heart and with many tears, not to cause you pain but to let you know the abundant love that I have for you" (2:4). Paul called for repentance. And, all glory to God, the Corinthian church did repent! As he would observe, "For even if I made you grieve with my letter, I do not regret it—though I did regret it, for I see that that letter grieved you, though only for a while. As it is, I rejoice, not because you were grieved, but because you were grieved into repenting. For you felt a godly grief, so that you suffered no loss through us" (7:8, 9). The majority came back to Paul and his gospel, but some still rejected his authority. Thus it was that Paul wrote the magnificent letter of Second Corinthians in A.D. 55 as he began to make plans to return for a third visit (cf. 2 Corinthians 12:14; 13:1).

So today we can read and study this letter, the most emotional of all the apostle's writings. Nowhere is Paul's heart so torn and exposed as in this letter. Second Corinthians bears a fierce tone of injured love, of paradoxically wounded, relentless affection. Toward the letter's end Paul will say, "And, apart from other things, there is the daily pressure on me of my anxiety for all the churches. Who is weak, and I am not weak? Who is made to fall, and I am not indignant?" (11:28, 29).

If you have ever invested your life in that of another, so that one turns to Christ (perhaps a child or a friend or a coworker or a relative) and then have had others lead that one astray, 2 Corinthians is for you. This book is about the nature of the gospel and authentic ministry. Those who really care about the gospel and the care of souls will find 2 Corinthians captivating. For those who don't care, this is about what your heart ought to be—and about what you ought to be about!

As Paul conveys his brief two-verse greeting to the Corinthians, he leaves no uncertainty as to what he is about—namely, to *preserve* his apostleship and to *preserve* the church.

Paul's Salutation (vv. 1, 2)

We see the purpose of Paul's writing in the two clauses of verse 1 with their distinct emphases on *apostle* and *church*: "Paul, an apostle of Christ Jesus by the will of God, and Timothy our brother, To the church of God that is at Corinth, with all the saints who are in the whole of Achaia."

Paul's high authority. From the distance of two millennia, it is easy to miss the uniquely high claims that Paul makes about his authority. By his disregarding the customary thanksgiving of a traditional greeting, Paul cut right to the quick, declaring that he was "an apostle of Christ Jesus"—thereby emphasizing that his call had come from the risen Christ on the Damascus road. Furthermore, Paul's explicit declaration that he was "an *apostle* of *Christ* Jesus" (rather than the more customary "of Jesus Christ") was carefully crafted to emphasize that he was a sent one from the Messiah Jesus, who was himself *the* unique Apostle sent from Heaven, in whom all the hopes and promises of the Old Testament found their fulfillment. And still more, as Messiah he was "Jesus" ("Jehovah is salvation")—God saving his people from their sins.[6]

The significance of Paul's being an apostle of *Messiah Jesus* is that Paul bore the apostleship of the Apostle-Messiah who personally commissioned him and his message. He was an apostle "by the will of God" in that the very "will of God that sent Jesus is the same will that Christ enacts in sending Paul to represent him as his 'Apostle'" (Hafemann).[7] Therefore, to reject the authority of the one who is an apostle of "Messiah Jesus by the will of God" is to reject the authority of God himself! Further, anyone who would dare to buck Paul's authority had, in effect, challenged God. This is awesome, terrifying authority.

The church's high position. The complement to Paul's exalted position is the exalted position of the church that he lifts up as he addresses it as "the church of God that is at Corinth, with all the saints who are in the whole of Achaia" (v. 1b). The interchangeable designations "saints" and "church of God" states the astonishing high truth about the believers of Corinth. But the terms are freighted with irony. "The saints," these holy ones, had sinned greatly against Paul. Clearly they were not saints because of their recent behavior, but solely because they were in Christ, the Holy One of God. Christ Jesus was their sanctification (cf. 1 Corinthians 1:30). And as to their designation as "the church of God," how ironic that was! They had treated Paul like dirt, but he called them the church of God!

The ironies were penetrating, but sweetly so, due to the grace of God. And these exalted truths about the Corinthians formed the ground for Paul's appeal, as we will see.

Paul's calling the Corinthians "the church of God that is at Corinth," or literally "the church of God that has its being in Corinth," suggests their continuity with God's people of the past when they assembled in God's presence to hear his Word from leaders like Moses. And now, in holy continuity with their forefathers, they were to hear and obey God's Word from his apostle.[8]

The power of Paul's argument would penetrate their souls precisely because they were *God's church* and not Paul's church! Though I have pastored College Church in Wheaton, Illinois, for a quarter of a century, it is not my church—it is the church of God that has its being in Chicago. The church is God's alone. And when we understand it as we should, we also understand that our mutual God-ordained function is to be an assembly of God's people in God's presence to hear and obey God's Word.

In respect to our application of 2 Corinthians, we must remember that this is God's Word for the church of God that has its being where we are planted. True, our culture is different from the first century, but it is our identity as "the church of God" that supplies the continuity and relevance of Paul's words. We share the same Father and the same Lord—we are brothers and sisters "with all the saints who are in the whole of Achaia."[9]

Second Corinthians is for us! From here on, Paul's passionate letter rides on two elevated designations—that of himself and that of the church. "The church of God" must listen to the "apostle of Christ Jesus by the will of God."

Paul's high hopes. Paul's salutation concludes with appropriately high hopes (his prayer-wish) for the Corinthian church: "Grace to you and peace from God our Father and the Lord Jesus Christ" (v. 2). It is impossible for us today to hear the word play here—Paul always replaced the Greek word for "Hello" *(charein)* with the Christian term for "grace" (*charis*). So when Paul's readers expected "Hello," Paul wished them "Grace."

And, of course, the greeting was "Grace . . . and peace" because peace/*shalom* always follows the loving favor of God.

It was a lovely wish, but as has been pointed out, "Paul's . . . wish takes on from the beginning an added sense of poignancy, and pain. Only those who accept Paul's greeting as an expression of his genuine apostolic authority will receive what 'God our Father and the Lord Jesus Christ' desire for them."[10]

Paul's Letter: Exalted Themes

The letter's character. The letter that ensues for the next 257 verses is passionate and uneven, and sometimes explosive. The most compelling defense of Paul's apostolate and ministry in all his letters extends from the middle of Chapter 2 and continues to the beginning of Chapter 7 (2:12—7:1). Then chapters 7—9 lay out the implications for the repentant Corinthians, while chapters 10—13 describe the implications for the unrepentant.

The entire text of the letter is dotted with magnificent expressions, from which I have listed a select few of my favorites to raise your anticipation.

> 2:15, 16: For we are the aroma of Christ to God among those who are being saved and among those who are perishing, to one a fragrance from death to death, to the other a fragrance from life to life. Who is sufficient for these things?
>
> 3:5: Not that we are sufficient in ourselves to claim anything as coming from us, but our sufficiency is from God.
>
> 4:17, 18: For this slight momentary affliction is preparing for us an eternal weight of glory beyond all comparison, as we look not to the things that are seen but to the things that are unseen. For the things that are seen are transient, but the things that are unseen are eternal.
>
> 5:10: For we must all appear before the judgment seat of Christ, so that each one may receive what is due for what he has done in the body, whether good or evil.
>
> 5:17: Therefore, if anyone is in Christ, he is a new creation. The old has passed away; behold, the new has come.
>
> 5:21: For our sake he made him to be sin who knew no sin, so that in him we might become the righteousness of God.
>
> 8:9: For you know the grace of our Lord Jesus Christ, that though he was rich, yet for your sake he became poor, so that you by his poverty might become rich.
>
> 9:7: Each one must give as he has made up his mind, not reluctantly or under compulsion, for God loves a cheerful giver.
>
> 10:3, 4: For though we walk in the flesh, we are not waging war according to the flesh. For the weapons of our warfare are not of the flesh but have divine power to destroy strongholds.
>
> 11:28, 29: And, apart from other things, there is the daily pressure on me of my anxiety for all the churches. Who is weak, and I am not weak? Who is made to fall, and I am not indignant?
>
> 13:14: The grace of the Lord Jesus Christ and the love of God and the fellowship of the Holy Spirit be with you all.

As you can see, 2 Corinthians provides us with passionate, living theology.

The letter's theme. The theme or melodic line of 2 Corinthians concerns the nature of ministry under the new covenant of Christ. The new covenant must be read against the backdrop of Exodus 32—34 and the Old Testament promises of the new covenant in Jeremiah 31 and Ezekiel 11, 36. Paul's use of these Scriptures and many other Old Testament texts trumpets his conviction that the new-covenant ministry has been inaugurated in Christ. Here, in no uncertain terms, is the pattern for all authentic ministry. Paul provides the litmus test for the real thing.

The letter's motif. The motif that keeps emerging throughout this epistle is that weakness is the source of strength and that suffering is the vehicle for God's power and glory. In 4:7–12 Paul describes gospel ministry in these terms:

> But we have this treasure in jars of clay, to show that the surpassing power belongs to God and not to us. We are afflicted in every way, but not crushed; perplexed, but not driven to despair; persecuted, but not forsaken; struck down, but not destroyed; always carrying in the body the death of Jesus, so that the life of Jesus may also be manifested in our bodies. For we who live are always being given over to death for Jesus' sake, so that the life of Jesus also may be manifested in our mortal flesh. So death is at work in us, but life in you.

In 6:3–10, he again describes his ministry in terms of suffering and weakness:

> We put no obstacle in anyone's way, so that no fault may be found with our ministry, but as servants of God we commend ourselves in every way: by great endurance, in afflictions, hardships, calamities, beatings, imprisonments, riots, labors, sleepless nights, hunger; by purity, knowledge, patience, kindness, the Holy Spirit, genuine love; by truthful speech, and the power of God; with the weapons of righteousness for the right hand and for the left; through honor and dishonor, through slander and praise. We are treated as impostors, and yet are true; as unknown, and yet well known; as dying, and behold, we live; as punished, and yet not killed; as sorrowful, yet always rejoicing; as poor, yet making many rich; as having nothing, yet possessing everything.

In 11:23–30, Paul provides his ministry qualifications by "boasting" in his sufferings as he begins his famous litany:

> Are they servants of Christ? I am a better one—I am talking like a madman—with far greater labors, far more imprisonments, with countless beatings, and often near death. Five times I received at the hands of

> the Jews the forty lashes less one. Three times I was beaten with rods. (vv. 23–25a)

And, of course, 12:9, 10 shares the famous declaration of Christ:

> But he said to me, "My grace is sufficient for you, for my power is made perfect in weakness." Therefore I will boast all the more gladly of my weaknesses, so that the power of Christ may rest upon me. For the sake of Christ, then, I am content with weaknesses, insults, hardships, persecutions, and calamities. For when I am weak, then I am strong.

This theology of weakness and suffering was foolish in new Corinth with its worship of self-made wealth and power. Only believing hearts could understand it—and they embraced it. Today it is no different in California, Illinois, or New York. Such thinking is incomprehensible—nuts!

And some (who actually claim to be in the church) likewise find it unbelievable as they preach a gospel of health and wealth. There is no room for Paul, no place for the new covenant, and no place for the surpassing power of Christ in their view.

Clearly, 2 Corinthians has a lot to teach us. And we have a lot to learn.

The point is, if Paul was who he said he was—"an apostle of Christ Jesus by the will of God"—if he is an apostle of the ultimate Apostle Messiah, Jesus—if his message then is the very Word of God—if to ignore him is to challenge God—then we had better listen if we fancy ourselves to be the church of God in continuity with the apostolic church.

We do believe it. He is *the* apostle. We are *the* church. His message is for us today, at the beginning of the third millennium.

The gospel does not ride on health and wealth but on weakness. The ministry of the Spirit is not one of splash and flash but of meekness and weakness. The gospel does not need the front pages of any paper. And when it brags, it brags of its weakness—and of God's power.

God's church, which listens to the word of the apostle of God, can expect two things: grace (the ongoing covenant love of God) and peace (his well-being that always accompanies his grace).

May God's grace and peace be multiplied upon God's people as we sit under his Holy Word as it comes from his magnificent apostle.

2

The Comfort of God

2 CORINTHIANS 1:3–7

DIETRICH BONHOEFFER WAS ONE OF A HANDFUL of German theologians to stand up to the Nazification of the German church. He was prominent in writing the famous Barmen Declaration, which rejected the infamous Aryan clauses imposed by Nazi ideology. Bonhoeffer's courage thrust him into the leadership of the Confessing Church along with other stalwarts like Martin Niemöller. Bonhoeffer went so far as to found an underground seminary in Finkenwald, Bavaria, which was closed by Gestapo chief Heinrich Himmler. This led to Bonhoeffer's joining the resistance movement and his being imprisoned by the Gestapo in April 1943. Bonhoeffer's *Letters from Prison* became a best seller after the war.

Among the letters is a beautiful poem written to his fiancée Maria von Wedemeyer entitled "New Year 1945." Stanza 3 is famous:

> Should it be ours to drain the cup of grieving
> Even to the dregs of pain,
> At thy command, we will not falter,
> Thankfully receiving all that is given
> By thy loving hand.[1]

Poignant words that became more so when, three months later, just as the war was ending, Bonhoeffer was hung in Flossenbürg prison.

Fast-forward to some eighteen years later, across the Atlantic in America, when another bride-to-be was grieving the death of her fiancé and found much comfort in Bonhoeffer's poem. Her fiancé, who died from injuries in a sledding accident, was the son of author Joseph Bayly and his wife Mary Lou. When she mailed Bonhoeffer's poem to them, Joe and Mary Lou also found comfort in "New Year 1945."

Twelve years after this (thirty years after Bonhoeffer's death), Joe Bayly received a letter from a pastor-friend in Massachusetts relating that he had visited a terminally ill woman in a Boston hospital for some period of time and had given her Joe's book of poems, *Heaven*, as comfort for her soul. The pastor said that the dying woman had stayed awake late the previous night to read it and told him of the comfort and help she had received from it. A few hours later she died. The woman, the pastor revealed, was Maria von Wedemeyer-Weller, Bonhoeffer's fiancée three decades earlier!

God's comfort circulates among his children—and sometimes it comes full circle, as it did from Dietrich Bonhoeffer to Maria von Wedemeyer in her grief to Joseph Bayly, Jr.'s grieving fiancée to Joe and Mary Lou Bayly in their grief and then back to Bonhoeffer's one-time fiancée as comfort in her dying hours.[2] Our text alludes to this astonishing cyclical nature of comfort—its mutuality—its overflowing nature.

By any estimation 2 Corinthians 1:3–7 frames the Bible's greatest text on comfort. The word "comfort" occurs no less than ten times in its noun and verb forms in this brief paragraph—essentially one-third of all thirty-one occurrences in the New Testament.[3] Paul says more about suffering, and more about comfort, than any other writer in the Bible. And it is here that he says the most about it.

There is a reason for this, and it was to answer critics who held that the sufferings that characterized Paul's life were evidence that he was not an apostle, because if he was the real thing he wouldn't be experiencing so much trouble. Paul's answer was that abundant suffering and abundant comfort are in fact signs of apostolic authenticity.

Celebration of the God of Comfort (v. 3)

In verses 3–7 Paul carefully crafts his words as he recasts the traditional opening words of the synagogue blessing in Christian terminology so as to celebrate God as the God of all comfort: "Blessed be the God and Father of our Lord Jesus Christ, the Father of mercies and God of all comfort" (v. 3).

The first of the nineteen synagogue benedictions then in use began, "Blessed art thou, O Lord our God and God of our fathers, God of Abraham, God of Isaac, and God of Jacob. . . ."[4] Paul takes it and identifies "the God of our fathers" as "the God and Father of our Lord Jesus Christ," thus testifying to the dramatic revelation of Christ to him on the Damascus road and his radical conversion. This Christianized Jewish blessing is original here in 2 Corinthians and appears also verbatim in Romans, Ephesians, and 1 Peter. In restating the synagogue blessing in Christian terms, Paul was evidently having a go at his Judaizing enemies, the fallen apostles in Corinth (cf. 11:22, 31). It was of the utmost importance for the apostle to establish in no uncertain terms that the God of Israel's patriarchs was the God and Father of the Lord Jesus Christ.

The synagogue prayer of Paul's day described God as "The Father of Mercies," but here Paul enlarges it to include "and God of all comfort"—the first of the ten references to comfort contained in this short paragraph. Paul's intentionality is immense! Chapters 40—66 of Isaiah repeatedly speak of the comfort or consolation of the Messianic age. Isaiah 40 begins, "Comfort, comfort my people, says your God. Speak tenderly to Jerusalem," and the final chapter, 66, says, "As one whom his mother comforts, so I will comfort you; you shall be comforted in Jerusalem" (v. 13). So when Christ came, the devout, including Simeon and Anna, were "waiting for the consolation of Israel" (Luke 2:25)—salvation and comfort. It was and is through Christ that the comfort of God the Father comes.

Here in our passage the idea of comfort is "to strengthen much," to encourage[5]—to stand by another and encourage him as he endures testing. Paul wanted his hearers to understand that the merciful Father is the author of *all* possible comfort and consolation. There is no enduring comfort apart from him.

Paul's own heartfelt celebration of God was for his deliverance from deadly peril in Asia (cf. 2 Corinthians 1:8–11), and then the gentle comfort brought to him by the return of Titus with good news about the Corinthian church (cf. 7:6, 7). For all this he passionately blessed God: "Blessed be the God and Father of our Lord Jesus Christ, the Father of mercies and God of all comfort" (1:3). How beautiful.

The explanation of God's comfort thus began with the celebration of God's comfort.

Paul's Apostolic Experience of God's Comfort (vv. 4, 5)

As we consider what Paul says in verses 4, 5 we must understand that Paul is referring to his own experience alone—that the plural "we" and "us" is what is sometimes called the "apostolic we."[6] This is made clear when we get to verses 6, 7 where there is a contrast between "we" (the apostle) and "you" (the Corinthians).

Description of God's comfort. So here in verse 4 Paul describes his own experience of comfort and how it graced the Corinthians: "who comforts us in all our affliction, so that we may be able to comfort those who are in any affliction, with the comfort with which we ourselves are comforted by God."

Paul was certainly one of the most afflicted men ever. He suffered cold, nakedness, beating, imprisonment, criminal assault, shipwreck, betrayal, desolation, desertion, and more. His was a life of perpetual death: "For we who live are always being given over to death for Jesus' sake" (4:11a). However, this said, he found that God comforted him in all his afflictions. Not in some but in "*all*" of them!

Every one of Paul's epic miseries was attended by God's comfort. His repeated imprisonments in Asia Minor, in Greece, and in Rome's dank Mamartine prison were venues of God's comfort. Through each of the forty lashes administered on five separate occasions, with the final lashes meant to bring him to the point of death, and through the torturous days of healing that followed each of the five beatings, he experienced the comfort of God. When he was stoned in Lystra with the largest stones being hurled upon his fallen body as the *coup de grace,* he experienced the comfort of God. Adrift like flotsam on the high seas (for the third time!) he knew the comfort of God again. When he was in danger from rivers—God's comfort, danger from robbers—God's comfort, danger from his own people—God's comfort, danger in the city—God's comfort, danger in the wilderness—God's comfort, danger from false brothers—God's comfort. "In toil and hardship, through many a sleepless night, in hunger and thirst, often without food, in cold and exposure" (11:27), Paul always experienced God's comfort. Never once was he without the comfort of God.

The result was that Paul was able to comfort those "in any affliction" (imagine, *any* affliction)—and he did so with the comfort with which he himself had been comforted by God.

How did Paul comfort others with the comfort with which he had been comforted by God? Overall by his example—as they observed his attitude and deportment in and through and after his sufferings. And then there were his prayers. And of course there were his gentle words of comfort, graced with authenticity and power, so that God's comfort was administered through him.

Affliction is essential. What we conclude here is that affliction was the key to Paul's effectiveness in ministry, and affliction is the key to effective ministry today. How countercultural this is. It even runs counter to so much "Christian" thinking that regards affliction as evidence of personal sin or deficient faith, and sleekness and ease as palpable evidence of divine blessing.

My own pastoral experience confirms Paul's insistence that afflictions have been good for me and for the ministry of the gospel—friends to authenticity and effectiveness.

Bishop Paul Barnett observes that God's comfort does not terminate in the one who receives it.

> God comforted Paul by the coming of Titus to Macedonia (7:6), just as Titus had previously been comforted by the Corinthians (7:7). Paul in turn will comfort the Corinthians (verse 6 [of chapter 1]), God's comfort thus having come full circle, from the Corinthians, through Titus to Paul, back to the Corinthians.[7]

This is something of what Maria von Wedemeyer-Weller experienced from Bonhoeffer to her to another grieving young woman to the Baylys and back to her. The circle all began with the experience of affliction and God's comfort overflowing to the comforted.

Explanation of God's comfort. Verse 5 supplies the reason why suffering equipped Paul to pass on God's comfort: "For as we share abundantly in Christ's sufferings, so through Christ we share abundantly in comfort too." Here the "sufferings" of Christ does not refer to the atoning sufferings of Christ but to the sufferings that come to those involved in the service of Christ (cf. 4:11, 12). They are "Christ's sufferings" because they come from following him and add to the fulfillment of the suffering destined for the Body of Christ (cf. Colossians 1:24). They are Christ's sufferings because he is *in* his people (cf. Acts 9:4, 5). C. S. Lewis solemnized this truth in the epitaph to *The Problem of Pain* where he quotes George MacDonald: "The Son of God suffered unto the death, not that men might not suffer, but that their sufferings might be like His." In this respect, Paul's prayer in Philippians 3:10, 11 is so right: "that I may know Him and the power of His resurrection and the fellowship of His sufferings, being conformed to His death; in order that I may attain to the resurrection from the dead" (NASB).

The metaphoric expression conveyed in the original of a flood in overflow is memorable—"For just as the sufferings of Christ overflow to us, so also through Christ, our comforting overflows."[8] The "for just as . . . so," especially in the Greek (*kathòs . . . houtos*), gives the sentence a solemn ring, accentuating the idea of overflow surplus—the comforting overflows. The emphasis of verse 5 is upon Paul's experience of overflowing comfort—a flood of consolation.

Most recently he had experienced this overflowing comfort in Asia where, he says, "We were so utterly burdened beyond our strength that we despaired of life itself. Indeed, we felt that we had received the sentence of death" (vv. 8b, 9a). But God delivered him with resurrection power (cf. vv. 9, 10). And more, God comforted Paul with a visit from Titus who brought him good news about the Corinthian church and their love for him (cf. 7:6, 7).

Note that Christ is the center and source of all comfort. Just as Paul's union with Christ was the source of his suffering, so also Christ was the source of his overflowing comfort.

The Corinthians' Experience of God's Comfort (vv. 6, 7)

The application of God's comfort. The overflowing nature of God's comfort anticipates its abundant application. We see this in Paul's direct statement to the Corinthians: "If we are afflicted, it is for your comfort and salvation; and if we are comforted, it is for your comfort, which you experience when you patiently endure the same sufferings that we suffer" (v. 6). Paul views both his experience of afflictions and his experience of comfort as contributing to the Corinthians' comfort. This is a dynamic way of looking at life because it endows all Christian living with elevated importance. The hard things we undergo as well as the comforts are all graces that together authenticate and empower ministry, so that those who truly desire to minister will patiently accept their lot from God and work on.

The thrust of Paul's apostolic ministry was not reciprocal but was a one-way street issuing in a flood of comfort to others. In this, he lived like Christ his Savior. Paul links the Corinthians' comfort to their patient endurance of sufferings: "it is for your comfort, which you experience when you patiently endure the same sufferings that we suffer" (v. 6b). The phrase "comfort, which you experience" is translated more literally as "comfort, which is energized":[9] "it is for your comfort, which is energized by patient endurance of the same sufferings that we suffer." Patient endurance of the same sufferings that Paul suffered will energize and activate the comfort of God.

Truly, Paul's patient endurance through multiple afflictions had been the key to his experiencing the comfort of God. Paul did not bolt from his circumstances or curse God for them but patiently endured them and thus found God energizing his comfort. What wisdom there is in this. As Peter would say, "But if when you do good and suffer for it you endure, this is a gracious thing in the sight of God. For to this you have been called, because Christ also suffered for you, leaving you an example, so that you might follow in his steps" (1 Peter 2:20b, 21).

Are you suffering afflictions because of your commitment to Christ? Do not run. Do not curse your circumstances. Instead patiently endure, and your comfort will overflow.

Confidence in God's comfort. Despite the Corinthians' disappointing history, their shameful questioning of Paul's apostleship, their infatuation with more attractive ministries and accommodating theologies, their temporary rejection of his authority—despite all this, Paul viewed the Corinthian church with unshakable confidence. "Our hope for you is unshaken, for we know that as you share in our sufferings, you will also share in our comfort" (v. 7).

Paul's confidence was embedded in the Corinthians' sharing in fellowship with him in both his sufferings and his comfort—because all believers have fellowship with Christ. As he wrote initially to the Corinthians, "God is faithful, by whom you were called into the fellowship of his Son, Jesus Christ our Lord" (1 Corinthians 1:9). Also, believers have fellowship in the Holy Spirit. As Paul's famous benediction has it, "The grace of our Lord Jesus Christ and the love of God and the fellowship of the Holy Spirit be with you all" (2 Corinthians 13:14). Indeed all believers have fellowship in the Holy Trinity, as John exclaimed: "indeed our fellowship is with the Father and with his Son Jesus Christ" (1 John 1:3b). This fellowship with the Father, Son, and Holy Sprit generates a fellowship in Christ's sufferings and thus leads to Paul's unshakable hope—"we know that as you share in our sufferings, you will also share in our comfort" (2 Corinthians 1:7b).

Despite the Corinthians' checkered past, Paul was sure they would rise to their divine fellowship, ultimately experiencing the full comfort of God. As Philip Hughes writes: "In the service of Christ . . . there may be disappointments, but there cannot be despair; there may be conflicts, but never doubt; there may be afflictions, but never without comfort."[10]

How Paul's exultant blessing resonates in our souls: "Blessed be the God and Father of our Lord Jesus Christ, the Father of mercies and God of all comfort" (v. 3). God our Father is the "God of all comfort." As "the Father of mercies," the most merciful Father, he is the author of all possible consolation.

I see this again and again as the people I shepherd testify to his comfort in the most disappointing and desperate times of life—even death. The Holy Spirit is near to them and speaks to their afflicted souls, and they breathe comfort.

For those who are afflicted and suffer for following Christ, this passage promises surpassing comfort. The truth is that God's comfort always exceeds our afflictions. "For as we share abundantly in Christ's sufferings, so through Christ we share abundantly in comfort too" (v. 5). Those who follow Christ know the greatest affliction—and the greatest comfort, a flood of comfort. "Blessed be the God and Father of our Lord Jesus Christ, the Father of mercies and God of all comfort" (v. 3).

3

Affliction and Resurrection

2 CORINTHIANS 1:8–11

WE COME TO THIS SECTION OF 2 CORINTHIANS with God's comfort ringing in our thoughts because Paul used the word ten times in the brief preceding paragraph—ten out of its 107 words in the Greek. This great paragraph is meant to echo in our hearts and to effect in us much comfort.

However, this said, we err if we do not carefully think through our application of what Paul says about comfort. God's comfort has primary and secondary levels of application. The primary application is to the Apostle Paul himself. As an apostle, Paul had been allotted an extraordinary amount of suffering, as God had commanded his messenger Ananias to tell Paul after Paul's conversion on the Damascus road. "Go, for he is a chosen instrument of mine to carry my name before the Gentiles and kings and the children of Israel. For I will show him how much he must suffer for the sake of my name" (Acts 9:15, 16). The apostles were foundational to the church, and their sufferings were essential to that foundation. There are no parallels to the founding apostles today. The application of *apostle* to church-founding missionaries (as is sometimes done) is a misuse of the term. We must also bear in mind that the preceding paragraph in 2 Corinthians 1 is largely a biographical defense of Paul's apostleship as he explains the outworkings of the comfort of God through his apostolate.

But there is also a second level of application to those who are doing apostle-like work—pioneer missionaries who are taking the gospel to hostile peoples, doing groundbreaking work in the inner cities of the world, ministering the gospel in dangerous places. This also includes those who shoulder leadership for the gospel and the church as they preach and challenge culture and convention regarding universalism and inclusivism and gnosticism and materialism, those who address the neglect of the poor and disabled, those who hold the church's feet to the fiery demands of the Scriptures. For such servants of Christ, the comforts here described have a deep relevance and application.

There are also Christians who serve God faithfully in their callings, though they are not pioneering the gospel or leading the church. All such Christians will find these words of comfort speaking to their condition. But to the noncommitted believer, who goes with the flow of culture, who risks nothing for Christ (and therefore does not share in Christ's sufferings) there is no application and no comfort offered here.

If you are the type of Christian who seeks your own comfort and tranquillity first so that on the one hand you resist the excesses of sin, but on the other you will not discomfort yourself for the gospel and the Body of Christ, if you seek only an untroubled life, this text is not for you. Paul has already been so clear: "For as we share abundantly in Christ's sufferings, so through Christ we share abundantly in comfort too" (v. 5). The comforts of this passage are for the committed. We must not make the mistake of applying Paul's words across the board to all Christians.

There are also other mistakes or misconceptions we must avoid. One is that if you follow hard after Christ you will encounter immense afflictions, and if you're not afflicted, it's because you're not following as you ought. Not so! We must remember that our individual afflictions are sovereignly bestowed by God's loving hand, as were Paul's. Some committed Christians lead far more tranquil and healthy lives than other believers with like commitments. We must also never make the foolish mistake of imagining that those who suffer more than others are more spiritual. Paul never glorified suffering as such. The Bible nowhere encourages people to seek suffering.

Along with this, if we live committed Christian lives, we must not do so waiting for the other shoe to drop, perpetually wincing and ducking at any hint of trouble. We all live under the good providence of God, and his unstinted goodness toward us never diminishes regardless of what comes our way. Here is what we must lay to heart: "For Paul, suffering is not intrinsically good, nor is it a Christian virtue. Rather, suffering is a page in the textbook used in God's school of faith."[1]

A Description of Affliction (vv. 8, 9a)

With the resounding comfort of God still sounding, Paul now relates a dramatic personal example of God's care for which he continues to bless God. "For we do not want you to be unaware, brothers, of the affliction we experienced in Asia. For we were so utterly burdened beyond our strength that we despaired of life itself. Indeed, we felt that we had received the sentence of death" (vv. 8, 9a).

The exact nature of what befell Paul in Asia remains a mystery. Some believe that it happened during the famous riots in Ephesus during the intense confrontation between Paul and a lynch mob under the sway of Demetrius the silversmith (cf. Acts 19:23ff.). Certainly the potential for violence was there, but Ephesus is unlikely. If it was in Ephesus, Paul would have said so, as that was the capital city of Asia. Also, the account in Acts 19 mentions no physical violence coming to Paul.

Some of the early church fathers thought this referred to Paul's fighting hand-to-hand with wild beasts in Ephesus, because they (wrongly) interpreted 1 Corinthians 15:32 literally instead of figuratively. Others imagine the affliction in Asia to be a life-threatening illness or an attack from his "thorn," his unknown ailment. But the language suggests a life-threatening event. Paul's graphic repetitions suggest a recent explosive instance of such intensity that it had death written all over it.[2]

Deathly despair. His despair is framed in memorable terms because the Greek words translated "For we were so utterly burdened beyond our strength" were also used to describe an overloaded ship riding low in the water[3] or a pack animal that pitifully falls in despair under its load[4] so that it cannot rise. Paul was so "utterly, unbearably crushed" (RSV) that he couldn't get up, as if he wore a leaden cape. Inertia gripped his being so much that he "despaired of life itself." His despair was so deep that he was literally "without a way" of escape.[5] There was no exit. "Indeed," he says of himself, "we felt that we had received the sentence of death" (v. 9a)—an *official* sentence of death[6]—which could have been handed down as an official verdict or as a divine reply to Paul's prayer for deliverance.[7] Either way, Paul conceded that he was done for, that it was over—he was being utterly crushed under an unbearable weight, helplessly awaiting death.

Perhaps you have experienced this from sudden trauma or disease, and you were utterly helpless. The sentence of death was written over you, and there was nothing you could do. My wife experienced this as she lay helpless, bleeding, feeling her life drain away, immobilized, speechless, unable to communicate with those who hovered over her, in a dark free fall. Paul sensed that despite all his remarkable earlier deliverances, his time had come. Think of it! Paul had had multiple life-threatening experiences—the stoning, five beatings that each took him to within an inch of his life, multiplied dangers and shipwrecks. But this affliction in Asia was the most damaging and debilitating. An inexorable, paralyzing weight had fallen on him in Asia, and there was no exit.

The Purpose of Affliction (v. 9b)

But there was a purpose in all of this, to which Paul gives a simple explanation: "But that was to make us rely not on ourselves but on God who raises the dead" (v. 9b). Suddenly the power of Christ's resurrection was brought to bear on Paul's deathly despair. There in Asia Paul's affliction (tantamount to death) was followed by a wondrous experience (tantamount to resurrection).[8] Notice that God's resurrection power is not described in the past tense ("God who *raised* the dead") but in the present ("God who *raises* the dead") because God continues to display that resurrection power in his delivering his children from impossible circumstances.

One of the older commentators remarks that "raises" is a "timeless present participle expressing a permanent attribute" of God.[9] God's nature is to raise the dead. In regard to this timeless truth St. Chrysostom wrote: "Notwithstanding that the resurrection is a future event, he shows that it happens every day; for when God raises up again a man whose life is despaired of, and who has been brought to the very gates of hell, He shows nothing other than a resurrection, snatching from the very jaws of death the one who had fallen into them."[10] So when we find ourselves in impossible circumstances as we follow Christ, remember that God, by nature, is a raiser of the dead. This truth is as old as Genesis, as old as Abraham's God, "who gives life to the dead and calls into existence the things that do not exist" (Romans 4:17).

Here the cycle of Christ's experience becomes the pattern for Paul and all serious Christians: affliction—death—resurrection. As a pastor I found this cycle to be true in my earliest experience in ministry when planting a church. It all began so well, and in the initial years it appeared that a solid work was in progress. But to my surprise and despair, it began to unravel. In retrospect some of the reasons are clear. A respected church leader was carrying on a secret life of sexual perversion. A church officer, responsible for financial affairs, was addicted to alcohol and drugs. Exotic legalism gripped others and set them at odds with healthy Christians. Converts, people we discipled, rejected sound doctrine and fell to asceticism. I was witnessing the death of a dream.

One dark summer night I bared all my death-like disappointments and afflictions to my wife, who responded unforgettably, "Hang on to my faith; I have enough for both of us." That dark night marked the beginning of a spiritual resurrection in my soul as we began to search the Scriptures as to the true meaning of ministry and success.[11]

Affliction—death—resurrection is the central law of life and ministry as afflictions draw you down to the end of yourself ("death") and then you look to Christ, finding yourself thrust upward in resurrection for further ministry. Paul will say in 2 Corinthians 4, "For we who live are always being given over to death for Jesus' sake, so that the life of Jesus also may be manifested in our mortal flesh" (v. 11). Christ's call to take up the cross and follow him is nothing less than a call to embrace this cycle. As C. S. Lewis said, "Nothing that has not died will be resurrected."[12] But death sets in motion the unstoppable process of resurrection.

Those who are student-age, who sense the stirrings of God's call to mission and ministry, sometimes romanticize the calling in their thoughts. And while there is genuine romance in following Christ, it is also a call to shoulder the cycle of Christ—life and death and resurrection. But how blessed are those who joyfully embrace this as they begin to follow Christ. The bottom-line purpose of Paul's deathly affliction was to make him rely not on himself but on God who raises the dead.

Who would have imagined that Paul would ever depend upon himself in light of the epic miseries and deliverances he had experienced. But apparently he still was tempted to practice self-reliance, and his experience in Asia helped steel him against this. As Paul would write a few chapters further on, "But we have this treasure in jars of clay, to show that the surpassing power belongs to God and not to us" (4:7). The apostle had come to live in utter dependence upon God.

The Certitudes of Affliction (v. 10)

The replay of Christ's death and resurrection in Paul's experience in Asia endowed him with immense certainty, as Paul emphasized in verse 10 with three repetitions of the word "deliver"—the first being *past* ("He delivered us from such a deadly peril"), the second being in the *near future* ("and he will deliver us"), and the third in the *ultimate future* ("On him we have set our hope that he will deliver us again"). As the Corinthians heard this read—"He delivered us . . . he will deliver us . . . he will deliver us again"—the certitude of deliverance from crushing circumstances gently freshened their souls. This is the endless refrain that comes to all committed believers—God by nature is the Deliverer, Redeemer, and Savior who raises the dead.

The one thing that you can be sure of as a child of God is that he will deliver you in the midst of your affliction as you call upon him. There is no doubt about this. True, he will not deliver us from all death situations in the near future of this life, but he will ultimately do so because he raises the dead.

This makes us, along with Paul, a people of hope—"On him we have set our hope that he will deliver us again."

> My hope is in the Lord
> Who gave himself for me,
> And paid the price of all my sin
> at Calvary.
> For me He died,
> For me He lives,
> And everlasting life and light
> He freely gives.
>
> Norman Clayton, 1945

Prayer and Affliction (v. 11)

Paul was confident in deliverance, but his confidence did not rest on God's past faithfulness alone, but on the prayer of believers, especially the Corinthians with whom he had shared so much. "You also must help us by prayer, so that many will give thanks on our behalf for the blessing granted us through the prayers of many" (v. 11). Here Philip Hughes's insights help us:

> Prayer is indeed a mystery, but it is stressed over and over again in the New Testament as a vital prerequisite for the release and experience of God's power. It is true that is it *God* who delivers, and that God stands in no need of human prayers before He can act on behalf of His afflicted servants. Yet there is the manward as well as the Godward aspect of such deliverance, and the manward side is summed up in the duty of Christians to intercede in prayer for their fellow-believers who are enduring affliction. . . . In prayer, human impotence casts itself at the feet of divine omnipotence. Thus the duty of prayer is not a modification of God's power, but a glorification of it."[13]

Paul fully understood the human side of deliverance and resurrection power—and that is why his letters bear repeated requests for prayer. "[Pray] also for me, that words may be given to me in opening my mouth boldly to proclaim the mystery of the gospel" (Ephesians 6:19). "For I know that through your prayers and the help of the Spirit of Jesus Christ this will turn out for my deliverance" (Philippians 1:19). "Pray also for us, that God may open to us a door for the word, to declare the mystery of Christ" (Colossians 4:3). "Finally, brothers, pray for us, that the word of the Lord may speed ahead and be honored" (2 Thessalonians 3:1).

Paul's request for prayer in 2 Corinthians 1:11 is beautiful and moving. "Many" in the phrase "so that many will give thanks" is literally "the faces" (the faces of many), thus picturing the upturned faces of the Corinthians to God as they offer thanks to him.[14] So we see that Paul ends verse 11 with thanks and praise to God, just as he began the section in verse 3. This is instinctively Paul—his heart's desire is that thanksgiving and praise be offered to God by all people (cf. 4:15).

What are we to make of all this? Essentially the following: The function of afflictions in the lives of those who aspire to be disciples of Christ is "to make us rely not on ourselves but on God who raises the dead" (v. 9). The shouldering of that affliction bears relation to the calling and mission of each follower of Christ. The apostolic burden was immense, and Paul was the most afflicted of men. Through the centuries and today, those called to lead the church in mission to the nations and cultures of the world have borne their share of affliction. And though we may not want to hear it, the suffering of pastors and missionaries is essential to mediating the gospel to God's people. The pattern of such lives is the same as that of Christ: *affliction* and downward trajectory, *death* at the bottom, and then *resurrection* and arching ascent in greater effectiveness for the gospel. Such lives have greater reliance upon God and, ironically, greater confidence in his deliverance.

Today the church needs pastors and missionary leaders who share the afflictions of Christ. Such an assertion may seem 2,000 years out-of-date or from another planet. Today's pastors are regularly taught to be CEOs and managers—anything but the above. But as lifelong pastor and New Testament scholar Bishop Paul Barnett concludes:

> Paul's experience of suffering and comfort in the course of his ministry is replicated in every generation in the lives of godly missionaries and pastors in their interrelationships with their congregations. While both minister and people suffer as they bear witness to Christ in an alien culture, there remains a distinctive role and therefore a distinctive suffering to the Christian leader. As the comfort of God is experienced in the life of the leader, so it will be passed on through ministry to the people.[15]

Let us pray fervently and frequently for God's ends, so that many upturned faces will give thanks for all the blessings granted us through the prayers of many.

4

Integrity and Ministry

2 CORINTHIANS 1:12—2:4

THERE IS NO DOUBT THAT THE BIBLE SETS THE BAR HIGH for those in spiritual leadership because sin committed by Christian leaders is in itself greater than the same sin committed by their followers. This truth is argued with compelling logic in *The Westminster Confession of Faith*.

Question 150

"Are all transgressions of the law of God equally heinous in themselves, and in the sight of God?"

Answer

"All transgressions of the law of God are not equally heinous; but some sins in themselves, and by reason of several aggravations are more heinous in the sight of God than others (cf. John 19:11; Ezekiel 8:6, 13, 15; 1 John 5:16; Psalm 78:17, 32, 56)."

Question 151

"What are those aggravations that make some sins more heinous than others?"

Answer

In briefest terms the four-part answer is this:

1. Some sins are more heinous than others due to the advantages of the offenders—"if they be of riper age, greater experience of grace, eminent for profession, gifts, place, office, guides to others, and whose example is likely to be followed by others"—their sins are more terrible.

2. Some sins are more heinous than others due to the parties they directly offend. Blasphemy of God is heinous, but also sins "against any of the saints, particularly weak brethren, the souls of them, or any other, and the common good of all or many" are particularly heinous.

3. Some sins are more heinous than others due to the nature and qual-

ity of the sin, that is if the sin is committed while fully knowing God's graces and requirements, and yet doing it anyway while admitting no reparation or fault.

4. Some sins are more heinous than others due to the "circumstances of time and place . . . if in public, or in the presence of others, who are thereby likely to be provoked or defiled."[1]

This is a good salutary truth and desperately needs to be followed in today's church. The ministry is a profession requiring the highest integrity, and those who do not measure up should remove themselves from leadership, or be removed.

This said, the higher demands of leadership leave the leader vulnerable to insinuations and false accusations by his people—and especially those who have a mind to question his leadership. People can be tough—like the purported churchgoers in a small town in northwest Scotland, of whom it was said that while others went to church to hear the gospel preached, they went to hear if the gospel was preached![2] Such hostile, quick-to-see-the-worst, graceless attributes are as old as the church, and especially the ancient church in Corinth, where the Apostle Paul had suffered unfounded criticism of his integrity and rejection by some.

The focus of the criticism recorded here was on Paul's changing his plans to visit the Corinthians. Initially he had promised to pay them an extended visit after passing through Macedonia, and perhaps even spend a winter there (cf. 1 Corinthians 16:5–9). But then, after a report from Timothy, he paid the Corinthians a brief painful visit, promising he would return. However, once away from Corinth, he decided to send a harsh corrective letter, indicating that he would visit them twice as he traveled to and from Macedonia on his way to Judea with an offering for the poor. These changes, from the perspective of Paul's detractors, were evidence that the Spirit of God was not with him. They argued that Paul's conduct should be consonant with the unchanging character of God and that his word should reflect a God who never lies. Paul, they charged, was double-minded and duplicitous. And some even insinuated that his announced extra visit was really to extract more money for himself.

Paul's tear-stained severe letter had won back most of the Corinthian church. But a group of intransigent, judgmental people still considered Paul to be deceptive, double-speaking, and deficient in character. How hurtful this was for Paul, because nothing could be further from the truth.

Affirmation of Integrity (1:12–14)

So Paul answers them with a brilliantly crafted introduction to the defense of his own integrity:

> For our boast is this: the testimony of our conscience that we behaved in the world with simplicity and godly sincerity, not by earthly wisdom but by the grace of God, and supremely so toward you. For we are not writing to you anything other than what you read and acknowledge and I hope you will fully acknowledge—just as you did partially acknowledge us, that on the day of our Lord Jesus you will boast of us as we will boast of you. (vv. 12–14)

Notice that Paul carefully framed his opening statement with repetitions of the word "boast" at the beginning and end and then used repetitions of the word "acknowledge" to conclude the statement, to fix before his hearers the truth of his good conduct. Further, Paul's choice of the word "boast" was a surprise because he himself abhorred boasting (cf. 1 Corinthians 1:29; 3:21; 4:7; 5:6), arguing that it can only be "in the Lord" (cf. 2 Corinthians 10:17)—which, of course, this was. Paul's unanticipated boast had his detractors' attention.

Paul's conscience. His boast was about his clear conscience—"the testimony of our conscience." Paul had heard their hurtful charges, but his conscience, which he knew would be judged by God, cleared him (cf. 1 Corinthians 4:5).

His conscience was clear because he had behaved with "simplicity" (or uprightness) and "godly sincerity," and he did so by the grace of God—and he did it literally in an overflowing manner to the Corinthians. Paul's conscience, his inner tribunal, unexceptionably declared that he had conducted himself with graced integrity toward the Corinthians.

In Paul's thought, conscience—a clear conscience, a good conscience—is foundational to ministry. Three times in his Pastoral Letters he referenced conscience, urging "love that issues from a pure heart and *a good conscience* and a sincere faith" (1 Timothy 1:5). He said that church leaders "must hold the mystery of the faith with *a clear conscience*" (1 Timothy 3:9). Substantiating his own ministry he said, "I thank God whom I serve, as did my ancestors, with *a clear conscience*" (2 Timothy 1:3). The rest of the New Testament testifies to Paul's empowerment through "a good conscience." He courageously took his stand before the Sanhedrin, looked them straight in the eye, and declared, "Brothers, I have lived my life before God in all *good conscience* up to this day" (Acts 23:1). And standing before Governor Felix he confidently declared, "So I always take pains to have a *clear conscience* toward both God and man" (Acts 24:16). To the Romans Paul voiced his amazing affirmation of love for his people as true because it was spoken with a clear conscience: "I am speaking the truth in Christ—I am not lying; my *conscience* bears me witness in the Holy Spirit" (Romans 9:1).

To the Corinthians, Paul audaciously boasts in his conscience. Paul has begun with an in-your-face repudiation of their charges.

Paul's hope. The apostle was also sure that he had communicated clearly in his most recent correspondence to the Corinthians (the so-called "severe" letter, 1 Corinthians 2:5; cf. 2 Corinthians 13:10), and that what he was now writing was consonant with what he had already written. So he boldly says, "For we are not writing to you anything other than what you read and acknowledge and I hope you will fully acknowledge—just as you did partially acknowledge us, that on the day of our Lord Jesus you will boast of us as we will boast of you" (1:13, 14). Paul believes that the truth of what he says will eventuate in their mutual boasting in each other in the consummation of all things in Christ. What a reversal—they will boast in him! Paul is absolutely sure of his integrity and that it will stand the final judgment. And that is why he stands so tall here. He is armed with faith and a clear conscience.

As one called to pastoral leadership, I have found this to be true. If my conscience is not entirely clear, I have trouble standing as I ought, but if I have a good conscience I can lead in confidence. Integrity is crucial to authority and power in ministry.

Paul's Integrity in Changing His Plans (1:15–22)

No vacillation in plans. Having defended his integrity Paul further defends himself against charges of vacillation:

> Because I was sure of this [i.e., that he had clearly communicated with them], I wanted to come to you first, so that you might have a second experience of grace. I wanted to visit you on my way to Macedonia, and to come back to you from Macedonia and have you send me on my way to Judea. Was I vacillating when I wanted to do this? Do I make my plans according to the flesh, ready to say "Yes, yes" and "No, no" at the same time? (vv. 15–17)

Paul had not equivocated. The apostle had changed his plans precisely to benefit the Corinthians with two visits as he went in and out of Macedonia, so they would have two experiences of grace. Likely the experiences of grace Paul is referring to are two opportunities to donate to the offering for the poor in Jerusalem, because in chapters 8—9, "grace" is used to describe the act of contributing to the collection.[3] Indeed, giving is a "grace" as it demonstrates that God has met your needs and that his grace has inclined you to give to others. Thus the Corinthians would get twice the benefit—they would be double-graced! In any event, Paul was not capricious in his plans but rather made them with graced intentionality.

Thus Paul posed two rhetorical questions to the Corinthians that both required negations. "Was I vacillating [literally, was I light, i.e., frivolous] when I wanted to do this?" No!

"Do I make my plans according to the flesh, ready to say 'Yes, yes' and 'No, no' at the same time?" That is, "do I make my plans in such a fleshly manner that I am ready to swear a double 'yes' and double 'no' at the same time?"[4] Absolutely not!

Paul was no impulsive lightweight. Like his Master, his yes was yes and his no was no. You could count on his word.

The evangelical Quakers of the seventeenth century were like this due to the radical integrity of their founder, George Fox. Fox was a towering man in his day, standing some 6'3'' in his cowhide suit (yes, his leathers), and even more imposing in character, dipping his hat to no man in cavalier England, but only to God. He spoke plain language, using the unpretentious thee's and thou's of the day, and spoke the truth as he saw it with unexceptionable integrity.

Fox declined all oaths, even in a court of law, giving only the simple affirmation that he was telling the truth. Fox's word was always truthful. And so it was for committed Quakers in the centuries that followed as they modeled a Christlike, Paul-like integrity, to the point that their word or handshake was superior to a legal contract. In this they were redolent with Pauline integrity.

Christ's integrity is Paul's integrity. The reason underlying this radical truth ethic for Paul was Christ himself. "As surely as God is faithful, our word to you has not been Yes and No. For the Son of God, Jesus Christ, whom we proclaimed among you, Silvanus and Timothy and I, was not Yes and No, but in him it is always Yes. For all the promises of God find their Yes in him. That is why it is through him that we utter our Amen to God for his glory" (vv. 18–20). Jesus Christ was and is the prophetic "Yes." Philip Hughes gives eloquent expression to the significance of Paul's statement:

> In Christ is the yes, the grand consummating affirmative, to all God's promises. He is the horn of salvation raised up for us by God, "as He spake by the mouth of His holy prophets which have been since the world began" (Lk. 24:44). The covenant promises addressed to Abraham and his seed are realized in His single person (Gal. 3:16). To the believer, therefore, Christ is all, not merely as fulfilling a word of the past, but as Himself being the very living Word of God, faithful and eternal. In Him all fullness dwells (Col. 1:19): wisdom, righteousness, sanctification, redemption are to be found in Him alone (1 Cor. 1:30). There is nothing which is not in Him, who is the First and the Last, the Beginning and End (Rev. 22:13).[5]

Because Christ is the grand consummating Yes—God's unambiguous, ultimate Yes—he is the ground and fulcrum of all Christian ethics. Those who are in Christ and embrace him as the Yes with all their hearts embrace truth—and truth-telling as a way of life. Nothing could be more dissonant and logically contradictory than to accuse the Apostle Paul (whose whole being was dedicated to preaching Christ) of playing with the truth! Paul's behavior was centered upon and in the character and actions of Christ.

If we say "Amen" to the truth about Christ as Paul calls us to in his conclusion—"That is why it is through him we utter our Amen to God for his glory" (v. 20b)—then we must also live lives of truth, of radical veracity.

Integrity lay at the heart of apostolic ministry. Truth was the medium. Sincerity was the evidence. Power was the outcome.

This still works today. When Billy Graham's preaching was filling Wembley Stadium, John Stott, then rector of All Souls in London, was asking himself, "why should it be . . . that our churches are half-empty and yet night after night thousands come to hear Billy Graham, 'and the answer I gave myself was this: I believe Billy was the first transparently sincere preacher these people have ever heard.'"[6]

The power of integrity! This is so needed today. We need preachers whose sermons are like thunder because their lives are like lightning![7]

Paul co-opts his critics. The logic of Paul's defense surely put his critics back on their heels. And it is here that he co-opted them, including them with himself as established together in Christ: "And it is God who establishes us with you in Christ, and has anointed us, and who has also put his seal on us and given us his Spirit in our hearts as a guarantee" (vv. 21, 22).

This description is stunning. The phrase "And it is God who establishes us with you in Christ" is in the present tense, describing an ongoing experience as Paul and his believing critics are being continually established in Christ. Yet the establishing rests on a single complete action that is stated as three closely related actions, each involving the Spirit. First, God has "anointed us," which in the original features a beautiful play on words that goes something like "God . . . christed us Christward," indicating that he has made us Christ's people, a messianic community.[8] Second, he has "put his seal on us," his sign of ownership that identifies us as his. This seal marks us out for redemption (cf. Ephesians 1:13; 4:30). Third, he has "given us his Spirit in our hearts as a guarantee." The initial installment guarantees the full inheritance to come.

This dazzling triad of the Spirit's work in establishing them together in Christ would thrill any earnest Corinthian and demonstrates how foolish the criticism of Paul was. After all, it was Paul's preaching that enabled them to be established in Christ. Rather than criticism, they all ought to be thanking Paul for his integrity of heart.

Again, Paul's Integrity in Changing Plans (1:23—2:4)

Remember, Paul's supposed vacillation (and lack of integrity) had come to the fore because he didn't pay a second visit to the Corinthians as he had promised. Instead he sent them a harsh letter. This was considered to be another evidence of his spineless failure of character. So now, for the Corinthians who still believed this line, Paul demonstrates that he changed his plans purely out of mercy and love.

The mercy motive. Paul's merciful heart shines in the paragraph beginning in verse 23, showing his desire to spare the Corinthians the pain that would have attended his coming:

> But I call God to witness against me—it was to spare you that I refrained from coming again to Corinth. Not that we lord it over your faith, but we work with you for your joy, for you stand firm in your faith. For I made up my mind not to make another painful visit to you. For if I cause you pain, who is there to make me glad but the one whom I have pained? And I wrote as I did, so that when I came I might not suffer pain from those who should have made me rejoice, for I felt sure of all of you, that my joy would be the joy of you all. (1:23—2:3)

Though he has apostolic authority, Paul frames his argument in gentle terms of their mutuality in Christ—"If one member suffers, all suffer together" (cf. 1 Corinthians 12:26). His smiling suggestion that he wouldn't have anyone to cheer him if he paid another painful visit was true. But, more, if he had come and they rebelled, that would have necessitated judgment, as he will threaten in his final warnings—"I warn them now while absent, as I did when present on my second visit, that if I come again I will not spare them" (2 Corinthians 13:2b). Far better to have written a severe letter than show up with the lash.

Merciful Paul was so like his Master who "is not slow to fulfill his promise as some count slowness, but is patient toward you, not wishing that any should perish, but that all should reach repentance" (2 Peter 3:9). "Just as God has extended one more opportunity for repentance and restoration to the world by separating the two comings of Christ, Paul too wanted to extend this same opportunity to the Corinthians" (Hafemann).[9]

The love motive. The Corinthians had been a source of much affliction and heartache to Paul, a truly excruciating part of what he termed "the daily pressure on me of my anxiety for all the churches" (11:28). And it had been while Paul was undergoing the unbearable affliction in Asia, when his strength began to fail and he despaired of life, that the Corinthians' criticisms heaped internal grief upon his external miseries.[10] These people whom he had wrestled into the kingdom through his early evangelistic disputations in Corinth and then instructed in the faith, and over whom he had prayed when they met opposition—these same people had savaged his character and motives, even questioning his apostleship. What hurt and grief to Paul's heart!

Nevertheless, Paul did not respond with angered rejection but with wounded love. "For I wrote to you out of much affliction and anguish of heart and with many tears, not to cause you pain but to let you know the abundant love that I have for you" (2 Corinthians 2:4). It was literally overflowing love that motivated and energized his severe letter and energizes him now as he defends his integrity to the Corinthians.

Paul's pastoral heart astonishes, so like that of the Lord amidst his abuse (cf. Luke 23:34).

The Apostle Paul's defense of his integrity is simply masterful.

Confidence. His initial uncharacteristic boast put them back on their heels as it announced a confidence born of a clear conscience as to how he had conducted his ministry—"with simplicity and godly sincerity, not by earthly wisdom but by the grace of God, and supremely so toward you" (1:12). Such was his confidence that he knew that at the resurrection he would become their boast and he would boast in them! Paul lived by the words that he commended to Timothy—"fight the good fight, holding on to faith and a good conscience" (1 Timothy 1:18, 19, NIV).

Grace. Paul's clear-conscience confidence was coupled with his desire for grace for the Corinthians. And that is why he altered his plans to visit them twice, to double-grace them. His change of plans was not irresponsible and capricious but rather showed graced intentionality under the direction of God.

Christ. Because Christ (the great consummating Yes to all that the Scriptures promise) was the center of Paul's life, Paul was radically truthful. Embracing Christ meant that Paul had taken truth-telling as a way of life. Duplicity and vacillation were not a part of the way he lived. His yes was yes, and his no was no. Christ was the ground and fulcrum of Paul's integrity.

Mutuality. Furthermore, God was establishing both Paul and the Corinthians together in Christ. This began with the Spirit's anointing them, sealing them, and giving himself as an earnest of what is to come. This mutuality demonstrated how fatuous and self-defeating their criticism was.

Mercy and love. Paul's change of plans was motivated by mercy. He cared enough to confront the Corinthian believers by letter, and he cared too much to visit them personally, because his presence likely would have necessitated judgment. Moreover, Paul's letter was motivated by his desire to let the Corinthians know of his overflowing love for them.

It is true that spiritual leadership demands integrity and exacts much from those who lead, for it is a call to character. And it is here that Paul excelled and could confidently boast in God's good providence.

The great apostle's soaring example of integrity should compel both leaders and their congregations to go to their knees, asking God for mercy and the grace to live out the apostolic ethic.

Leaders ought to humbly hold their consciences up to the ultimate—to God's Word—so that he grounds their lives and leverages a life of truth.

All God's people must seek this for themselves and for their leaders, for it has everything to do with preaching the gospel and bringing glory to God.

5

Forgiveness and Ministry

2 CORINTHIANS 2:5–11

AFTER THE APOSTLE PAUL'S DEFENSE of his integrity, which he so brilliantly grounded in conscience, grace, truth, mutuality, mercy, and love (cf. 2 Corinthians 1:12—2:4), he then turned in 2:5–11 to the one who attacked him, but not as we might expect. Paul pled for forgiveness for the offender because he had already suffered the discipline of the church.

It had happened like this: When Paul learned from Timothy's visit to Corinth that there were troubles in the church, Paul paid the Corinthians an unscheduled visit, presuming that he would quickly fix things and be on his way. To his surprise, he was opposed to his face. Apparently a leader of the Corinthian church publicly assailed Paul while the church passively observed (cf. 2 Corinthians 12:11). The attacker evidently had come under the sway of Paul's opponents who had recently come to Corinth. As to the nature of the insults, we surmise that they had to do with Paul's integrity—namely, that he was dishonest and double-minded and lacking in courage. Also, it was likely charged or insinuated that he was appropriating the collection for the poor in Jerusalem for his own needs. Moreover, all this was probably laced with *ad hominem* comments about his ministerial effectiveness. In any event the humiliating surprise attack, coupled with a lack of support by the church, had so taken Paul aback that he elected to leave Corinth for a time.

It was in the wake of this rejection that Paul wrote his severe, painful letter, poignantly described in the opening verses of chapter 2. The letter did its work, as Paul reflects later in 7:8–13a:

> For even if I made you grieve with my letter, I do not regret it—though I did regret it, for I see that that letter grieved you, though only for a while.

> As it is, I rejoice, not because you were grieved, but because you were grieved into repenting. For you felt a godly grief, so that you suffered no loss through us. For godly grief produces a repentance that leads to salvation without regret, whereas worldly grief produces death. For see what earnestness this godly grief has produced in you, but also what eagerness to clear yourselves, what indignation, what fear, what longing, what zeal, what punishment! At every point you have proved yourselves innocent in the matter. So although I wrote to you, it was not for the sake of the one who did the wrong, nor for the sake of the one who suffered the wrong, but in order that your earnestness for us might be revealed to you in the sight of God. Therefore we are comforted.

The majority of the Corinthians repented. And though it does not say what they did with the offender, the consensus is that they cast him from the fellowship of the church, because this best fits the following account and is consistent with a previously mentioned case of discipline in Corinth (cf. 1 Corinthians 5:1–13). And, glory to God, the offender repented and sought forgiveness.

There was only one problem—the Corinthians hadn't forgiven him and had no desire to do so! How true to life, and the church universal! The church is loath to exercise church discipline against an unrepentant sinner. And then when it finally steps up to its responsibility and does it, it finds it difficult to forgive and restore the repentant sinner.

This disinclination to forgive, this tendency to turn away from those who have caused pain and embarrassment (despite their repentance), loomed as an approaching shipwreck for the church. Failure to forgive would have put the church out of step with its gracious Savior and could well have sunk the Good Ship Grace.

Churchwide Pain (v. 5)

The assault upon Paul had inflicted a churchwide pain that Paul carefully delineates: "Now if anyone has caused pain, he has caused it not to me, but in some measure—not to put it too severely—to all of you" (v. 5). Paul's sensitivity here is implicit as he avoids naming the offender because identifying the culprit by name would not contribute to the man's desired restoration. And even more, Paul takes care to minimize his misery caused by his attacker, saying of the pain, "he caused it not to me." Was Paul's discounting of his pain untruthful or disingenuous? Not at all, because Paul had a scriptural view of personal pain as it relates to the whole church. Thus he emphasizes that the pain—"not to put it too severely [or not to exaggerate[1]]—[is] to all of you." Everyone had suffered pain when Paul was abused.

In his initial letter to the Corinthians Paul had explained, "If one member suffers, all suffer together; if one member is honored, all rejoice together" (12:26). And later in 2 Corinthians he will reference the same interconnectedness: "Who is weak, and I am not weak? Who is made to fall, and I am not indignant?" (11:29). Clearly, there is profound spiritual commonality between all true believers.

For Paul, the church was not a club offering trial memberships, and *the Body of Christ* was not a churchy slogan.[2] They were a community of brothers and sisters with radical interconnected relationships—relationships that the writer of Hebrews so eloquently celebrates in 12:22–24:

> But you have come to Mount Zion and to the city of the living God, the heavenly Jerusalem, and to innumerable angels in festal gathering, and to the assembly of the firstborn who are enrolled in heaven, and to God, the judge of all, and to the spirits of the righteous made perfect, and to Jesus, the mediator of a new covenant, and to the sprinkled blood that speaks a better word than the blood of Abel.

No, the church was not a club, but rather an eternal community with cosmic relationships.

Paul would never have countenanced the free-riding ecclesiastical hitchhikers of today, much less the McChurch consumers who attend one church for the preaching, send their children to a second church for the youth group, and participate in another church's small groups—people who live without commitment, without accountability, without discipline, without the Lord's Table.

For Paul, the church was central to Christian existence. He never conceived of Christians living apart from the visible church. Rather, Christians lived in such profound relationship that the pain of one was truly felt by all. And the drubbing that Paul suffered was a misery for all. As Francis Thompson mused in "The Mistress of Vision," "Thou canst not stir a flower / Without troubling of a star."

Today's church needs to take back the seriousness of the doctrine of the church and live out the profound mutuality of the Body of Christ. We must take to heart that the commitments of praying for the church, participating in the regular services and ministries of the church, supporting its ministries and missions with our resources, and submitting to the constituted leadership are not options but rather Biblical imperatives.

Forgive the Sinner (vv. 6–8)

Paul, for the sake of the offender, has discounted his own pain and has explained its churchwide effect. Now he asks the church to forgive the man and restore him to fellowship: "For such a one, this punishment by the majority is enough, so you should rather turn to forgive and comfort him, or he may be overwhelmed by excessive sorrow. So I beg you to reaffirm your love for him" (vv. 6–8).

Again Paul's pastoral sensitivity comes to the fore. The punishment—the extended exclusion from the church—has been "enough." Paul's fear that the offender "may be overwhelmed by excessive sorrow" conjures up the picture of a terrible end because "overwhelmed" is literally "to swallow up"[3] and is an allusion to the judgment of Korah when Moses prophesied that the earth would swallow up the rebellious:

> And as soon as he had finished speaking all these words, the ground under them split apart. And the earth opened its mouth and swallowed them up, with their households and all the people who belonged to Korah and all their goods. So they and all that belonged to them went down alive into Sheol, and the earth closed over them, and they perished from the midst of the assembly. And all Israel who were around them fled at their cry, for they said, "Lest the earth swallow us up!" (Numbers 16:31–34)

Paul sensed that the excommunication had left the man so drowning in despondent sorrow that he was in danger of being sucked down into the earth in death. Perhaps he was even contemplating suicide.

Again, this poor excluded man understood the mountainous doctrine of the church. And he could not bear to live apart from the benefits and comforts of the Body of Christ. He feared for his own soul. How unlike some people I have encountered over the years who blithely brushed off church discipline and traveled a few miles to another church where they continued on without history and accountability and fear of God—in pursuit of the ostensibly "Christian" life. The irony is that in fearing nothing they may well meet an end not unlike that of Korah.

For Paul, forgiveness was of paramount importance for the sinner and for the church, and he concludes the thought by saying, "So I beg you to reaffirm your love for him" (v. 8)—by a formal act of the congregation. Paul did not merely beg the Corinthians to forgive the sinner—he viewed it as a matter of obedience: "For this is why I wrote, that I might test you and know whether you are obedient in everything" (v. 9). Obedience to God's Word demands doing the hard work of church discipline, and then the hard work of forgiving.

Our Forgiveness (vv. 10, 11)

To clinch his appeal to forgive the offender, Paul cites his own example as a model for the Corinthians: "Anyone whom you forgive, I also forgive. What I have forgiven, if I have forgiven anything, has been for your sake in the presence of Christ" (v. 10). Just as Paul had minimized the pain that the offender caused him, he minimizes his own forgiveness of the man with the dismissive "if I have forgiven anything," as if it were no big deal. The implicit message was, "I, the offended, did it, and you can do it too." And he adds that the forgiveness was for the Corinthians' sake—"your sake in the presence of Christ." The fact was, if the Corinthian church refused to forgive the penitent sinner, a poison would clog the way of grace. The Corinthians' refusal to forgive could have killed the church. The church was already suffering from its corporate mercilessness. Paul's message was: "My Corinthian brothers and sisters, it was for your sake (in addition to the offender's) that I forgave him. So now, you forgive him too!"

Christ's forgiveness. What we must see is that the power to forgive was given to Paul "in the presence of Christ" (literally, "in the face of Christ"), as Christ looked on in approval and empowerment. Jesus Christ taught that unwillingness to forgive is evidence of not having experienced his forgiveness. When we pray the Lord's Prayer, we ask him to effect this reality: "forgive us our debts, as we also have forgiven our debtors" (Matthew 6:12). The Lord drives the truth home in no uncertain terms in the next sentence after the great prayer: "For if you forgive others their trespasses, your heavenly Father will also forgive you, but if you do not forgive others their trespasses, neither will your Father forgive your trespasses" (6:14, 15). This "forgiven people forgive" teaching was so integral to Jesus' teaching that he devoted an entire teaching to it in the Parable of the Unforgiving Servant, which concludes, "'So also my heavenly Father will do to every one of you, if you do not forgive your brother from your heart'" (Matthew 18:35).

John Wesley once had the occasion to drive this daunting truth home. He had offended the British General Oglethorpe who exploded, "I never forgive!" To which Wesley replied, "Then, Sir, I hope you never sin."

By invoking the lordship of Christ, Paul also focuses our hearts on Christ as the one who not only demands that we forgive but empowers us to do so. You have been liberated to do so. And any honest attempt to bow to Christ in this will be met with the high voltage of unremitting grace.

Satan's ploy. Paul concludes his plea to forgive the sinner with the hard reality that an unforgiving heart has been duped by Satan—"so that we would not be outwitted by Satan; for we are not ignorant of his designs" (v. 11). Again, the young church in Corinth could have been shipwrecked by refusing to obey God by forgiving the repentant sinner who had caused so much pain. If they had let him stew in his despondency, they would have cooked their own souls. And Satan could then have put a fork in the church of Corinth.

We are no different as individuals and as churches. If there are people whom we refuse to forgive despite their repentance and pleas, we had better consider whether we are of the faith.

True Christian forgiveness is, as Paul declared, a matter of obedience "in everything" (v. 9). Brother and sister in Christ, you can do it. The late Corrie ten Boom recalled in her book *The Hiding Place* a postwar meeting with a guard from the Ravensbrück concentration camp where her sister had died and where she herself had been subjected to horrible indignities:

> It was at a church service in Munich that I saw him, the former S.S. man who had stood guard at the shower room door in the processing center at Ravensbrück. He was the first of our actual jailers that I had seen since that time. And suddenly it was all there—the roomful of mocking men, the heaps of clothing, Betsie's pain-blanched face.
>
> He came up to me as the church was emptying, beaming and bowing. "How grateful I am for your message, Fraulein," he said. "To think that, as you say, He has washed my sins away!"
>
> His hand was thrust out to shake mine. And I, who had preached so often to the people in Bloemendaal the need to forgive, kept my hand at my side.
>
> Even as the angry, vengeful thoughts boiled through me, I saw the sin of them. Jesus Christ had died for this man; was I going to ask for more? *Lord Jesus*, I prayed, *forgive me and help me to forgive him.*
>
> I tried to smile, I struggled to raise my hand. I could not. I felt nothing, not the slightest spark of warmth or charity. And so again I breathed a silent prayer. *Jesus, I cannot forgive him. Give me Your forgiveness.*
>
> As I took his hand the most incredible thing happened. From my shoulder along my arm and through my hand a current seemed to pass from me to him, while into my heart sprang a love for this stranger that almost overwhelmed me.[4]

Christians, you can do it! God's Word says, "Be kind to one another, tenderhearted, forgiving one another, as God in Christ forgave you" (Ephesians 4:32). And again, "Put on then, as God's chosen ones, holy and beloved, compassion, kindness, humility, meekness, and patience, bearing with one another and, if one has a complaint against another, forgiving each other; as the Lord has forgiven you, so you also must forgive" (Colossians 3:12, 13).

6

Triumphal Procession in Christ

2 CORINTHIANS 2:12–17

THE RECENT DEATH OF MY MOTHER at age eighty-three strongly suggests to me that I may join her in a couple of decades—if her genes have anything to say about it. And, of course, this doesn't factor in disease or trauma. Morbid thoughts? I don't think so. Notwithstanding our love for our family and friends, and the loss they will feel at our departure, if one one-hundredth of what the Scriptures say about Heaven is true, it is a wonder that when we get old we hang on to life as we do. So I embrace the statistical realities of a possible score of years.

It is actually a sweet thing to grow old as a Christian. It is always "far better" to be with the Lord (Philippians 1:23). Death, as C. S. Lewis said, is "Chapter One of the Great Story . . . which goes on forever and ever in which every chapter is better than the one before."[1]

But there is another spiritual reality that we ought to embrace but that is not so easy to do. That reality is this: A vibrant, useful spiritual life is a death march in which the marcher repeatedly dies. It is the path pioneered and mastered by Christ. And it is the course that Paul strode as he said, "I die every day!" (1 Corinthians 15:31). It is the course celebrated in the triumphal procession, which is at the heart of the passage before us.

Paul's Suffering (vv. 12, 13)

As we have seen, Paul's enemies criticized him for everything—and one of their criticisms was that Paul was always vacillating and changing his plans, which, to them, was evidence that his ministry was fleshly and definitely not of God (cf. 1:15–17; but cf. vv. 18–20). So here again the apostle gives his reasons for his change of plans: "When I came to Troas to preach the gospel of Christ, even though a door was opened for me in the Lord, my spirit was not at rest because I did not find my brother Titus there. So I took leave of them and went on to Macedonia" (2:12, 13).

Excruciating anxiety. Poor Paul had been so taken aback by the surprise opposition during his second visit to the church in Corinth that though he was the church's founder, he cut short his visit and retreated to Ephesus where he wrote a tearful, severe reproach to the Corinthians. Then, anxious to hear how they had received it, he dispatched Titus to Corinth to find out and traveled to Troas where they had agreed to rendezvous.

Paul was suffering from pastoral anxiety—which is the trademark province of all spiritual leadership. My pastoral mentor, Verl Lindley, who is now retired after fifty years of ministry, was asleep one night when his wife, Lois, awoke to find him hunched up on his hands and knees at the foot of the bed. His arms were cupped as if he was embracing something, and he was muttering. She cried, "Verl! What on earth are you doing?" "Shhh," he answered, still asleep. "I'm holding a pyramid of marbles together, and if I move, it's going to tumble down." The classic pastoral nightmare. There were a lot of marbles at stake for Paul because he realized that if matters didn't get straightened out in Corinth, the future of that whole apostolic church was jeopardized. So Paul waited on pins and needles for Titus's return.

As he waited in Troas, his ministry flourished remarkably. We know this because an open door is the same metaphor used to describe his extraordinary ministry in Ephesus—founding the church and spreading the gospel throughout Asia (cf. 1 Corinthians 16:8, 9; Acts 19:1–10). The ministry in Troas burgeoned while Paul waited and waited—and this doubled his anxiety. He was desperate to hear from Titus, and reluctant to leave the work of God—he was torn.

Paul's anxiety was excruciating. In fact, this experience in Troas was at the center of the most trying of all of Paul's sufferings. And Paul described it as the crown of his incredible sufferings in 11:28 where he says, "And, apart from other things, there is the daily pressure on me of my anxiety for all the churches." Paul agonized—"my spirit was not at rest because I did not find my brother Titus there" (2:13a).

Finally, when he could no longer stand the torment, he said good-bye to the open door: "So I took leave of them and went on to Macedonia" (v 13b). And even when he got to Macedonia, the anguish continued, as we see in 7:5 where he reveals, "For even when we came into Macedonia, our bodies had no rest, but we were afflicted at every turn—fighting without and fear within." Paul even became depressed in Macedonia (cf. 7:6)! This was a tough, tough time for the apostle.

Paul's Triumph (v. 14)

Paul uses this brief account of his tough time in Troas to set up a mighty restatement of his central theme: "But thanks be to God, who in Christ always leads us in triumphal procession, and through us spreads the fragrance of the knowledge of him everywhere" (2:14).

Triumphal procession. In order for us to understand what Paul is saying, we must visualize what the apostle has in mind in the technical term "triumphal procession." The Roman triumphal procession of Paul's day was the result of a long development that went back to the pre-Roman Etruscan dynasties.[2] A triumph of the first order featured the conquering general riding in a triumphal chariot drawn by four horses (and in some triumphs, even elephants).[3] He was clothed in a purple toga and a tunic stitched with palm fronds. In his hand he carried a scepter crowned by an eagle, and his face was tinted red in reference to the god Jupiter.[4]

In Paul's day, triumphal processions were conducted with grand theatrical pomp, always with a train of conquered subjects in a vast vanguard. Appian described General Pompey's third triumph in 61 B.C. as follows:

> [I]n the triumphal procession were two-horse carriages and litters laden with gold or other ornaments of various kinds, also the son of Hystaspes, the throne and scepter of Mithridates Eupator himself, and his image, eight cubits high, made of solid gold, and 75,100,000 drachmas of silver coin; also an infinite number of wagons carrying arms and beaks of ships, and a multitude of captives and pirates, none of them bound, but all arrayed in their native costumes.[5]

After this, Appian provides a long list of various kings, satraps, and generals led in procession. Add to this the pagan priests burning incense and musicians and cultic rhythms, and we have the picture.

The question is, what did this picture of the triumphal procession mean to Paul—how did he see himself in relation to it? The answer is, not as a victorious soldier (as some have thought), but as a conquered subject! Startling as this idea may be, the application goes beyond that to frankly shocking—because conquered enemies (or a representative group of them) were put to death at the end of the processional as a sacrifice to the Roman gods.[6] Thus Paul viewed himself as *God's captive being led to death*. This is confirmed by the only other occurrence of the Greek word translated "triumphal procession" in the New Testament, in Colossians 2:15 where God, having conquered the rulers of this age, has led them in triumphal procession and a public display of their destruction.

Understanding this, Scott Hafemann (whose doctoral thesis was centered on this text) says:

> Paul's metaphor in 2:14 may be "decoded" as follows: As the enemy of God's people, God had conquered Paul at his conversion call on the road to Damascus and was now leading him, as a "slave of Christ" (his favorite term for himself as an apostle), to death in Christ, in order that Paul might display or reveal the majesty, power, and glory of God, his conqueror.[7]

This understanding best fits the context and tenor of 2 Corinthians since suffering is a constant motif, and death is shorthand (metonymy) for suffering. This is evident from the beginning as we see the eight references to suffering or affliction with which the book opens in 1:3–11. As we read on, Paul will dramatically restate the idea in 4:8–12:

> We are afflicted in every way, but not crushed; perplexed, but not driven to despair; persecuted, but not forsaken; struck down, but not destroyed; always carrying in the body the death of Jesus, so that the life of Jesus may also be manifested in our bodies. For we who live are always being given over to death for Jesus' sake, so that the life of Jesus also may be manifested in our mortal flesh. So death is at work in us, but life in you.

And again in 6:9 he will say, "as unknown, and yet well known; as dying, and behold, we live; as punished, and yet not killed." And finally, death to self is the requirement for all who would follow Christ, because Christ himself said, "If anyone would come after me, let him deny himself and take up his cross and follow me" (Matthew 16:24).

The bottom line is this: Suffering/death (which is part and parcel with the cross) is the very thing God uses to make himself known. Therefore, Paul's driving point is that his suffering, pictured here as being led to death in the Roman procession, is the medium through which God is revealing himself.

Fragrance. As to the effectiveness of this ministry, it is diffuse and universal. "But thanks be to God, who in Christ always leads us in triumphal procession, and through us spreads the fragrance of the knowledge of him everywhere" (v. 14). The triumphal procession (during which the incense offered to the gods wafted over the processional) left its aroma lingering over the spectators long after the parade had passed by. So it was with the fragrance of Paul's ministry, so redolent with suffering and death. The apostolic procession smelled of God and his lingering grace.

Odors and fragrances are intrusive. You can be driving seventy miles an hour, and if a skunk has suffered displeasure along the highway in the last two hours, you will know it. Or perhaps you've had the experience of driving with your windows up and the air on and pulling up behind a car in which a man is smoking a cigar—and smelling it!

A friend of mine went to the post office on the military base to pick up an expected letter from his fiancée. In spite of his insistence, he was told repeatedly that it was not there. Why was he so sure that it was? Because he could smell his fiancée's perfumed missive. And he got the letter!

So it is when your life bears the crushed fragrance of suffering and daily death. As God led Paul in triumphal procession, the fragrance of God wafted over the ancient world. It could not be shut out. Grace lingered in its train. Even the imperial palace smelled it—and all the saints from Caesar's household will one day greet us (cf. Philippians 4:22).

Perhaps you have been sensing the dissonance of this as it interfaces with life around us—it is all so contrary to how we would like to consider the Christian life and Christian ministry. We would much prefer riding in the chariot with the conquering general (God himself!) while the fragrance of our triumph wafts out to the masses and gospel tracts rain down on the fortunate. But that is not the way it happens—the gospel emanates from our weaknesses and death.

Regarding Christian ministry, who do most people prefer to follow? What train do they readily jump on? Surely not that of the weak and dying. The preferred train is that of personality and performance and success. The "successful" ministry rides on *savoir faire* and a message dependent on technique and technology and knowing how to create "worship environments" and effect the latest in corporate management.[8]

Such ministry leaves no place for Christ because our Lord said, "'Take up your cross and follow me.'" The fragrance of Christ can only come through being led in triumphal procession as captives of the cross.

The Aroma of Christ (vv. 15, 16a)

The thought of incense introduced in verse 14 is further developed as Paul uses a fresh word for fragrance that is here rendered "aroma" or "sweet aroma," sometimes used as a woman's name, Euodia (cf. Philippians 4:2). As faithful followers of Christ, Paul and the apostles were the sweet aroma of Christ rising up to God, irrespective of the human response to their message. As they preached, the smoke of Christ's sacrifice ascended to God, well-pleasing to him. Thus, the primary audience in Heaven was glorified.

But the aroma also had a horizontal and mutually exclusive effect upon the people who heard—"to one a fragrance from death to death, to the other a fragrance from life to life" (v. 16a). The smell of incense would have had different connotations to the victors and to the captives in the procession—namely, life and death. The apostolic witness would be "a fragrance from life to life" for those who believed and "a fragrance from death to death" for those who rejected it. Truly, the effect of Christ's coming is either death or life, as Simeon had said when he held the baby Jesus in his arms: "Behold, this child is appointed for the fall and rising of many in Israel" (Luke 2:34). Those who believe on the Son have eternal life, but those who do not obey the Son will not see life, for the wrath of God abides on them (cf. John 3:36).[9]

It was just like that at my mother's funeral as my son preached Christ. Most smelled a fragrant aroma of grace; the funeral was a celebration of life. But some experienced "a fragrance from death to death." The same aroma is to one ineffable sweetness but to another an unpleasant odor. How is the aroma of Christ to you?

Paul's Sufficiency (vv. 16b, 17)

Given the call to follow Christ in his triumphal procession, captive to death, emblematic of suffering and weakness, and given the life-and-death effect of following Christ, the question naturally rises, "Who is sufficient for these things?" (v. 16). The automatic response is, "No one!" Paul would never claim self-sufficiency, but further, his sufficiency was in Christ, as he will state specifically in 3:5: "Not that we are sufficient in ourselves to claim anything as coming from us, but our sufficiency is from God."

Therefore, Paul affirmed his sufficiency *negatively* and *positively*. Negatively, he declared, "For we are not, like so many, peddlers of God's word" (2:17a). This denial was pointed at his detractors who actually did trade in the Word because the word "peddle" references traders who would dilute their wine with water or use false weights—all suggesting tampering with the Word or watering it down for personal gain. Paul never watered down God's Word to make it more palatable. He never looked to see which way the wind was blowing. He never practiced the homiletics of consensus. He never held back.

In point of fact, his suffering came from the fourfold positives of his personal integrity in communicating God's Word. First, he and his cohorts did it "as men of sincerity." His preaching, to use the Puritan William Ames's words, came "out of the inward affection of the heart without any affectation." Whenever Paul spoke, he was wholly sincere. His was an eloquence of the heart. Second, Paul spoke "as commissioned by God"—literally, "as *from* God." As he would later say, "God . . . gave us the ministry of reconciliation . . . entrusting to us the message of reconciliation" (cf. 5:18, 19). Paul was "an apostle of Christ Jesus" (1:1). His commission came from Messiah Jesus—and that is how he preached. Third, Paul ministered the Word "in the sight of God" (2:17)—literally, "before God." Thus, he did it humbly and with trembling and with no thought of praise. He was not like the Boston clergyman who prayed such a self-consciously ornate prayer that Monday's paper described it as "the most eloquent prayer ever offered to a Boston audience." God was Paul's audience. Fourth, Paul spoke "in Christ"—that is, in union with Christ. His preaching flowed from his incorporation in Christ.

Paul's fourfold integrity produced a sufficiency that was from God and set the standard for all who would minister. As Paul Barnett summarizes:

> All ministers must be as committed to the canon of the gospel as Paul was. That this verbal message is the word of God demands that those who speak it incarnate the integrity of God in their lives, mindful that they do so in the sight of the God before whose tribunal they must stand (see on 5:10). And, like Paul, they speak out of the fullness of a relationship with Christ, that is, as those "in Christ."[10]

I'm reminded of the lines we all know:

> Only one life,
> 'Twill soon be past,
> Only what's done for Christ
> Will last.

That is true. And truly I have no trouble accepting the brevity of life, be it a score of years or much less. I, in fact, embrace it.

But there is a parallel principle that is far more daunting—and that is to embrace the triumphal procession (which is at the heart of this great letter) and live its death principle to the fullest.

The way to live is to understand that weakness, suffering, and death are the means by which the fragrance of the knowledge of Christ wafts to the ends of the earth. And then to be like Paul and not fight it, but embrace it!

> Only what's done for Christ
> Will last.

7

Credentials of Ministry

2 CORINTHIANS 3:1–3

I REGULARLY RECITE TO MYSELF AND OTHER PREACHERS that though we can never *perfectly* embody the truth that we preach, we must be subject to it, long for it, pursue it, and, through prayer and repentance, make it as much a part of our lives as possible. It is imperative that this happen so that when we preach we will do so with utter, passionate sincerity like that of the Apostle Paul.

Of course, it's one thing for the preacher to desire this integrity and sincerity for himself and quite another to claim to have achieved it as Paul did in defending himself when he declared, "For we are not, like so many, peddlers of God's word, but as men of sincerity, as commissioned by God, in the sight of God we speak in Christ" (2:17). Notwithstanding the fact that it was all true of Paul and that he had said it in frank and honest defense of his ministry, Paul realized that he had left himself open to charges that he had heard before—charges of pride and alleged self-congratulation.

So the apostle immediately followed with a brace of questions calculated to mute his detractors and elevate his credentials: "Are we beginning to commend ourselves again? Or do we need, as some do, letters of recommendation to you, or from you?" (3:1). It wasn't that Paul believed that using letters of recommendation was wrong. Just the opposite, because the slow and unreliable communications of the ancient world necessitated letters of introduction and commendation. Paul often wrote recommendations himself on separate occasions commending Timothy to others (cf. 1 Corinthians 16:10, 11), and then Titus (cf. 2 Corinthians 8:22ff.), and then Phoebe (cf. Romans 16:1, 2), and even Timothy and Epaphroditus together (cf. Philippians 2:19–30). The book of Philemon is, in effect, a letter of recommendation. Nonetheless, such letters could easily be exaggerated or misleading—possibilities that Paul alludes to with the use of the anonymous designation "some" in his second question,

"Or do we need, as some do, letters of recommendation to you, or from you?" (v. 1b). It is generally agreed that the "many" who are "peddlers of God's word" (2:17) and the "some" here are the same people[1]—it is these shady characters who use and abuse written recommendations.

Given the situation, Paul's point is that he himself needed no such letters of recommendation, and that such letters would be ridiculous in the light of his lengthy association with the Corinthians. Paul, in effect, declares the absurdity of the idea that he needed human commendations so that he could then present his true credentials—*credentials of the heart authored by Christ and the Holy Spirit.* In presenting his credentials, Paul gives us the indispensable credentials of all true gospel ministry.

Paul's Letter (v. 2)

The apostle's opening assertion, "You yourselves are our letter of recommendation" (v. 2a), while no doubt cheering his supporters, would have caught his detractors off guard. What a novel idea—that the Corinthians were Paul's living, breathing letters of recommendation. It was a pulsing, metaphorical suggestion of powerful application: people as letters. A beautiful echo of this truth is found in Polycarp's second-century Epistle to the Philippians where he addresses the members of the church as those "among whom the blessed Paul laboured, who were his letters in the beginning."[2]

Here in 2 Corinthians, Paul's full sentence courses with significance: "You yourselves are our letter of recommendation, written on our hearts, to be known and read by all" (v. 2). The apostolic plural, "our hearts," means that Paul has the Corinthians written on his heart, the most interior and secret dimension of his being.[3] The heart in Biblical thought is the center of inner life and the seat of all functions of the soul. It is the place to which God turns and his Spirit speaks.[4] There at the epicenter of his being Paul has the Corinthians. They had been inscribed on his heart at the time of their conversion. And, as the Greek has it, they were written permanently on his heart, so that they could not slip away or be forgotten.[5]

I personally know what Paul describes here, because there are people written on my heart who are, so to speak, my spiritual children—and they are permanently there. Not a week goes by when I am not aware of them. They are living validations of my calling and ministry.

The superiorities of these living, breathing letters are explicit and implicit in Paul's description. They are incontrovertible evidence of the power of the gospel and the fruit of ministry. Written letters may easily mislead, but living letters will reveal the truth. Living heart letters are also more intimate. As Philip Hughes says, "This is a letter engraved in his heart, not flourished in his hand or carried in his luggage. It is something far more intimate than an external document of paper and ink, and at the same time far more permanent. It could not be forgotten, nor mislaid."[6] And such letters are accessible to all people because they are "known and read by all." The letters written with pen and ink will be read only by a limited number of people. But lives are read by all, even the illiterate. The church in Corinth was an open letter of Christ to the world, a declaration of his power and love for the whole world.

Also, by Paul's creation of this dynamic metaphor—"You yourselves are our letter"—the apostle shifted the proof of his apostleship from himself onto the shoulders of the Corinthians. If Paul is not genuine, then they are bogus. Paul is no longer on the defensive but is now on the offensive.[7]

Christ's Letter (v. 3a)

Having done this, Paul took care to make sure that the Corinthians understood that he was not the author of the letter: "And you show that you are a letter from Christ" (v. 3a). A letter of recommendation must always come from a third party, and the ultimate third-party recommender is Christ, the Messiah himself. By claiming Messiah as the author, Paul was able to claim higher authority for his credentials than his enemies could claim for theirs.[8]

Thus Paul's role was secondary, that of delivery—"a letter from Christ delivered by us." Since the literal meaning of "delivered" is "ministered," this suggests that Christ is the author and Paul is the scribe who ministers or serves by the preaching of the gospel.[9] Calvin says of this:

> [Paul] says that it was *ministered* by himself, likening himself, as it were to the ink and the pen. In other words, he makes Christ the Author and himself the instrument in order that his detractors may understand that they have Christ Himself to deal with if they go on speaking maliciously against His apostle.[10]

The effect of all this is stunningly remarkable. Paul has the Corinthians embedded as living letters in the deep interior of his heart, but they were written by Messiah himself.

The Spirit's Letter (v. 3b)

As Paul points to Christ as the ultimate author, his thinking courses back to the stone tablets of the old covenant upon which the Law was inscribed by the finger of God. So now he asserts the glorious superiority of the new covenant: "And you show that you are a letter from Christ delivered by us, written not with ink but with the Spirit of the living God, not on tablets of stone but on tablets of human hearts" (v. 3). God had promised Israel centuries before through the prophet Ezekiel that a time was coming when he would change their hearts: "And I will give them one heart, and a new spirit

I will put within them. I will remove the heart of stone from their flesh and give them a heart of flesh, that they may walk in my statues and keep my rules and obey them. And they shall be my people, and I will be their God" (Ezekiel 11:19, 20). This promise was reiterated by Ezekiel in the more personal second person "your": "And I will give you a new heart, and a new spirit I will put within you. And I will remove the heart of stone from your flesh and give you a heart of flesh" (36:26).

Paul's description of writing on "tablets of human hearts" was an explicit reference to Jeremiah 31, which so remarkably prophesies about the new covenant that was later inaugurated by Christ. The occasion of Jeremiah's prophecy was the reign of Josiah in 600 B.C. when—after the rediscovery of the Law and a time of national repentance and a public covenant to keep the Law—Israel *again* failed! In the midst of this tragic failure, God promised a new covenant—not conditional like the old, but unconditional—totally dependent upon the word of God:

> "Behold, the days are coming, declares the LORD, when I will make a new covenant with the house of Israel and the house of Judah, not like the covenant that I made with their fathers on the day when I took them by the hand to bring them out of the land of Egypt, my covenant that they broke, though I was their husband, declares the LORD. For this is the covenant that I will make with the house of Israel after those days, declares the LORD: I will put my law within them, and I will write it on their hearts. And I will be their God, and they shall be my people." (vv. 31–33)

The problem with the old covenant was that it was external. Its laws were written on stone (cf. Exodus 32:15, 16). As such they provided no internal power to live them out. Of course, there were great benefits in memorizing God's Word. Psalms 1 and 119 eloquently testify to the benefit of knowing the Law, because it can guide and influence the heart. But inscribing the heart was far beyond the power of unaided man. Something far more radical was needed—a spiritual heart operation.

Dr. Christiaan Barnard, the first surgeon ever to do a heart transplant, impulsively asked one of his patients, Dr. Philip Blaiberg,

> "Would you like to see your old heart?" At 8 p.m. on a subsequent evening, the men stood in a room of the Groote Schuur Hospital in Johannesburg, South Africa. Dr. Barnard went up to a cupboard, took down a glass container and handed it to Dr. Blaiberg. Inside that container was Blaiberg's old heart. For a moment he stood there stunned into silence—the first man in history ever to hold his own heart in his hands. Finally he spoke and for ten minutes plied Dr. Barnard with technical questions. Then he turned to

take a final look at the contents of the glass container, and said, "So this is my old heart that caused me so much trouble."

He handed it back, turned away and left it forever.[11]

This is a window into what Christ does. We remain the same people, but our hearts become radically new. God has written his laws within us. He has made us to be "partakers of the divine nature" (2 Peter 1:4). True, we still battle with our fleshly nature, but as members of Christ's Body, our spiritual inclinations are matched to God's laws (cf. John 14:15–17; 16:12, 13). They are no longer external and foreign to us but internal. "Therefore, if anyone is in Christ, he is a new creation. The old has passed away; behold, the new has come" (2 Corinthians 5:17).

Here we must note that along with a new heart the new covenant promised a new relationship, a new knowledge, and a true forgiveness. In addition to inscribing the Law on hearts, God promised, "And I will be their God, and they shall be my people" (Jeremiah 31:33b). In a transcendent sense, God is God to everyone who lives as he sustains them in all of life. But there is a tender, truer relationship of heart to heart, spirit to spirit—so that "I will be their God, and they shall be my people" is true in a deeper, more soul-satisfying way than those on the outside can imagine. "I will be their God" means God gives himself to us. And "they shall be my people" means he takes us to himself.

Also, along with writing God's Law on our hearts, he provides a new knowledge of himself. "And no longer shall each one teach his neighbor and each his brother, saying, 'Know the LORD,' for they shall all know me, from the least of them to the greatest, declares the LORD" (Jeremiah 31:34a). The old covenant was given corporately to Israel, including many among Israel who did not know God personally. But those who now experience the new covenant come one by one as they are born of God. Jesus defined eternal life: "And this is eternal life, that they know you the only true God, and Jesus Christ whom you have sent" (John 17:3). So those who partake of the new covenant all know Christ "from the least of them to the greatest." No one needs to say, "Know the LORD" to them, though, at the same time, "Know the LORD" remains an invitation to the whole world.

And, of course, those who have had the Spirit write on their hearts have true forgiveness—"'For I will forgive their iniquity, and I will remember their sin no more'" (Jeremiah 31: 34b). This is what the old covenant could not do. Under the old covenant, sins were never completely forgiven. Sinners then were covered, waiting for and pointing to true forgiveness through Christ's death. What good news the gospel is!

So God offers a new heart ("I will put my law within them, and I will write it on their hearts"), a new relationship ("And I will be their God, and they shall be my people"), a new knowledge ("And no longer shall each one teach his neighbor and each his brothers, saying, 'Know the LORD,' for they shall all know me, from the least to the greatest"), and a true forgiveness ("For I will forgive their iniquity, and will remember their sin no more").

The new covenant promises a new heart, a new relationship, a new knowledge, and true forgiveness! All of this, this vast ministry of the Spirit, was what Paul had brought to the Corinthians with the full-blown realities of the new covenant.

The Apostle Paul didn't need letters of recommendation from anyone. The Corinthians were his letter, and they were written on the very core of his soul, eternally. They could never be cast from his heart, much less forgotten. In fact, the apostle looked to the Corinthians' salvation as validation of his own ministry. And more, the letters in Paul's heart were "known and read by all." Though the letters were written in Paul's heart, he was not the author—Christ was! The Corinthian believers were missives of the Messiah. Paul had merely inscribed them through his preaching of the gospel.

And, again, all of this was nothing less than the long-awaited ministry of the new covenant done in the fullness of the Spirit. Paul goes on to say:

> Such is the confidence that we have through Christ toward God. Not that we are sufficient in ourselves to claim anything as coming from us, but our sufficiency is from God, who has made us sufficient to be ministers of a new covenant, not of the letter but of the Spirit. For the letter kills, but the Spirit gives life. (vv. 4–6)

Paul was credentialed, qualified, and sufficient for ministry.

Paul's presentation of his *credentials of the heart* supplies us with the credentials for true gospel ministry. Paul began by embracing his place in the triumphal procession to his death. As he put it later, "always being given over to death for Jesus' sake, so that the life of Jesus also may be manifested in our mortal flesh" (4:11). He did not try to manage the process but received it as from God's hand. So must we.

Thus Paul's life was redolent with the aroma of Christ. As he marched in his place, he was the fragrance of life to those who believed and the odor of death to those who rejected Christ, just as we must be.

His distinctive was that he did not peddle God's Word but preached it purely and with passionate sincerity, just as we are called to do.

His letters of commendation were living letters, as ours must be—written on the very center of his being, as it must be with us—written by Christ and humbly ministered, as we must do—fulfilling the promises of the new covenant, as does our divine calling.

8

Sufficient for Ministry

2 CORINTHIANS 3:4–6

VANCE HAVNER, beloved preacher, pastor, and evangelist during my early years of ministry, recalls the beginning of his itinerant ministry:

> Here I was, about to begin a full-time traveling ministry which meant sleeping in a different bed every week, changing food and climate, always getting adjusted and never getting adjusted—and utterly exhausted before I started! Any adviser would have called it sheerest folly. I felt more like quitting instead of undertaking a most demanding work which many strong men have tried and been unable to continue. If ever there was a chance to prove that God's strength is made perfect in weakness and that when we are weak we are strong, this was it. The Lord had the strength and I had the weakness so we teamed up! It is an unbeatable combination.[1]

And it was, as all who heard his inimitable, soul-searching messages will attest. In relation to what the Apostle Paul says about sufficiency for ministry in the brief text before us, Vance Havner's words serve as a cheerful invitation to apply the apostle's wisdom to our lives and ministries.

Frankly, Paul was confident about power and effectiveness in his ministry because, as he had just said, the Corinthians were "a letter from Christ" written by "the Spirit of the living God" (v. 3). With such living, breathing letters he had every reason to be confident, and so Paul summarizes, "Such is the confidence that we have through Christ toward God" (v. 4). Because his confidence is "through Christ" and not through any power of his own, and because his confidence is "toward God," it focuses on nothing earthly as its source or end.[2] Paul was supremely God-confident. And Paul confidently fought for the gospel and advised his gospel partners to be "not frightened in anything by your opponents . . . a clear sign to them of their destruction, but of your salvation" (Philippians 1:28).

Paul's Personal Insufficiency (v. 5a)

Confidence, however, is one thing; claims of self-sufficiency are quite another. So Paul was quick to renounce any measure of self-sufficiency, saying, "Not that we are sufficient in ourselves to claim anything as coming from us" (v. 5a). Paul was quite sincere. As Calvin emphasized, "this disclaiming of all merit is not . . . pretended modesty but he says what he really feels from the heart."[3] Thus with a fine irony Paul asserts that his confidence was rooted in his personal inadequacy—there was no self-generated capacity in him adequate to do ministry.

By emphasizing his insufficiency, Paul is consciously alluding to Moses' insistence of his inadequacy when God called him to lead Israel. His demurral and God's response were as follows:

> But Moses said to the LORD, "Oh, my LORD, I am not eloquent, either in the past or since you have spoken to your servant, but I am slow of speech and of tongue." Then the LORD said to him, "Who has made man's mouth? Who makes him mute, or deaf, or seeing, or blind? Is it not I, the LORD? Now therefore go, and I will be with your mouth and teach you what you shall speak." But he said, "Oh, my LORD, please send someone else." Then the anger of the LORD was kindled against Moses and he said, "Is there not Aaron your brother, the Levite? I know that he can speak well. Behold, he is coming out to meet you, and when he sees you, he will be glad in his heart. You shall speak to him and put the words in his mouth, and I will be with your mouth and with his mouth and will teach you both what to do. He shall speak for you to the people, and he shall be your mouth, and you shall be as God to him. And take in your hand this staff, with which you shall do the signs." (Exodus 4:10–17)

Subsequently, Moses' unparalleled leadership proved that in spite of his natural insufficiency, God made him sufficient. This pattern (human insufficiency—divine sufficiency) became the pattern for the calls of the great prophets of Israel. Gideon's insufficiency ("Please, Lord, how can I save Israel? Behold, my clan is the weakest in Manasseh, and I am the least in my father's house," Judges 6:15), was met with the Lord's sufficiency ("And the LORD said to him, 'But I will be with you, and you shall strike the Midianites as one man,'" v. 16). Isaiah's insufficiency ("Woe is me! For I am lost; for I am a man of unclean lips, and I dwell in the midst of a people of unclean lips; for my eyes have seen the King, the LORD of hosts!," Isaiah 6:5), was countered by one of the Lord's seraphim bearing a burning coal with which he touched Isaiah's mouth (cf. vv. 6, 7). Jeremiah's insufficiency ("Ah, Lord God! Behold, I do not know how to speak, for I am only a youth," Jeremiah 1:6) was allayed by the Lord ("But the Lord said to me, 'Do not say, "I am only a youth"; for to all to whom I send you, you shall go, and whatever I command you, you shall speak,'" v. 7). Ezekiel's innate sense of insufficiency was remedied by a vision of the glory of the Lord when the awesome wheels within wheels "full of eyes all around" approached his prostrate body, and God commanded him to stand, speak his words, and eat the scroll (cf. Ezekiel 1:1—3:11). When God's call came, human insufficiency became the ground of God's sufficiency.

So we see that if the Lord called Moses despite his inarticulateness, then no one can claim the prophets' excuses (Gideon's military weakness, Isaiah's sin, Jeremiah's youth, or Ezekiel's trepidation), or the weaknesses we may offer, as valid reasons to duck God's respective call. As Scott Hafemann so piquantly observes, "Indeed, the call of Moses demonstrates that these very obstacles are an essential part of the call itself, illustrating clearly that God's grace, not the prophet's strength, is the source of his sufficiency."[4] In a word, our weaknesses are part of, and the ground of, God's call to serve him. Vance Havner is right. Our weaknesses and his strength form an unbeatable combination!

The most eloquent statement of this truth that I know of comes from Oswald Chambers:

> God can achieve his purpose either through the absence of human power and resources, or the abandonment of reliance on them. All through history God has chosen and used nobodies, because their unusual dependence on him made possible the unique display of his power and grace. He chose and used somebodies only when they renounced dependence on their natural abilities and resources.[5]

A calligraphy of Chambers's words sits framed opposite my desk as a constant reminder and call to believe this at all times and to live out my ministry in consonance with this truth. This is because the great challenge is to believe this when I am most aware of my insufficiencies.

Paul's God-Given Sufficiency (vv. 5b, 6)

Truly, only a man who, like the Apostle Paul, is humbly aware of his complete weakness can know and prove the total sufficiency of God's grace. Thus Paul is able to balance his negative declaration, "Not that we are sufficient in ourselves," with the positive counterpoint, "but our sufficiency is from God" (v. 5). And Paul goes on to explain that his sufficiency comes from two things: 1) the sufficiency of the new covenant and 2) the sufficiency of the Spirit.

New-covenant sufficiency. First, the ministry of the new covenant of Christ was and is a ministry of transformation, whereas the old covenant of Moses did not bring about transformation. The old covenant began auspiciously, as Exodus describes it, with the giving of the Ten Commandments (cf. Exodus 19, 20), the reading of the Book of the Covenant (cf. Exodus 20:18—23:33), and the people's unanimous response, "All the words that the LORD has spoken we will do" (24:3). Following the people's promise, everything of significance was doused with the blood of the inaugural sacrifices—half the blood on the altar and the other half on the people and the Book of the Covenant (cf. 24:6, 8). The reason for this blood-drenching was to emphasize the seriousness of sin and to teach that the payment for sin is death.

But the weakness of the old covenant became immediately apparent. The people who doubly promised "All the words that the LORD has spoken we will do," and again, "All that the LORD has spoken we will do, and we will be obedient" couldn't do it for one day (24:3, 7)! This is because though the old covenant law was good, it was an *external* ordinance, and the blood of animal sacrifice could not take away sin.

So it was that after generations of repeated failure, God promised a new covenant to Jeremiah, recorded in 31:31–34, which prophesied the contours of transformation:

> Behold, the days are coming, declares the LORD, when I will make a new covenant with the house of Israel and the house of Judah, not like the covenant that I made with their fathers on the day when I took them by the hand to bring them out of the land of Egypt, my covenant that they broke, though I was their husband, declares the LORD. For this is the covenant that I will make with the house of Israel after those days, declares the LORD: I will put my law within them, and I will write it on their hearts. And I will be their God, and they shall be my people. And no longer shall each one teach his neighbor and each his brother, saying, "Know the LORD," for they shall all know me, from the least of them to the greatest, declares the LORD. For I will forgive their iniquity, and I will remember their sin no more.

The promise of *internal* renewal (the Law within, an intimacy with God, a personal relationship with God, and true forgiveness) all prophesied radical transformation.

Then, centuries later when Christ came to the final hours of his life and held up the cup at Passover saying, "This cup that is poured out for you is *the new covenant* in my blood" (Luke 22:20), it was as if he laid his hand on that passage in Jeremiah and said, "This day this Scripture is fulfilled before your eyes." Jesus Christ effects the radical transformation of the new covenant by his shed blood. Millions upon millions of such transformations have been worked in the lives of men and women for two millennia, and we ourselves share the flow of transformation in Christ.

Paul's point, in respect to himself, is that at the moment of his conversion and calling he had been made a minister of the new covenant.[6] At the apostle's conversion Christ had said:

> I am Jesus whom you are persecuting. But rise and stand upon your feet, for I have appeared to you for this purpose, to appoint you as a servant and witness to the things in which you have seen me and to those in which I will appear to you, delivering you from your people and from the Gentiles—to whom I am sending you to open their eyes, so that they may turn from darkness to light and from the power of Satan to God, that they may receive forgiveness of sins and a place among those who are sanctified by faith in me."(Acts 26:15–18)

Also Ananias, Christ's emissary to Paul, had said, "The God of our fathers appointed you to know his will, to see the Righteous One and to hear a voice from his mouth; for you will be a witness for him to everyone of what you have seen and heard" (Acts 22:14, 15).

The apostle could never get over the thrill of this. As he later wrote to Timothy, "I thank him who has given me strength, Christ Jesus our Lord, because he judged me faithful, appointing me to his service, though formerly I was a blasphemer, persecutor, and insolent opponent" (1 Timothy 1:12, 13).[7]

And herein lay Paul's adequacy. It was totally of God—"but our sufficiency is from God, who has made us sufficient to be ministers of a new covenant" (3:6). Like Moses and the Old Testament prophets after him, Paul also was made "sufficient in spite of insufficiency by the grace of God" (Hafemann).[8] This universal principle has been the experience of God's choice servants—for example, Hudson Taylor who wrote, "God chose me because I was weak enough. God does not do his work by large committees. He trains somebody to be quiet enough, and little enough, and then uses him."[9] Paul's insufficiency provided the ground for God's grace. But more, Paul was not a prophet, but an apostle of Christ. Paul's ministry was like that of a prophet, but he was an apostle of Messiah Jesus (cf. 1:1).[10]

Paul lived out his ministry with the unlimited sufficiency of the new covenant. The transforming power of the gospel attended all his ministry—transformation in many places including Antioch, Ephesus, Corinth, and even Rome—always with astonishing inward change. And so it has always been for those who embrace their weakness and God's new-covenant power.

Holy Spirit sufficiency. The corresponding promise to Jeremiah's prophecy of the new covenant was Ezekiel's promise of the Spirit:

> And I will give you a new heart, and a new spirit I will put within you. And I will remove the heart of stone from your flesh and give you a heart of flesh. And I will put my Spirit within you, and cause you to walk in my statutes and be careful to obey my rules. (Ezekiel 36:26, 27)

And Paul references this promise as we see in verse 6 in its entirety: "who has made us sufficient to be ministers of a new covenant, not of the letter but of the Spirit. For the letter kills, but the Spirit gives life." The problem with the old covenant was that the written Law (here called "the letter") provided no power to obey it because it was not accompanied by the empowering work of the Holy Spirit.

The Law wasn't bad. In fact, it was the holy, just, and good expression of God's will, and innately spiritual (cf. Romans 7:12, 14). And the Law itself did not kill. Rather it was the Law without the Spirit (the Law as "letter") that killed.

However, under the new covenant inaugurated by Christ, that condition changed for the better by means of the Holy Spirit who writes "not on tablets of stone but on tablets of human hearts" (v. 3b) and therefore enables the obedience of which Ezekiel prophesied: "And I will put my Spirit within you, and cause you to walk in my statutes and be careful to obey my rules" (36:27). St. Augustine eloquently observed, "*There* it was on tables of stone that the finger of God operated; *here* it was on the hearts of men. *There* it was outwardly that the law was registered, so that the unrighteous were terrified by it; *here* it was inwardly given, so that we might be justified by it."[11] And William Tyndale enthused, "For when Christ is preached, and the promises which God hath made in Christ are believed, the Spirit entereth the heart, and looseth the heart, and giveth lust to do the law, and maketh the law a lively thing in the heart."[12]

Paul had an incalculable advantage over Moses. Moses was charged to minister the Law to a stiff-necked people who would not obey it, but Paul was called to minister in the transforming power of the Spirit to a people who would be empowered to keep the Law as members of the new covenant.[13] What a glory it is to proclaim the gospel of the new covenant in Christ's blood—to proclaim radical transformation ("If any man in Christ, new creation!," 2 Corinthians 5:17, literal translation)—to proclaim the Spirit's empowerment to keep God's statutes—to preach complete forgiveness. Called to preach the gospel—could anything be more grand and glorious than this?

The dual sources for Paul's sufficiency for ministry were the new covenant's radical transformation of heart coupled with the life-changing, enabling power of the Holy Spirit—"Not that we are sufficient in ourselves to claim anything as coming from us, but our sufficiency is from God, who has made us sufficient to be ministers of a new covenant, not of the letter but of the Spirit. For the letter kills, but the Spirit gives life" (vv. 5, 6). Paul's weakness and the Lord's strength—it was an unbeatable combination, as it has always been, from the least to the greatest.

In August 1955 Canon H. K. Luce of Durham wrote a letter to *The Times* deploring Billy Graham's recent invitation to preach at Cambridge University. Billy Graham's approach, he argued, would be "unthinkable before a university audience . . . it would be laughed out of court." This provided a long and lively correspondence in England's great newspaper.[14]

Though Billy, age thirty-six, was unusually experienced, the thought of conducting a mission at Cambridge weighed heavily upon him. His biographer William Martin notes:

> Graham, ever insecure about his lack of advanced theological education, dreaded the meetings and feared that a poor showing might do serious harm to his ministry and affect 'which way the tide will turn in Britain.' Had he been able to do so without a complete loss of face, he would have canceled the meetings or persuaded some better-qualified man to replace him.[15]

And, indeed, Billy, writing in his own biography forty years later, quotes his own personal letter to John Stott that confirms his trepidation:

> I have been deeply concerned and in much thought about our Cambridge mission this autumn. . . . I do not know that I have ever felt more inadequate and totally unprepared for a mission. As I think over the possibility for messages, I realize how shallow and weak my presentations are. In fact, I was so overwhelmed with my unpreparedness that I almost decided to cancel my appearance, but because plans have gone so far perhaps it is best to go through with it. . . . However, it is my prayer that I shall come in the demonstration and power of the Holy Spirit.[16]

Thus the great evangelist chronicled his weakness and his need of the Spirit's power. Billy's arrival in Cambridge was unsettling. The opening night of the Cambridge Mission was Sunday, November 6, the day after Guy Fawkes Day, a day of fireworks, bonfires, and general revelry. As Billy spoke to his team in the Debating Hall of the Union, a firecracker was tossed through an open window despite a strong police presence around the building. Billy also met with C. S. Lewis, newly arrived in Cambridge, and the conversation went well, though Lewis's parting remark was unsettling: "You know you have many critics, but I have never met one of your critics who knows you personally."[17] Had Lewis met *anyone* who knew Billy personally?

The meetings were held in Great St. Mary's, the university church in the epicenter of Cambridge. And as young Billy sat in his Geneva gown and doctoral hood, every gallery and niche of the church was occupied.

Graham preached for three nights, but the results were modest. His sermons were, by his own estimation, too academic. He knew that he was not getting through to the students' hearts. He felt he was preaching to please his audience rather than the Holy Spirit. So Billy Graham sought the Lord.

Then came the breakthrough. Following his third sermon, the day after his thirty-seventh birthday, Billy Graham set aside his university-focused sermons and preached to ordinary human souls.[18] Billy Graham's weakness plus the all-sufficient, transforming gospel of the new covenant plus his dependence upon the Holy Spirit wrought a mighty ministry in Cambridge. Afterward John Stott wrote his praying congregation, "History will begin to show, but only eternity will finally reveal, how much was accomplished during that week."[19] I happen to know of another great evangelist who came to Christ that week—David Watson.

Those whom God uses have always been aware of their insufficiency and weakness, be it Moses or Gideon or Isaiah or Jeremiah or Ezekiel or Paul or Peter or John. And it was their insufficiency that invited the sufficiency of God.

God is not looking for gifted people or people who are self-sufficient. He is looking for inadequate people who will give their weakness to him and open themselves to the ministry of the Holy Spirit and the transforming grace of the new covenant as it is ministered by Christ Jesus himself.

If God is calling you, do not hide behind your weakness. I don't know what he may be calling you to do—it may be a worldwide mission, it may be teaching a Sunday school class, it may be ministering to children, it may be reaching out in your neighborhood, it may be stepping up at work. But if he's calling you, don't hide behind your weakness—your weakness is the ground for his calling. Follow God, and he will use your weakness as an occasion for his power.

And if you are feeling terrifying stirrings within your soul as he nudges you outside your comfort zone, where you will be out of your depth (but you know that he is calling you), give your weakness to him and accept his sufficiency.

This is the way it was for Moses and for all the prophets and for the apostles and for all who follow in their stead—everyone who serves the Lord. God uses people who are weak because of their unique ability to depend upon him.

9

A More Glorious Ministry

2 CORINTHIANS 3:7–18

IT IS UNIVERSALLY AGREED that Paul's teaching in the third chapter of 2 Corinthians amounts to a commentary on Exodus 32—34, the account of God's response to Israel's breaking its promise to keep the Law. At Sinai, Israel had twice promised that the people would keep *all* the words of the Law (cf. Exodus 24:3–7). But before Moses could descend the mountain with the divinely inscribed tablets, Israel had broken its promise by worshiping Aaron's golden calf. And Moses angrily dashed the commandments to pieces at the foot of Sinai (cf. Exodus 32:19). Israel's sin was of such proportion that the nation's complete annihilation by God was only averted by Moses' intercessions (cf. 32:11–14, 31–34).

However, the breaking of the covenant was not without consequences—monumental consequences. God's presence would no longer accompany Israel, as God explained: "If for a single moment I should go up among you, I would consume you" (33:5). Thus God's presence withdrew from the people as Moses pitched the tent of meeting "outside the camp, far off from the camp" (v. 7). There, in the separated "tent of meeting," with a pillar of cloud rising over the entrance, Moses would speak to God (cf. vv. 9–11).

During Moses' celebrated intercession in verses 14–16, he asked that God's presence would go with him, and God promised to grant his request (v. 17). And it was then that God promised to show Moses his glory (cf. vv. 18–23). So Moses cut two new stone tablets and ascended Sinai again, where the Lord descended in a cloud, hid Moses in a cleft in the rock, and proclaimed his glory as he passed by, allowing Moses to see the afterglow of his presence (cf. 33:19–23; 34:5–7). As Moses worshiped, his singular petition was for God's presence: "If now I have found favor in your sight, O Lord, please let the Lord go in the midst of us" (34:9a). Following Moses' prayer came the second giving of the Law. "So he was there with the LORD forty days and forty nights. He neither ate bread nor drank water. And he wrote on the tablets the words of the covenant, the Ten Commandments" (34:28).

As to Moses' repeated requests for the Lord's glorious presence among God's people, surprise! Moses *himself* became the mediator of God's presence and glory to Israel.

> When Moses came down from Mount Sinai, with the two tablets of the testimony in his hand as he came down from the mountain, Moses did not know that the skin of his face shone because he had been talking with God. Aaron and all the people of Israel saw Moses, and behold, the skin of his face shone, and they were afraid to come near him. But Moses called to them, and Aaron and all the leaders of the congregation returned to him, and Moses talked with them. Afterward all the people of Israel came near, and he commanded them all that the LORD had spoken with him in Mount Sinai. And when Moses had finished speaking with them, he put a veil over his face. Whenever Moses went in before the LORD to speak with him, he would remove the veil, until he came out. And when he came out and told the people of Israel what he was commanded, the people of Israel would see the face of Moses, that the skin of Moses' face was shining. And Moses would put the veil over his face again, until he went in to speak with him. (vv. 29–35)

The people were correct to be so fearful of Moses' unveiled countenance because it indicated God's presence and consuming judgment. Moses therefore veiled his face to protect Israel from being destroyed. And we must add that is the only reason he veiled his face. His veiling was not, as some suppose, to hide the fading glory but, again, to protect Israel. As Scott Hafemann explains:

> Moses' veiled mediation of God's glory permits his presence to remain in Israel's midst without destroying her. In this regard, Moses' veiling himself is an act of mercy. At the same time, the very fact that Moses must veil his face is an act of judgment because of the hardness of Israel's heart. This veil not only preserves Israel from being destroyed; it also keeps her from being transformed.[1]

This understood, Paul's defense and argument in 2 Corinthians 3:7–18 is essentially this: Moses' ministry of the old covenant did not provide Israel the immediate and continual access to the glorious presence of God that came through Paul's ministry of the new covenant. Thus Paul's ministry is more glorious!

So we can see that frail, humble Paul dared to place his ministry above that of Moses. His method here is first to compare the glory of the two ministries (vv. 7–11) and then to state his conclusions in the remaining verses (vv. 12–18).

The Greater Glory of Paul's Ministry (vv. 7–11)

Paul begins with three comparisons that follow the Hebrew light-to-heavy (lesser-to-greater) form of argument.

More glory. The first is in verses 7, 8. *Lesser:* "Now if the ministry of death, carved in letters on stone, came with such glory that the Israelites could not gaze at Moses' face because of its glory, which was being brought to an end . . ." *Greater:* ". . . will not the ministry of the Spirit have even more glory?" The Law came with great glory. It was so great that it exercised a ministry of judgment and death on Israel, which could not keep the Law for even a day! That is why the people feared to gaze upon the reflected glory on Moses' face—and why its effect (judgment) was continually being "brought to an end" by Moses' repeated veilings of the glory.[2]

Therefore, if Moses' ministry came by such glory that it had to be veiled, how much more glorious is Paul's unveiled "ministry of the Spirit" that constantly exposes God's people to his glory and transforming power.

Again glory. The following lesser-to-greater comparison reads: *Lesser*: "For if there was glory in the ministry of condemnation, the ministry of righteousness . . ." *Greater*: ". . . must far exceed it in glory. Indeed, in this case, what once had glory has come to have no glory at all, because of the glory that surpasses it" (vv. 9, 10). "The ministry of condemnation" refers to the effects of Moses' ministry among Israel following the worship of the golden calf. Paul's "ministry of righteousness" lines up with what the prophets foretold about the ministry of the Spirit: "And I will give them one heart, and a new spirit I will put within them. I will remove the heart of stone from their flesh and give them a heart of flesh, that they may walk in my statutes and keep my rules and obey them" (Ezekiel 11:19, 20; cf. 36:24–29).

Today there is no condemnation for those who are in Christ Jesus, as Paul declares in Romans 8. The old covenant was indeed glorious itself. But the effect of the new covenant is so much more glorious in its ministry of righteousness—the abiding locus of God's glory is in Paul's ministry.

More glory again. The third comparison caps Paul's argument for the surpassing glory of his ministry. *Lesser:* "For if what was being brought to an end came with glory . . ." *Greater:* ". . . much more will what is permanent have glory" (v. 11). In contrast to Moses' ministry of glory that was "continually being rendered inoperative,"[3] the glory of Paul's ministry is permanent—and therefore far more glorious.

Paul's three-pronged logic declares, first, that his ministry is more glorious than that of Moses because of its unlimited exposure to God's glory; second, that his ministry is surpassingly glorious because it is a ministry of righteousness; and third, his ministry is superior to Moses' because his ministry is permanent.

How stunning! The Apostle Paul, who embraced weakness and death as the ground for power in his ministry (cf. 2:14–17), has the temerity to place himself above Moses as to the surpassing glory of his ministry.

What a sobering declaration to Paul's detractors in any age. Think twice (three times!) when you hear the urbane jibes tossed Paul's way by popular culture. It is a puzzle to me when I hear Christians being dismissive of Paul who was *the* competent minister of the new covenant.

The Surpassing Effects of Paul's Ministry (vv. 12–18)

This driving contrast between Moses' and Paul's ministries intensifies as Paul applies the contrasts, focusing on the effects of the two ministries.

Boldness. Because of the superiority of his ministry Paul is bold: "Since we have such a hope, we are very bold, not like Moses, who would put a veil over his face so that the Israelites might not gaze at the outcome of what was being brought to an end" (vv. 12, 13) or "nullified." Moses repeatedly veiled his face so that the hard-hearted Israelites might not gaze at "the outcome" (i.e., the judgment) of that which was being rendered ineffective by the veil.[4] But Paul preached with barefaced boldness because he knew that the glory of the new-covenant ministry was not to be veiled.

Paul always got it straight and gave it straight—with no cant or double-talk. He may have come to the Corinthians in fear and trembling and much weakness, but when he spoke it was with fearless candor.[5]

Unveiling. Long after Moses and his veil were no more, a veil of hardness covered the hearts of Israel, as Paul explains: "But their minds were hardened. For to this day, when they read the old covenant, that same veil remains unlifted, because only through Christ is it taken away. Yes, to this day whenever Moses is read a veil lies over their hearts" (vv. 14, 15). Paul witnessed the veiling in his day when, despite the weekly Sabbath readings of Moses, the people's *hearts* remained veiled.

The veil was not, and is not, intellectual but rather moral—a heart-veil. "The 'veil [that] covers [Israel's] heart' (v. 15b) does not refer to a cognitive inability because of a lack of a special spiritual endowment, but to a volitional inability as a result of a hardened disposition."[6] Today those who accept the message of Scripture will go where the text leads, which is always to the Messiah who takes the veil away.

So Paul declares, "But when one turns to the Lord, the veil is removed" (v. 16). Do you remember when the veil was lifted by Christ from your heart? It happened to me on the very day I believed as I read Romans 10:9, 10: "If you confess with your mouth that Jesus is Lord and believe in your heart that God raised him from the dead, you will be saved. For with the heart one believes and is justified, and with the mouth one confesses and is saved." As I read this, it was as if the words lifted from the page and streamed up through my eyes and into my heart. That night other texts, before incomprehensible, were filled with light. The half-century old red pencil markings on the India paper pages of my tiny Bible testify to the veil's lifting. And over the years I have come to see the Messiah ever more clearly as the central theme and coming consummation of all of Scripture.

Has the veil been removed from your heart? Have the Scriptures become alive? Does Christ make sense to you? Or perhaps this is just beginning to happen to you. Then pray, asking Christ to strip away the veil. If you do, I can promise you, on the basis of God's Word, that he will.

Freedom. The dramatic picture of Christ's hand lifting the veil from our darkened hearts pulses with liberation and freedom and, of course, reality. So Paul declares, "Now the Lord is the Spirit, and where the Spirit of the Lord is, there is freedom" (v. 17). "Lord" can either refer to God the Father or Christ the Son.[7] But what is emphasized here is the close identification between the Lord and the Spirit. So Moses' experience of the Lord (Yahweh) in the Tent of Meeting is equivalent to the experience of the Spirit in Paul's ministry.[8]

Unveiled before God, Moses was liberated to love and serve God and his people. Here in 2 Corinthians Paul's emphasis is that the freedom to obey the Law comes from the power of the Spirit—"where the Spirit of the Lord is, there is freedom"—and that this is authentic freedom. Through the work of the Holy Spirit there is liberation to do the right thing, to consider others first, to love others as we ought, to forgive the unforgivable, to return good for evil. And more, to "love the Lord your God with all your heart and with all your soul and with all your mind and with all your strength" (Mark 12:30). Thus, "Where the Spirit of the Lord is, there is freedom." Indeed!

Transformation. The culminating effect of Paul's ministry is transformation. "And we all, with unveiled face, beholding the glory of the Lord, are being transformed into the same image from one degree of glory to another. For this comes from the Lord who is the Spirit" (v. 18). When Moses removed his veil in the Tent of Meeting and spoke with the Lord face to face, he experienced a *physical* transformation when his face became luminous. At the same time he underwent a sanctifying *moral* transformation as, being exposed to God's presence and revelation, his character and will became so marked with God's image that he lived in profound obedience to God's glorious revelation and in fact delivered the Ten Commandments to his people.

Moses' temporary exposure to the glory of the Lord worked a mighty transformation in and upon him. But the new-covenant ministry of Paul is even more transforming because our exposure is constant and continuous (there is no veil). And more, it works in the reverse order of Moses' experience, first by effecting a *moral* transformation into God's image as all "are being transformed into the same image from one degree of glory to another" (v. 18). We express the image of God by living according to the commandments, which express his nature. The change is progressive, so that willing exposure to the sunlight of God's presence will burn his image ever deeper into our character and will. And ultimately, at Christ's appearance, we will undergo a *physical* transformation in glory. This is what Paul's ministry offered, and this is the grand and great difference between his and Moses' ministry.

The old covenant had no such power. However, I have seen this power countless times when the most impossibly proud or impossibly profane or impossibly self-centered or impossibly malicious or impossibly cruel or vile or self-righteous have been transformed and are being transformed into the image of Christ.

And one day they will be like Christ. A. J. Gossip, the celebrated Scottish preacher, remembered Principal Rainy's ringing challenge at the Communion Table in Edinburgh:

> 'Do you believe your faith?' he asked; 'do you believe this I am telling you? Do you believe a day is coming, really coming, when you will stand before the throne of God, and the angels will whisper together and say, 'How like Christ he is'? That is not easy to believe. And yet not to believe is blasphemy. For that, not less than that, is what Christ promises.[9]

Christians, do you believe your faith? Do you believe that the veil has been lifted by Christ? Do you believe that he has freed you to love him and others as you ought? Do you believe that Christ is transforming you now and that one day you will be like him?

Knowing yourself (as I know myself) you may find this challenges your belief. But not to believe is blasphemy. For this is what Christ promises.

10

Doing Ministry

2 CORINTHIANS 4:1–6

C. H. SPURGEON, in his classic *Lectures to My Students*, in the chapter properly titled "The Minister's Fainting Fits," describes the pressures upon the Christian minister to lose heart.

> Our work, when earnestly undertaken, lays us open to attacks in the direction of depression. Who can bear the weight of souls without sometimes sinking to the dust? Passionate longings after men's conversion, if not fully satisfied (and when are they?), consume the soul with anxiety and disappointment. To see the hopeful turn aside, waxing more bold in sin—are not these sights enough to crush us to the earth? The kingdom comes not as we would, the reverend name is not hallowed as we desire, and for this we must weep. How can we be otherwise than sorrowful, while men believe not our report, and the divine arm is not revealed? All mental work tends to weary and to depress, for much study is a weariness of the flesh; but ours is more than mental work—it is heart work, the labour of our inmost soul. . . . Such soul-travail as that of a faithful minister will bring on occasional seasons of exhaustion, when heart and flesh will fail.[1]

Such pressures were not unique to the Victorian ministry because weary hearts have been common to the ministerial calling from the beginning. Spurgeon's words will find sympathetic resonance in any heart acquainted with ministry.

No one has ever experienced more of what Spurgeon so aptly describes than the Apostle Paul. Consider the litany of deadly ministerial pressures that Paul describes in chapter 11 capped by his concluding comment, "Apart from other things, there is the daily pressure on me of my anxiety for all the churches. Who is weak, and I am not weak? Who is made to fall, and I am not indignant?" (vv. 28, 29). This summary remark makes Spurgeon's pressures pale by comparison. And more, the specifics of the personal attacks in Corinth against Paul (which Paul references in Chapter 4) were especially galling—namely, that his ministry was weak and fading, that he was dishonest, that he effectually corrupted God's Word, and that he hindered the preaching of the gospel. These were hurtful, wicked, unfounded accusations, and especially so in light of Paul's integrity.

But did Paul faint under these attacks? In no way! Rather, he defends the integrity of his ministry with a point-by-point response to his detractors. And as a result he gives the church a dynamic profile of how the ministry of the gospel ought to be done.

With Heart (v. 1)

Paul's opening response—"Therefore, having this ministry by the mercy of God, we do not lose heart"—references the surpassingly glorious ministry of the new covenant as compared to Moses' ministry under the old covenant in that it effects a removal of the veil of unbelief, the liberation of the Holy Spirit, and transformation into the image of the Lord. Having a ministry of such splendor left Paul with no place for faintheartedness but only for boldness (cf. 3:12).

Paul was perpetually conscious that he had this ministry "by the mercy of God," given to him at the moment of his conversion on the road to Damascus when he was knocked to the ground by the flash of Christ's glory and was commissioned to go to the Gentiles (cf. Acts 9:3–9, 15–17).[2] Such mercy! And he could never get over it. As he later wrote to Timothy as the chief of sinners, "I thank . . . Christ Jesus our Lord, because he judged me faithful, appointing me to his service, though formerly I was a blasphemer, persecutor, and insolent opponent. But I received mercy . . ." (1 Timothy 1:12, 13). His apostleship was solely due to God's mercy. Therefore, the combination of this mercy and the astonishingly surpassing glory of his ministry heartened him and kept him from losing heart.

Paul's critics imagined that the difficulties and reversals that dogged his ministry had disheartened him, as they would any man. But Paul was energized for ministry. In a couple more paragraphs he will reaffirm this, saying, "So we do not lose heart. Though our outer nature is wasting away, our inner nature is being renewed day by day" (4:16).

Spurgeon was right in delineating discouragement as one of the ministry's great risks. Loss of heart can bring disaster. But these two things will ground our hearts: 1) God's merciful call, and 2) the surpassing glory of the gospel ministry.

> He stands in Christ's stead; his message is the Word of God; around him are immortal souls; the Saviour, unseen, is beside him; the Holy Spirit broods over the congregation; angels gaze upon the scene; and heaven and hell await the issue."
>
> Matthew Simpson[3]

What glory! How heartening!

With Forthrightness (v. 2)

In addition to being heartened and energized by God's gift of ministry at his conversion,[4] Paul naturally embraced forthrightness as his method of ministry.

No subterfuge. This involved the rejection of all deceit: "But we have renounced disgraceful, underhanded ways" (v. 2a)—literally, "the hidden things of shame," the kinds of things people do but only under cover, and with shame if exposed.[5]

Specifically, Paul adds, "We refuse to practice cunning"—"a cunning readiness to adopt any device or trickery for the achievement of ends which are anything but altruistic" (Hughes).[6] This is Machiavellian cunning in which "the end justifies the means" regardless of the means employed.[7] Paul uses the same word "cunning" again in 11:3 where he describes Satan's work saying, "the serpent deceived Eve by his cunning." This is the slyness and stealth of the dark side. Such cunning will stop at nothing. The cunning ploys vary, but the same self-interest pervades.

I once received an expensive brochure that featured eight separate pictures of a self-styled "evangelist" designed to instill confidence in his power. It featured photos of him praying by a waterfall and praying with his hands on a pile of letters asking for prayer. Another photo showed him holding a baby. In another he was shaking the hand of a poor man. But what really got my attention was the offer of a specially blessed handkerchief that had been dipped in the Jordan River and that, if prayerfully applied, would bring healing. The cost? About twenty-five dollars in today's economy.

Such conduct was anathema to Paul. He had renounced cunning when he was called to ministry, and he had never come close to it. Moreover, his rejection of trickery was an oblique attack on his accusers' underhanded, behind-the-back attempts to bring him down.

Nor did Paul "tamper with God's word." He did not falsify it or water it down.[8] Such tampering invariably edits God's Word and exalts the preacher. When Henry Irving's version of Shakespeare appeared, a reviewer wrote, "His productions at the Lyceum Theater, London, interpreted Irving rather than Shakespeare. Everything was done with lavish care. Nothing was cut, except Shakespeare."[9] So it is with much preaching: nothing is cut but the Bible. This is the methodology of crass liberalism, which operates on the premise that what the text states can, by no means, be true.[10]

But it is far more common for the evangelical preacher to edit God's Word: 1) by removing the text from its context, and using it to say whatever the preacher likes, 2) by moralizing the text, so that it is reduced to an ethical maxim that fits any religion, 3) by using the text to promote hobbyhorses, and 4) by dogmatic insistence that the text says things it does not truly say. This homiletical hocus-pocus has subtle roots such as the desire to be clever and popular or synthetically relevant or intellectually respectable or to make the gospel more acceptable. But most often God's Word gets watered down by the preacher's laziness. He simply will not do the hard work to engage and preach a text in its context.

Openness instead. In stark contrast, Paul embraces openness and candor: "but by the open statement of the truth we would commend ourselves to everyone's conscience in the sight of God" (v. 2b). Paul would admonish Timothy, "Do your best to present yourself to God as one approved, a worker who has no need to be ashamed, rightly handling the word of truth" (2 Timothy 2:15). "Rightly handling" is based on the Greek word *orthos* ("straight"). So Paul was charging Timothy "to impart the truth *without deviation, straight, undiluted*"[11]—to get it straight and give it straight!

Thus, by forthright openness of his ministry Paul solicited the approval of all, because he was convinced that when people were true to their consciences, they would be compelled to acknowledge that his ministry was one of integrity. The further fact that he conducted his straight-on ministry "in the sight of God" means that his ultimate concern in everything was God's approval (cf. 1 Corinthians 4:3, 4; 2 Corinthians 5:10). God was his primary audience; thus Paul preached the undiluted Word of God with bold simplicity and clarity.

With Penetrating Perception (vv. 3, 4)

As Paul preached the simple gospel, he perceived the interior reasons for its rejection:

> And even if our gospel is veiled, it is veiled to those who are perishing. In their case the god of this world has blinded the minds of the unbelievers, to keep them from seeing the light of the gospel of the glory of Christ, who is the image of God. (vv. 3, 4)

Veiled. Recently I heard a member of my congregation tell how she had repeatedly explained the gospel to another woman who simply did not get it, though she apparently wanted to. So finally she said to the woman, "You have a veil over your heart. And you need to pray that God will remove it." A few weeks later the woman called, elated, as she explained that she had gone to bed the night before perplexed, but when she awoke that morning everything was clear. The veil was gone forever.

Nothing had been wrong with the gospel. The gospel had been veiled *to* the woman because it was veiled *in* her. The veil was in her heart and mind, not over the gospel. As Calvin put it, "the blindness of unbelievers in no way detracts from the clearness of the gospel, for the sun is no less resplendent because the blind do not perceive it."[12]

Blinded. Paul knew firsthand what it was like to be blinded to the truth because he had been in the bonds of darkness before being dazzled by the glory of Christ on the Damascus road. But from the apostle's conversion onward, the light of Christ filled his existence. His mission, in fact, became, "to open their eyes, so that they may turn from darkness to light and from the power of Satan to God" (Acts 26:18).

Because Christ was the image of God, he possessed and shined forth God's glory. Colossians 1:15 states of Christ, "He is the image [*ikon*] of the invisible God." Hebrews 1:3 explains of Christ, "He is the radiance of the glory of God and the exact imprint of his nature." This is why the Apostle John concludes the prologue of his Gospel by saying, "No one has ever seen God; the only God [Jesus Christ], who is at the Father's side, he has made him known" (1:18). And later we read that Jesus said, "Whoever has seen me has seen the Father" (14:9).

If you don't get it, if the glory of Christ sounds like so much mystical jargon, if the gospel doesn't make sense to you, you need to ask God to remove the veil. I can promise you that if you do, the logic of the gospel and the transforming glory of Christ will become the clear, organizing reality of your existence.

By Exalting Christ (v. 5)

The antidote to the veil of blindness is lifting up Christ, to which Paul gives timeless, proverbial expression: "For what we proclaim is not ourselves, but Jesus Christ as Lord, with ourselves as your servants for Jesus' sake" (v. 5). The phrase "Jesus Christ as Lord" is shorthand for the gospel.

First, "Jesus" (i.e., "the Lord saves"), the name given to the Son of God at his incarnation, signifies that the Lord's salvation came when Jesus was born. That is why aged Simeon swept baby Jesus into his arms when they brought him into the temple and declared, "Lord, now you are letting your servant depart in peace, according to your word; for my eyes have seen your salvation" (Luke 2:29, 30). Second, the title "Christ" (i.e., "the Anointed," "the Messiah") speaks of his being the fulfillment of Old Testament prophecy—". . . that Christ died for our sins in accordance with the Scriptures, that he was buried, that he was raised on the third day in accordance with the Scriptures" (1 Corinthians 15:3, 4). Third, "Lord" declares the fact that the crucified Christ has been exalted by God through the resurrection to the position of lordship in Heaven and that he is the ruler of the world. Ultimately the entire cosmos will confess this: ". . . so that at the name of Jesus every knee should bow, in heaven and on earth and under the earth, and every tongue confess that *Jesus Christ is Lord*, to the glory of God the Father" (Philippians 2:10, 11).

Jesus Christ is no princelet or kinglet, and not merely a king, but "King of kings and Lord of lords" (Revelation 19:16). Thus when you confess that "Jesus Christ is Lord" you at once confess his *incarnation* and his *Messiahship* and his *lordship,* sealed by his glorious resurrection as he now forever reigns.

Believing that Jesus is Lord is indispensable to salvation. Remember the text through which I was saved? It was Romans 10:9, "because, if you confess with your mouth that *Jesus is Lord* and believe in your heart that God raised him from the dead, you will be saved." When I confessed this, it was due to the regenerating work of the Holy Spirit in my life because, as Paul says in 1 Corinthians 12:3, "No one can say 'Jesus is Lord' except in the Holy Spirit."

The question of all questions is: do you believe in Jesus Christ as Lord in all that phrase demands? If so, the Spirit of God is operative in your soul.

The corollary to such a view of Christ is that Paul (along with all true ministers of the new covenant) did not and do not proclaim themselves but declare only that they serve the church for Jesus' sake. "Paul was a minister, not a master; a servant, not a lord" (Hughes).[13] Truly, no man can fancy himself great and at the same time declare that God is great. The proclamation that "Jesus Christ is Lord" is the province of the humble alone.

Paul's proverbial declaration stands as a rebuke to any minister of the gospel who aspires to greatness or fame. Any preacher who fails to preach "Jesus Christ as Lord" or fails to be a servant "for Jesus' sake" has forsaken the apostolic ministry of the new covenant.

With Creation Confidence (v. 6)

Paul was no armchair theorist writing theological abstractions. He knew what it was to be blind and then to see. His encounter on the Damascus road at high noon when he "saw on the way a light from heaven, brighter than the sun" (Acts 26:13) that was in fact "the light of the knowledge of the glory of God in the face of Jesus Christ" (v. 6)—that was the moment when the veil was stripped away, and his blind heart saw, and he was transformed.

And more, Paul knew that his experience was a paradigm of what every believer has quietly experienced in Christ. All believers were blind before they saw. And the same Spirit who opened Paul's eyes opens the eyes of all who will believe.

And here's the driving point: it is nothing less than God's creational power that does it! "For God, who said, 'Let light shine out of darkness,' has shone in our hearts to give the light of the knowledge of the glory of God in the face of Jesus Christ" (v. 6). The God who said, "Let light shine out of darkness," so that the darkness of the primeval world was banished by light, is the one who does it for us. Think of it. The God of creation, who first called light out of darkness, is the only one who has the power to overcome our blindness. And he does it with a word!

"Let there be light!"
thus spoke the Lord;
thus we were made
and thus restored.
Christ's conquering Word
created all;
our shining hope:
his sovereign call.

John Piper, 1976[14]

There is no one beyond the creative and re-creative power of God. He who spoke the worlds into existence and with a word birthed light and plants and birds and sea creatures and animals and us—this God can illumine us and transform us from glory to glory with a word. No one is beyond his love. No one is beyond his grace. And no one is beyond his creational power.

The symmetries and beauty of Paul's thought in this paragraph are remarkable. Paul's defense of himself as a minister of the new covenant has given us an exposition of how the ministry of the gospel ought to be conducted.

- Paul ministered with *heart* because in God's mercy he was met at Damascus and was called to minister to the Gentiles. The new-covenant ministry's surpassing glories of liberation and transformation energized him. And because of the ministry's grandeur and the astonishing mercy of his having been given the ministry, Paul did not lose heart.
- The apostle also ministered with *forthrightness*. Paul would have nothing to do with secretive cunning and trickery. And he never diluted or altered God's Holy Word. Rather, Paul got it straight and gave it straight, appealing with confidence to the consciences of men.
- Paul also ministered with *perception* in respect to the veiled and blind condition of the unbelieving. And Paul's own experience of transformation informed him of what was necessary for men to believe.

• The apostle therefore ministered by *lifting Christ up*. Preaching Jesus Christ as Lord left no doubt about the full work of the incarnate Son, the Messiah, and his lordly sovereignty established by his resurrection. When a man or woman exalts Christ, there is no room for self-exaltation. Instead of self-promotion, there is servanthood.

• Lastly, Paul ministered with *divine confidence*. "For God, who said, 'Let light shine out of darkness,' has shone in our hearts to give the light of the knowledge of the glory of God in the face of Jesus Christ" (v. 6). Nothing less than creation power is applied to blind souls. There was, and is, no one beyond the grace of God.

Paul's heart, Paul's forthrightness, Paul's perception, Paul's exaltation of Christ, and Paul's gospel confidence are meant to inform and strengthen our ministering hearts.

And having such a ministry, we will not lose heart!

11

The Power of New-Covenant Ministry

2 CORINTHIANS 4:7–12

CLAY JARS WERE THE THROWAWAY CONTAINERS of the ancient world, so that their life spans were generally a few years at the most. They were used to store and transport water and olive oil and wine and grain and even family treasures. Earthenware jars were an anonymous part of everyday living as they were used for cooking and eating and drinking and storing leftovers. Every domestic archaeological excavation site contains their remains, called ostraca, from the Greek word for pottery. No one took note of clay jars any more than we would of a fast-food container. They were simply there for convenience. It was no great tragedy when such vessels were broken. They were cheap and easy to replace.

As such, jars of clay provided Paul with a penetrating metaphor for his and his followers' humanity. Indeed Adam was formed out of the dust of the ground, and to dust he returned (cf. Genesis 2:7; 3:19). As clay jars we are all frail, weak, transitory mortals.

Declaration of Power (v. 7)

This understood, Paul's famous declaration pulses with meaning: "But we have this treasure in jars of clay, to show that the surpassing power belongs to God and not to us" (v. 7). The "treasure" is the illuminating power (described in the preceding verse as "the light of the knowledge of the glory of God in the face of Jesus Christ") that God provides with the full creation power with which he spoke things into existence. This "treasure," this creational, transforming gospel power, has been committed to insignificant, fragile followers of Christ—men and women who, like Paul, are all clay pots.

The reason for this is so there would be no mistake about where the power comes from—"to show that the surpassing power belongs to God and not to us." This is not a pious *pro forma* acknowledgment of Paul's (and our) limitations as compared to the greatness of God. This is not a casual admission. This is Christian realism. Christians are never powerful in themselves but are only vessels in which God's power is exhibited. Paul is speaking primarily of himself, but the truth he teaches is true for every follower of Christ. Our utter frailty and weakness provides the ground for God's power.

At the end of this letter Paul rejoices that his weakness makes him a conduit for God's power: "But he said to me, 'My grace is sufficient for you, for my power is made perfect in weakness.' Therefore I will boast all the more gladly of my weaknesses, so that the power of Christ may rest upon me" (12:9). And in Chapter 4 the breaking up of our clay vessels through the crushing circumstances of life allows "the light of the knowledge of the glory of God in the face of Jesus Christ" (v. 6) to shine forth in full creational, gospel power. In all of this, then, Paul is graphically and categorically stating that our weakness is essential to and necessary for the display of his power.

It is easy to misread what Paul says here so that we interpret it as the means of enhancing *our* power. Thus we may imagine that as we embrace our weakness God will pour his power into us so that we become powerful. The natural equation is: My weakness plus God's power equals *my* power.

But that is *not* what Paul is saying. Rather, he teaches that as we embrace our weakness, God fills us with his power so that his power is manifested through us. We do not become powerful. We remain weak. We do not grow in power. We grow in weakness. We go from weakness to weakness, which is to remain vessels of his power—ever weak and ever strong.

Someone once asked St. Francis how he was able to accomplish so much. He replied, "This may be why: The Lord looked down from heaven and said, 'Where can I find the weakest, littlest man on earth?' Then he saw me and said, 'I've found him, and he won't be proud of it. He'll see that I am only using him because of his insignificance.'" "But we have this treasure in jars of clay, to show that the surpassing power belongs to God and not to us" (v. 7). Have we embraced our weakness as a way of life—and as the invitation to his surpassing power?

Paradoxes of Power (vv. 8, 9)

Now in verses 8, 9 the apostle gives four parallel paradoxes that all illustrate Paul's experience of the clay pot axiom in his own life—namely, that weakness invites strength. The paradoxes are autobiographical of Paul's constant experience.[1] At the same time they touch on the biography of the committed Christian disciple. They also provide a panorama of Christian history through the centuries and even describe some people we have known.

This is one of the grand rhetorical moments in Paul's writings. Each paradox is lapidary in its polish and balance and follows the same pattern hinging on the identical emphatic adversative "but not."[2] And the paradoxes together present an ascending intensity of weakness countered with power.

First, "We are afflicted in every way, but not crushed" (v. 8a). The earthen vessel of Paul's life was "afflicted" in the radical sense of pressured, which is best represented by the word *squeezed*. Any number of the catastrophes that befell Paul could have exerted intense compressions. But his pressured weakness was ever met with God's power, and he was "not crushed." Merrill Tenney's unpublished translation brilliantly expresses it: "We are squeezed but not squashed." Perfect! Paul, clay vessel that he was, was astonishingly resilient but never squashed.

Second, he was "perplexed, but not driven to despair" (v. 8b). In Greek these words form a rhyming word play (*aporoúmenoi . . . exaporoúmenoi*) as the second word intensifies the first.[3] Various attempts have been made to capture the word play in English—"at a loss, but not at a loss" (Tasker), "in despondency, yet not in despair" (Plummer), "confused but not confounded" (Hughes).[4] But again, Dr. Tenney seems to get it best: "bewildered but not befuddled." Fragile as Paul's humanity was when confronted with difficulties and loss, he was never befuddled and despairing. It was said of Napoleon that he had an unquestioned magic for victory, but no technique for defeat. The great general riding his beautiful mount at Austerlitz became the despairing horseman slouching in retreat from Moscow.[5] But Paul had a technique for defeat and weakness in "the surpassing power [that] belongs to God."

Was he perplexed at times? Yes, but not driven to despair. Was he bewildered at times? Yes, but not befuddled. Later Paul would charge Timothy, "But you, keep your head in all situations, endure hardship, do the work of an evangelist, discharge all the duties of your ministry" (2 Timothy 4:5, NIV). And this Paul himself did, as God's strength was perfected in his weakness.

Third, Paul was "persecuted, but not forsaken" (v. 9a). Paul knew what it was to be persecuted (literally, "pursued" or "hunted down"), but he was never forsaken *by God*, as the Old Testament background of this word indicates.[6]

God cannot forsake his chosen vessels. When Jesus prophetically cried from the cross, "My God, my God, why have you forsaken me?" (Psalm 22:1; cf. Mark 15:34), he knew that he would not be abandoned to the grave. And, more, God will not forsake any of his people, for they are redeemed by his Son. Paul was absolutely confident of God's abiding presence regardless of how or where he was hounded.

Fourth, the intensity of the paradoxes peaks in the final expression, "struck down, but not destroyed" (v. 9b). "Struck down" means struck down by a weapon—"whacked" as we might say. But Paul was not destroyed. Rather he was quickly back on his feet. We know of one of these events in Lystra when Paul was hunted down and ritually stoned (a ghastly, cruel event), capped by his body being dragged outside the city to rot. But to the astonishment of his disciples, Paul popped open an eye and led them back into Lystra (cf. Acts 14:19, 20)! Again Tenney's rendering catches the idea: "knocked down, but not knocked out." Incredible strength in the midst of total weakness.

You can catch the intensity of Paul's paradoxes by stacking the sufferings he endured in the earthen vessel of his body (using Tenney's rendering): "squeezed . . . bewildered . . . pursued . . . knocked down." What abject weakness! But we have God's surpassing power: "not squashed . . . not befuddled . . . not abandoned . . . not knocked out." What astonishing power! Again, "we have this treasure in jars of clay, to show that the surpassing power belongs to God and not to us" (v. 7). It wasn't that Paul in each case reached down into his soul, sucked it up, and became *the man*. It was never *his* strength. It was God's. Paul's weakness was the occasion for God's power. Paul remained an earthen pot, and a cracked pot at that, as his crumbling flesh allowed the power of God to shine so brightly.

The Principle of Power (vv. 10, 11)

As Paul deepens his point, he goes on to instruct the Corinthians that his experience of power through weakness was, in effect, like that of Jesus in his death (weakness) and his resurrection (power). He sums up his paradoxical experiences with a radically Christ-focused statement: "always carrying in the body the death of Jesus, so that the life of Jesus may also be manifested in our bodies" (v. 10).

Death. To understand this we must note very carefully that the word rendered "death" here refers to the *process of dying* rather than to the final state of death. So C. K. Barrett explains that "Paul's meaning is that one who observed his life as a Christian apostle . . . would see constantly repeated a process analogous to the killing of Jesus."[7] Paul carried about in his body the dying of Jesus as he lived out his missionary calling. Paul concluded his letter to the Galatians by saying, "From now on let no one cause me trouble, for I bear on my body the marks of Jesus" (6:17). Paul got those marks in four kinds of suffering when he was "squeezed" and "bewildered" and "pursued" and "knocked down"—they were the dying of Jesus. Indeed, Jesus by virtue of his solidarity with Paul knew those sufferings. In fact,

Jesus could have said to Paul's persecutors, "Why are you persecuting me?" just as he had once said it to Paul on the Damascus road (cf. Acts 9:4; cf. Colossians 1:24).

Life. Though bearing in his body the killing of Jesus was a part of Paul's experience of ministering the new covenant, it was not an end in itself. We who serve Jesus share in his dying "so that the life of Jesus may also be manifested in our bodies" (v. 10b).

This refers both to the here and now and to the life hereafter. Those who observed Paul saw the life of Jesus in the amazing power that was displayed through Paul's weakness as he was "not squashed" and "not befuddled" and "not abandoned" and "not knocked out." In the same way, the life of Jesus is manifested in the lives of those who truly follow him. And ultimately these realities will be full-blown in our final deliverance from mortality in the great resurrection of the dead.

To emphasize these great truths, Paul repeats himself again in stronger terms: "For we who live are always being given over to death for Jesus' sake, so that the life of Jesus also may be manifested in our mortal flesh" (v. 11). It is the same language used to describe Jesus' being handed over to his enemies (cf. Mark 9:31; 10:33).[8] The sufferings of those who follow Christ are not haphazard but are part of the divine plan for the spread of the gospel. It remains God's will that his frail jars of clay be used to show that the surpassing power belongs to God.

The Surprise of Power (v. 12)

Paul concludes this astonishing paragraph with an unexpected twist because, by the way Paul has been structuring his thought, we would expect him to say something like, "So death is at work in us, but life is also at work in us." But surprisingly, he says, "So death is at work in us, but life in you."

This is, of course, the great principle of the cross. Christ died that we might live. The great exchange of the gospel is: Christ's life for ours. And those who are used most to spread the good news of Christ embrace death as the operational principle of ministry. When George Muller, pastor and provider for thousands of children, was asked his secret, he hung his head and said, "There was a day when I died." Then he hung it lower and said, "Died to George Muller." Jesus said,

> Truly, truly, I say to you, unless a grain of wheat falls into the earth and dies, it remains alone; but if it dies, it bears much fruit. Whoever loves his life loses it, and whoever hates his life in this world will keep it for eternal life. If anyone serves me, he must follow me; and where I am, there will my servant be also. If anyone serves me, the Father will honor him. (John 12:24–26)

It's humbling to take to heart the fact that we are clay pots, and as such we are fragile and transitory, vessels of weakness. It's humbling to accept that Paul's declaration, "But we have this treasure in jars of clay, to show that the surpassing power belongs to God and not to us" (v. 7) is not a formula for *our* power. The equation for power is: my weakness plus God's power equal's *God's* power. It's humbling to hear that all my acknowledgment of weakness will not make *me* strong—embracing weakness leads to more weakness.

But it is also so beautiful and so liberating to know that God's power in our lives does not come from our pursuit of power. How wonderful to know that "we have this treasure in jars of clay, to show that the surpassing power belongs to God and not to us." Bless God for the powerful resiliency this brings! So that we are

> squeezed but not squashed,
> bewildered but not befuddled,
> pursued but not abandoned,
> knocked down but not knocked out.

How beautiful that this reflects the life of Jesus in us, "always carrying in the body the death of Jesus, so that the life of Jesus may also be manifested in our bodies" (v. 10). How heartening to know that when you live this way, death is at work in us but life is at work in those whom God has called us to serve. What a glory that the power of new-covenant ministry comes by embracing weakness.

What a word for the church today—with our human idolatries and our exaltation of human beings. The power of the gospel comes in our weakness, not in our strength, not in our greatness, but in the fact that we are clay pots—and cracked ones at that!

12

"Futures" and Steadfastness

2 CORINTHIANS 4:13–18

THE APOSTLE PAUL HAS JUST EXPLAINED in the preceding paragraph (4:7–12) how his weakness occasioned God's power, so that he was:

> squeezed but not squashed,
> bewildered but not befuddled,
> pursued but not abandoned,
> knocked down but not knocked out.

This weakness-power principle was, in effect, the life-death principle of Christ himself—so that Paul was carrying in his body the dying of Jesus with the result that the life of Jesus was manifested in his mortal flesh. The effect was that as death was at work in him, life was at work in his hearers. Paul's weakness was definitely the ground of God's power.

Now, beginning in verse 13, Paul explains what sustained him to continue preaching—his faith in God. Paul does this by citing a brief line from Psalm 116:10, the heart of Psalm 116:[1] "Since we have the same spirit of faith according to what has been written, 'I believed, and so I spoke,' we also believe, and so we also speak" (v. 13). For Paul, a brief reference like this served as a pointer to the full context of the Psalm upon which he based his statement of faith. Significantly, Psalm 116 describes a time when the writer (King David) almost died (cf. vv. 3, 8, 15), but God delivered him from death (cf. vv. 8–10). David "believed" that God had delivered him and therefore "spoke" of it (v. 10). As this statement in verse 10 is the center and pivot of the Psalm, it places faith at its very heart.

The Apostle Paul felt a spiritual kinship with King David because, like him, Paul had been also delivered from death (cf. 2 Corinthians 1:8–10; 4:7–11; 11:23ff.). Paul had likewise believed, and so he also spoke—as he preached "God's word" (4:2), "the gospel" (4:4), and "Jesus Christ as Lord" (4:5).[2] Thus Paul's gospel ministry rested squarely on God's Word and his experience of God's deliverance from death, which was in grand continuity with the experience of the suffering righteous of the past. It is from this platform of faith that Paul spoke with unflinching certitude and power.

This said, we must understand that while the foundation of Paul's faith was in the past, Paul now goes on to show that the focus of his faith was on the future. What heartened him for the battle and fortified him to preach Christ Jesus in every circumstance was his dynamic certainty and confidence about the future. It will become ever so clear in this passage that what Paul longed for and believed about the future had everything to do with how he lived in the present. And it is exactly the same for us. Our beliefs and hopes for the future exert a control that dictates how we live our present lives. Our "futures" determine the present.

Confidence in Resurrection (vv. 14, 15)

Future resurrection. The first reason Paul puts forth for his unflinching preaching amidst the squeezings and bewilderments and houndings and knockdowns of ministry is his utter confidence in future resurrection: "and so we also speak, knowing that he who raised the Lord Jesus will raise us also with Jesus and bring us with you into his presence" (vv. 13b, 14). The resurrection was, in fact, central to Paul's preaching of the gospel, as he told the Corinthians: "For I delivered to you as of first importance what I also received: that Christ died for our sins in accordance with the Scriptures, that he was buried, that he was raised on the third day in accordance with the Scriptures" (1 Corinthians 15:3, 4). The resurrection was the triumphant half of the gospel, and the reflexive refrain of Paul's lips was, "Remember Jesus Christ, risen from the dead, the offspring of David, as preached in my gospel" (2 Timothy 2:8). The book of Acts records the Athenians' bemusement at Paul "because he was preaching Jesus and the resurrection" (Acts 17:18).

Here in 2 Corinthians Paul's description pictures the resurrection as a joyous, shared event that includes "Jesus," "us" (Paul and company), and "you" (the Corinthians) (v. 14). The resurrection of the Corinthians (and all believers) is as sure as the resurrection of Jesus himself, as Paul had earlier told the Corinthians: "For as in Adam all die, so also in Christ shall all be made alive. But each in his own order: Christ the firstfruits, then at his coming those who belong to Christ" (1 Corinthians 15:22, 23). The apostle's abiding confidence is that he, along with all believers, is only a step behind the Lord.[3] Paul would have loved the bold confidence of the three-hundred-year-old tombstone epitaph for Mr. Isaac Greentree:

> Beneath these green trees rising to the skies,
> The planter of them, Isaac Greentree, lies;
> The time shall come when these green trees shall fall,
> And Isaac Greentree rise above them all.[4]

For Paul, this confident hope in the future resurrection was what gave him strength to persevere. As Tim Savage has observed:

> It is . . . because [Paul] believes in a future resurrection of the dead that he is presently willing to carry about in his body the dying of Jesus (4:10–11). It is because he trusts in a future exaltation that he submits now to the condition of a "slave" (4:5). It is because he looks forward to a future heavenly life that he is willing to die daily (1 Corinthians 15:31). It is because he anticipates reigning with Christ in the future that he can speak so boldly in the present (2 Corinthians 4:13). Without faith in a future resurrection Paul's present suffering would be not only intolerable, but also meaningless (1 Corinthians 15:30–32). He would, on his own admission, be a man most to be pitied (1 Corinthians 15:17–19).[5]

So we can see that what Paul believed about the future had everything to do with the way he lived. And more, the difference between Paul and many Christians lies right here. Many Christians do not truly believe in a future resurrection. Or if they do, they see it as a distant, fuzzy event with no relevance for today. Certainly they do not see it as the grand cosmic certainty that they will actually share with Christ. And they don't believe it with the intensity of Paul.

How, and in what terms, we conceive of the future is a decisive question. For most Christians, the contemplation of retirement trumps the contemplation of their ultimate destiny. For most, eschatology (i.e., the study of the last things) is defined by a single word—*retirement*. Far more energy and thought is given to enhancing the health and wealth of the final twenty years of earthly existence than to eternal existence. Clearly, we are called to focus on future resurrection and exaltation if we have any desire to live as we ought.

Future doxology. A complementary reason behind Paul's tenacity in ministry is the ultimate praise and glory of God: "For it is all for your sake, so that as grace extends to more and more people it may increase thanksgiving, to the glory of God" (v. 15). Ultimate praise—doxology! On one occasion Charles Spurgeon was explaining the gospel to a woman who, on the verge of belief and salvation, exclaimed, "Oh, Mr. Spurgeon, if the Lord saves me, he shall never hear the end of it!" How right she was. That is what happens when grace extends to more and more people.

Paul's spiritual math was impeccable. In the here and now the more people who come to Christ, the more people there are to "with one voice glorify the God and Father of our Lord Jesus Christ" (Romans 15:6). But Paul was also looking beyond the now to the endless future described in Revelation when the math will explode:

> After this I looked, and behold, a great multitude that no one could number, from every nation, from all tribes and peoples and languages, standing before the throne and before the Lamb, clothed in white robes, with palm branches in their hands, and crying out with a loud voice, 'Salvation belongs to our God who sits on the throne, and to the Lamb!'" (Revelation 7:9, 10)

Eternal doxology!

Paul's "futures"—the future resurrection and the future doxology—are what steadied and steeled him to keep the course. They are the reasons that he wasn't squashed or befuddled or abandoned or knocked out. Thus we see that our "futures" have everything to do with the way we live. How are your "futures"? As to retirement, it's not a matter of whether you're *saving* for retirement; it's a matter of whether you're *living* for retirement. Certainly we ought to be prudent, but what folly to spend all our energies investing in this world just so we can have a brief stay in Leisure World!

Confidence in Transformation (vv. 16–18)

Aging and decay can be disheartening, and especially so for those without hope of resurrection and transformation. The Greco-Roman culture of Paul's day gave voice to remarkable expressions of despair. The Greek poet Aeschylus declared, "there is death once and for all and there is no resurrection." The Roman Marcus Aurelius held that at death all that is left is "dust, ashes, bones and stench."[6] Very contemporary expressions, are they not?

Sir Frederic K. Catherwood, Christian businessman and onetime chairman of the European Parliament, once sat at lunch with one of Britain's greatest scientists, at that time president of The Royal Society of Britain, and the two discussed the Bible and Christianity. The aged scientist remained firm in his unbelief. Catherwood writes:

> Only three or four years later, a few months before his death, I saw the same man in the library of our club, a gaunt, gloomy, silent figure, hunched over the fire, staring into nothing, face to face with oblivion. When I left the

> club some time later, he was standing in the rain without a coat. I offered him a lift; he told me not to bother. He had come to the end, and nothing seemed to matter any more.[7]

Given the Apostle Paul's age and his battered ministerial history, one might presume a similar despair for the old apostle. Far from it. He purposefully concludes, "So we do not lose heart" (v. 16a), which was a reiteration of what he said at the beginning of the chapter: "Therefore, having this ministry by the mercy of God, we do not lose heart" (v. 1). And with this, the apostle now gives his reasoning for this conclusion—in a word, his hope in *transformation*, ultimate future transformation.

Assured of inner reward. The primary reason that Paul remained upbeat about life and ministry is given in an easy-to-remember saying: "Though our outer nature is wasting away, our inner nature is being renewed day by day" (v. 16b). Our bodies are wearing down minute by minute. If you want to see the difference that age makes, take two tennis balls (one fresh from the can and the other plucked from the leaves with fifteen sets on it) and drop them side by side. Watch them bounce. You'll see the difference! Then examine them together, the one firm, bright, optic yellow, the other gray, with bald spots and spongy to the touch.

But Paul isn't describing physical decay as such. "Outer nature" (literally, "outer man") does not refer to the body, and "inner nature" (literally, "inner man") does not refer to the soul. There is no body/soul dichotomy here. Both "outer man" and "inner man" refer to the *whole person*. "Outer man" refers to our status in Adam as part of this present age; "inner man" refers to our status in the last Adam, Christ.[8] Therefore, Paul is saying that the old sinful man is "wasting away" (being deconstructed!), while our new self in Christ is "being renewed" (reconstructed!) "day by day."

The process of deconstruction and reconstruction is taking place right now as our new self "is being renewed in knowledge after the image of its creator" (Colossians 3:10). And the final reconstruction will occur at Christ's appearing when the whole person will be redeemed and conformed to the likeness of the last Adam, God's Son (cf. Romans 8:28, 29). Thus Paul was heartened because amidst the stresses and perplexities of apostolic ministry, the old nature was deconstructing, and he was being reconstructed in the image of Christ. No faint heart here! The transformation is far too glorious and encouraging to allow that.

And we ought ourselves to be heartened because Paul's experience is a template for our life in Christ. The deconstruction is typically messy, but daily transformation is beautiful.

Heavy glory. An added reason why Paul does not lose heart amidst his life's pressures is found in his statement, "For this slight momentary affliction is preparing for us an eternal weight of glory beyond all comparison"

(v. 17). Earlier, when Paul began this letter, he stated that the "affliction" he had experienced in Asia had left him "weighed down beyond measure" (literal Greek, 1:8). The weight of his affliction was real and, in fact, almost killed him. However, here in 4:17 Paul reemploys the same words "weight" and "beyond measure," but in this context to minimize the deadly weight of affliction he had experienced in Asia.

Instead of the weight of affliction, there is now the "weight of glory." And, whereas the Asian affliction had "weighed him down beyond all measure," the "weight of glory" is doubly beyond measure,[9] that is to say, "out of all proportion"[10]—exponential glory! For Paul, "The affliction which once felt like a lethal weight around his neck now seems weightless in comparison to his eternal load of glory."[11] Philip Hughes concludes, "Affliction for Jesus' sake, however crushing it may seem, is in fact light, a weightless trifle, when weighed against the mass of that glory."[12] This is theological reality for all those who through grace have become children of God. When the apostle suffered affliction, he did not focus his thoughts on how heavy the affliction was but on how heavy the glory would be because of the affliction. If we, in the midst of our affliction, will see it as it is, we will find our voices again and sing songs in the night.

The truth is that our momentary afflictions are "*preparing*" us for an eternal load of glory out of all proportion. Are you going through a tough time? The afflictions will pass. Believe it. Don't lose heart. And more, embrace the fact that the fires are burning away the dross so that a load of glory will be yours.

Future perspective. Paul endured because he looked past the transitory moment to the future—"as we look not to the things that are seen but to the things that are unseen. For the things that are seen are transient, but the things that are unseen are eternal" (v. 18). Everything we see with our eyes is temporary. There is nothing we can look at that is not transient, from the possessions we own to earth itself to the farthest star to the tiniest microbe.

But the unseen is eternal—God himself (Father, Son, and Holy Spirit)—the souls of our brothers and sisters in Christ—the promises of God yet to be fulfilled—Heaven itself.

The tragedy of our times is that men and women have lost their eyes for the unseen and believe and hope and work in the visible. But Paul focused on the unseen things to come. Paul's hope was set in the future resurrection. For him the grave was empty. The certitude of the resurrection was inevitable and compelling. It determined the way he lived. Because of it, he bore in his body the dying of Jesus and lived as a slave to others and willingly died daily. Paul could unwaveringly hear the far-off song of eternal doxology from every tongue and tribe. And the strains of future doxology kept him on course. His "futures" shaped his life and destiny.

Alongside Paul's hope in future *resurrection* was his hope in future *transformation*. He did not lose heart because his old sinful man was "wasting away" in blessed deconstruction while his new self in Christ was "being renewed day by day." And he looked forward to his final transformation at Christ's appearing. He remained heartened because the weight of the afflictions of ministry were nothing compared to the weight of glory for which they were preparing him. And he endured because he looked past the transitory to the eternal. He knew, to quote Lewis, that "whatever is not eternal is eternally out of date."

Because Paul's focus was on the future resurrection and transformation, he was:

> squeezed but not squashed,
> bewildered but not befuddled,
> pursued but not abandoned,
> knocked down but not knocked out.

It's axiomatic: our future hopes determine how we live in the present. The question is: how are our "futures"?

What are you living for? It's never too late to get it right. Don't waste your life.

13

More Beyond

2 CORINTHIANS 5:1–10

WHEN SPAIN HAD EXTENDED HER CONQUESTS to the ends of the then-known world and controlled both sides of the Mediterranean at the Straits of Gibraltar (the fabled Pillars of Hercules), her coins proudly pictured the Pillars framing a scroll inscribed with the Latin words *Ne Plus Ultra*—"No More Beyond." The Pillars gated the end of the earth. But "In 1492 Columbus sailed the ocean blue" and discovered the New World. The proud nation then admitted her ignorance and struck the negative *Ne* from her coinage, leaving the words *Plus Ultra*—"More Beyond."

The change from the myopic "No More Beyond" to the expansive "More Beyond" effected a revolution in world culture, global economy, and geopolitics. The change also serves as a handy example of what is needed in the spiritual geography of modern men and women, because so many live in the stifling delusion that there is no more beyond. Most, including many Christians, live as if "this is it"—as in the Looney Tunes *finis*, "That's all, folks!"

At the same time, *Plus Ultra* perfectly describes the Apostle Paul and the ultimate focus of the whole of Scripture and the intensive focus of this section of 2 Corinthians. We will see that 5:1–10 is in driving continuity with 4:13–18, where we saw that Paul's confidence in future resurrection and transformation was what enabled him to minister with such resiliency and steadfastness (cf. 4:7–12). Again we must emphasize that our "futures" (what we focus on) determine the way we live. The ongoing challenge is to embrace the *Plus Ultra* of future resurrection life with everything that is in us.

Paul begins this section of his argument with a confident assertion of the future resurrection of the body: [1] "For we know that if the tent, which is our earthly home, is destroyed, we have a building from God, a house not made with hands, eternal in the heavens" (v. 1). It was natural for Paul to liken his present body to a tent because tent-making was his missionary avocation. A tent, he well knew, was both vulnerable and temporary and therefore a fitting metaphor for the body. And his switch of metaphors for the body from "tent" to "a building from God" was meant to emphasize the coming change from a temporary body to a permanent resurrection body. In fact, the image that Paul appears to have had in mind was the tabernacle tent that was superseded by the temple building. Just as the tabernacle was the temporary dwelling of God until the building of a permanent temple in Jerusalem, so also Paul's mortal body is merely temporary and will be replaced by an imperishable resurrection body.[2]

And more, just as there was continuity between the tabernacle and the temple, there is continuity between the mortal body and the imperishable body of the resurrection. This is Paul's explicit teaching in Philippians 3:20, 21: "But our citizenship is in heaven, and from it we await a Savior, the Lord Jesus Christ, who will transform our lowly body to be like his glorious body, by the power that enables him even to subject all things to himself." This same thought informed Paul's earlier lyrical expression to the Corinthians:

> Behold! I tell you a mystery. We shall not all sleep, but we shall all be changed, in a moment, in the twinkling of an eye, at the last trumpet. For the trumpet will sound, and the dead will be raised imperishable, and we shall be changed. For this perishable body must put on the imperishable, and this mortal body must put on immortality. (1 Corinthians 15:51–53)

Just as Christ's glorified resurrection body was in continuity with his incarnate body, so also will be ours. The body that was knitted together in our mother's womb, our congenital body in which we now live, will be resurrected and will exist transformed in eternal continuity (cf. Psalm 139:13–15).

This continuity affirms the goodness of God's physical creation. As Wayne Grudem explains:

> We will live in bodies that have all the excellent qualities God created us to have, and thereby we will forever be living proof of the wisdom of God in making a material creation that from the beginning was "very good" (Gen. 1:31). We will live as resurrected believers in those new bodies and they will be suitable for inhabiting the "new heavens and a new earth in which righteousness dwells" (2 Peter 3:13).[3]

We ought to joyfully pinch ourselves in acknowledgment of what awaits our bodies!

Paul was confident that the things he was experiencing in the present (his outer nature wasting away, while his inner man was being renewed day by day—the momentary affliction—his focus on the eternal unseen) would have their fulfillment when his scarred, weathered, disintegrating body experienced glorious resurrection—"a building from God, a house not made with hands, eternal in the heavens" (v. 1). There was "More Beyond" for Paul's body. He was sure of it!

With Confident Longing (vv. 2–5)

Groanings. Paul's confidence in the future resurrection expressed itself in deep, longing, anticipatory groans.

> For in this tent we groan, longing to put on our heavenly dwelling, if indeed by putting it on we may not be found naked. For while we are still in this tent, we groan, being burdened—not that we would be unclothed, but that we would be further clothed, so that what is mortal may be swallowed up by life. (vv. 2–4)

A pastor once received a letter from a nine-year-old girl that said, "Dear Pastor, I hope to go to heaven someday, but later than sooner. Love, Ellen."

Out of the mouths of babes! Ellen speaks for almost everyone. We all want to go to Heaven, but later as opposed to sooner. However, as we have come to expect, this isn't the way Paul thought. Paul hoped to get there sooner rather than later.

Paul's initial expression is intrinsically positive: "For in this tent we groan, longing to put on our heavenly dwelling"—a groaning of anticipation. His longing is like the groaning for future glory that he expressed in the three complementary groans in Romans 8.

The first groan is that of *creation*:

> For the creation waits with eager longing for the revealing of the sons of God. For the creation was subjected to futility, not willingly, but because of him who subjected it, in hope that the creation itself will be set free from its bondage to decay and obtain the freedom of the glory of the children of God. For we know that the whole creation has been groaning together in the pains of childbirth until now. (vv. 19–22)

Creation's "eager longing" is based on the idea of craning the neck forward in expectation. J. B. Phillips paraphrased this, "The whole creation is on tiptoe to see the wonderful sight of the sons of God coming into their own." There are anticipatory groans for glory all around us.

While creation groans, *Christians* groan too: "And not only the creation, but we ourselves, who have the firstfruits of the Spirit, groan inwardly as we wait eagerly for adoption as sons, the redemption of our bodies" (v. 23). We groan for our adoption as sons, which will be completed at the redemption of our bodies. We groan because of the experience of living in mortal, sinful flesh. But we groan positively as we have "the firstfruits of the Spirit"—the initial down payment of the eternal. We are on tiptoe along with creation, waiting for our deliverance.

Creation groans, we groan, and even *the Holy Spirit* groans: "Likewise the Spirit helps us in our weakness. For we do not know what to pray for as we ought, but the Spirit himself intercedes for us with groanings too deep for words" (v. 26). The Holy spirit expresses the longings we feel but cannot articulate. So we see that because of the greatness of the coming glory and because of our weakness, we groan. But we are not alone, for we are surrounded by the sympathetic groanings of creation and even of the Holy Spirit. And one day our groanings will be transmuted into praises in glory!

Paul's groanings were like those of a child waiting for Christmas. He groaned in his earthly tent as he dreamed pleasant dreams of the gift of his new heavenly dwelling.

The apostle's longing was not for death as such, but to be clothed with his heavenly dwelling because by being clothed in his new resurrection body, he would "not be found naked"—that is, exposed to the shame of judgment for sins he might commit.[4] So he further groans to be fully clothed with his resurrection body and thus to be vindicated and beyond judgment: "For while we are still in this tent, we groan, being burdened—not that we would be unclothed, but that we would be further clothed, so that what is mortal may be swallowed up by life" (5:4). "Swallowed up by life" is his allusion to the completion of redemption described in Isaiah 25:8, and also in 1 Corinthians 15:54—"When the perishable puts on the imperishable, and the mortal puts on immortality, then shall come to pass the saying that is written: 'Death is swallowed up in victory.'"

Guarantee. The reason Paul groaned longingly for his resurrection body is God himself and God's gift of the Holy Spirit: "He who has prepared us for this very thing is God, who has given us the Spirit as a guarantee" (v. 5). Paul's groaning was a gift from God. The "guarantee" (Greek, *arrhabōn*) of the Holy Spirit is the word used in modern Greek for an engagement ring, which pledges and guarantees the marriage day.[5] So we understand that the Holy Spirit's wondrous work of transformation in Paul's life (cf. 3:18; 4:16) served as a guarantee of the ultimate transformation that would take place at the resurrection of his body. The Holy Spirit's renovative work on Paul's life assured him of the *Plus Ultra*—that there was more beyond. Again, his longing for his resurrection body was a gift from God.

Do you groan in this body, longing for your heavenly dwelling? I can say that as my understanding of the Scriptures has deepened with the years and therefore my experience of the Spirit, the more I groan for my heavenly dwelling. C. S. Lewis said:

> There have been times when I think we do not desire heaven, but more often I find myself wondering whether in our heart of hearts, we have ever desired anything else. . . . It is the secret signature of each soul, the incommunicable and unappeasable want, the thing we desired before we met our wives or made our friends or chose our work, and which we shall still desire on our deathbeds when the mind no longer knows wife or friend or work.[6]

> But trailing clouds of glory do we come
> From God, who is our home.
>
> William Wordsworth

Confident Attitude (vv. 6–8)

Because Paul was confident about the future regardless of the trials of the present, he was "always of good courage" (v. 6a), or, more accurately, "courageous." By any estimate, he was one of the bravest, most resilient souls of all history. I am personally in awe of the apostle. I can think of no revolutionary in ancient or modern history who can match him. It was the sheer weight of his "futures," his focus upon the *Plus Ultra*, that provided the ballast for his heroic, epic voyages.

Reality. As a result, Paul faced reality with cheerful optimism. "We know that while we are at home in the body we are away from the Lord, for we walk by faith, not by sight" (vv. 6b, 7). Paul knew that Christ was always with him and that he was in perpetual communion with him. Nevertheless, Paul's residence in his present body meant that in one sense he was away from the Lord and the ultimate fellowship of intimacy. So Paul lived by faith in the promises of God's Word—"for we walk by faith, and not by sight" (v. 7).

Paul set his sight on the unseen. He focused on the coming "weight of glory" (4:17) rather than on his afflictions. He was not concerned that his outer man was wasting away because he saw the unseen—his inner nature was undergoing daily renewal. Paul's faith in the unseen beyond controlled his entire existence.

Preference. His abiding preference—indeed, his passionate longing—was to be with Christ: "Yes, we are of good courage, and we would rather be away from the body and at home with the Lord" (v. 8). We misunderstand if we conceive of his desire in mere geographical terms. Paul desired ultimate fellowship with the Lord. Certainly in his earthly body he *knew* the Lord, as does every believer. But to be "at home with the Lord" encompasses warmth of fellowship that is wholly active and reciprocal with live face-to-face exchange.[7] Paul sees this in his future and thus longs assuredly for his resurrection body in which he will be at home with the Lord.

We must not fail to miss a telling implication—which is that Paul does *not* desire a prolonged life on earth! In fact, he told the Philippians, "My desire is to depart and be with Christ, for that is far better" (Philippians 1:23). The conviction of *Plus Ultra* radically alters our values and desires for the present.

I recall Joe Bayly, who was no stranger to death (having lost three children early in life), saying that in light of the promises that await us, it is a mystery that we Christians go to the medical extremes that we do to hang on to life.

Confident Resolve (vv. 9, 10)

This hope of imminent person-to-person communion with Christ naturally evokes an ongoing resolve to please him—"So whether we are at home or away, we make it our aim to please him" (v. 9). My three-year-old golden retriever, Daisy, provides me with a canine example of the desire to please because that is all my dog wants to do. Daisy dutifully watches me and listens for my voice inflections or gestures that indicate my pleasure. Her posture seems to say, "Just tell me what you want and I'll do it!" Daisy doesn't bark. She doesn't jump up. She doesn't paw the door or screen to get out. She doesn't steal food, and she doesn't beg. She just stares at the door until I am overcome with guilt. Daisy worships me.

Actually, she's not perfect. She demands affection. And while she doesn't go into the off-limits living room when I'm home, she does sneak in to peer out of the window to see which way her master has gone. So when I'm away from home, I'm not sure that she always makes it her aim to please me. Bad dog!

A sentimental example from the lips of a dog-lover? Yes! But this is instructive.

Daisy isn't very smart. She doesn't understand abstractions. She doesn't think much beyond her toys and her next meal and how to get a scratch between the ears. She can't read. She has no eschatology—no doctrine of the future, of resurrection, of judgment and reward. Daisy's *Plus Ultra* is the next dog biscuit. But though she has no doctrine of future reward, she wants to please her master.

How much more we should want to please Christ Jesus, our Master. We understand that he is eternal God, that he loved us so much that he died for us, that he was resurrected on the third day, that he has prepared a resurrection body for us, that he is going to take us to himself for all eternity, that the *Plus Ultra* is not a biscuit but the immeasurable "riches of his grace" (Ephesians 1:7). And this understanding ought (and must!) make us resolve that "whether we are at home or away, we make it our aim to please him" (v. 9).

And if that is not enough to effect our resolve, there is one other eschatological item: "For we must all appear before the judgment seat of Christ, so that each one may receive what is due for what he has done in the body, whether good or evil" (v. 10). Upon command, Christ had stood before the judgment seat (*bēma*) of Pilate (cf. Matthew 27:19), and likewise Paul had stood before the judgment seat of Gallio (cf. Acts 18:12).

Beyond history, at the great resurrection, there will be compulsory attendance at the cosmic *bēma* of Christ. There every child of God will give full account of what he has done in the body, the tent of this life. And all will be judged with unfailing scrutiny as our works and hearts are evaluated to determine not our destiny (which for believers is with God) but to evaluate our works, as earlier described by Paul:

> Now if anyone builds on the foundation with gold, silver, precious stones, wood, hay, straw—each one's work will become manifest, for the Day will disclose it, because it will be revealed by fire, and the fire will test what sort of work each one has done. If the work that anyone has built on the foundation survives, he will receive a reward. If anyone's work is burned up, he will suffer loss, though he himself will be saved, but only as through fire. (1 Corinthians 3:12–15)

That is a daunting thought, but Paul is implicitly confident because he has made it his aim to please God while in his earthly body. How is it with us? Will there be enduring architecture or monumental ashes?

The opinion of modernism and postmodernism is *Ne Plus Ultra!*—"No More Beyond." Materialist dogma says there is nothing beyond the physical universe.

But Christ's dogma is *Plus Ultra*—"the things that are seen are transient, but the things that are unseen are eternal" (4:18). What lies beyond is the future resurrection of our bodies. And if we are sure of our *Plus Ultra*, we groan with Christmas-like anticipation for our resurrection bodies. We groan for that day when we will be delivered from nakedness, the judgment upon Adam. Our longing is sweetened by the Spirit's wedding ring, his inimitable work in our souls. Thus we are of good courage. We walk by faith, not by sight, and therefore see the unseen. We long to be at home with the Lord. Regardless, we aim to please him, for judgment is coming.

So, fellow believers, we know how we ought to live. But the practical question is: Do we live on the dark side of today's Pillars of Hercules as if there is "No More Beyond," or in Christ's radiantly expansive "More Beyond"?

The answer will determine how we live and how we will fare at the judgment seat of Christ.

14

Paul's Driving Motivations

2 CORINTHIANS 5:11–15

IN 1926, FRESH-OUT-OF-HARVARD news correspondent John McCook Roots sat in a waterfront room in Canton. With him was the mysterious Communist revolutionary, Mikhail Borodin. The two men watched the junks sailing by, backlit by a brilliant Pearl River sunset as they discussed the subject of missionaries in China. Borodin's personal secretary was a diminutive Vietnamese, later known to the world as Ho Chi Minh. Borodin had been an adviser to the recently deceased Sun Yat-Sen, and now he was an intimate adviser to the legendary Chou En-Lai. Missionaries were naturally a disputed subject.

After a long silence in the conversation, Borodin, still gazing out the window, began murmuring, half to himself. "'You know,' he mused, 'I used to read the New Testament. Again and again I read it. It is the most wonderful story ever told. That man Paul. He was a *real* revolutionary. I take off my hat to him!'" He then made a symbolic gesture as his black hair momentarily fell over his face.[1] Borodin, the shadowy revolutionary, knew the real thing when he saw it—a sad concession from one of Communism's tragic figures. The devoted Communist Borodin died in a Siberian labor camp in 1951.

The question that our text evokes and answers is: What motivated Paul's radically revolutionary life? What drove him to live and die as he did for the gospel? The answer is memorably paradoxical, for it involves opposites—fear and love.

Fear of Judgment (vv. 11–13)

Paul had just announced the inevitable post-resurrection appointment for all of God's children: "For we must all appear before the judgment seat of

Christ, so that each one may receive what is due for what he has done in the body, whether good or evil" (v. 10). And, as Paul voiced it, he himself felt its fearful weight on his own soul because as an apostle he would have to give a strict account at the judgment seat for how he lived out his apostolic calling. James, the Lord's brother, expressed parallel sentiments: "Not many of you should become teachers, my brothers, for you know that we who teach will be judged with greater strictness" (James 3:1).

Fear evokes persuasion. Thus Paul begins this paragraph by saying, "Therefore, knowing the fear of the Lord, we persuade others" (v. 11a). It isn't that Paul was terrified or afraid, as we commonly use the words, but rather that he was awed by the thought of standing before a Being so holy, so morally superior, so removed from evil that in his presence all human boasting, all human pride, and all human arrogance would vanish as he stands in speechless humility before the One beyond understanding and with trembling lips gives full account of himself.[2] This fear of the Lord drove Paul to "persuade others"—that is, to persuade the Corinthians of his gospel and the integrity of his person as an apostle. In theological terms, eschatological fear motivated Paul to carry out his calling.

Paul's choice of the word "persuade" is revealing because Paul was aware that it connoted the persuasive techniques of Greco-Roman rhetorical tradition[3] that he outright rejected in his first letter to the Corinthians:

> And I, when I came to you, brothers, did not come proclaiming to you the testimony of God with lofty speech or wisdom. For I decided to know nothing among you except Jesus Christ and him crucified. And I was with you in weakness and in fear and much trembling, and my speech and my message were not in plausible words of wisdom, but in demonstration of the Spirit and of power, that your faith might not rest in the wisdom of men but in the power of God. (1 Corinthians 2:1–5)

Nevertheless, he used the word "persuade" in 2 Corinthians 5:11 to describe what he did in response to the tremulous prospect of the judgment seat of Christ. Thus we see that while Paul rejects the persuasive techniques of the rhetoricians, he does not reject the need to persuade. Significantly, Luke uses the same word "persuade" several times in Acts to describe Paul's evangelizing activities (cf. Acts 17:4; 18:4; 19:8, 26; 26:28; 28:23).[4] So we understand here in 2 Corinthians that as Paul says, "Therefore, knowing the fear of the Lord, we persuade others," he uses the emotive word "persuade" to describe his intense evangelizing activities as they are intertwined with his efforts to persuade his hearers of his integrity of ministry.

Persuasion in perspective. Paul knew, of course, that he didn't have to persuade God, so he immediately says, "But what we are is known to God"

(v. 11b). Paul's character had been and still is laid bare to God, and remains so. But Paul's character was held in low regard by those Corinthians who had been poisoned by the slurs of Paul's enemies regarding his integrity and qualifications. Hence Paul's additional comment, "and I hope it is known also to your conscience" (v. 11c).

Deep down, the Corinthians were aware of the character of Paul's ministry from when he was with them and how he proclaimed not himself but Christ as Lord and himself their servant (cf. 4:5), calling them to "be reconciled to God" (5:20) with sincerity and integrity (cf. 1:12–14; 2:17; 4:2).[5] He hoped, therefore, that the moral faculties of their consciences would connect the dots and that he would become known and remain known to them as the man of integrity that he truly was.

Expressing himself like this, Paul was aware that his detractors would probably accuse him of boasting in the dubious manner of the Greek rhetoricians. So he covered himself: "We are not commending ourselves to you again but giving you cause to boast about us, so that you may be able to answer those who boast about outward appearance and not about what is in the heart" (v. 12).

Paul's words are tinged with irony. His enemies, he said, boasted "about outward appearance" (literally, "in the face," and not in the heart), a conscious reference to God's advice to Samuel in choosing David over Saul: "Do not look on his appearance or on the height of his stature, because I have rejected him. For the Lord sees not as man sees: man looks on the outward appearance [LXX, "face"], but the Lord looks on the heart" (1 Samuel 16:7). Paul's opponents *boasted in the face*—the sheer externalities of oratorical appearance, rhetorical eloquence, extravagant commendatory letters, rich honoraria, and impressive display. In contrast, Paul says, "I'll give you cause to boast about me—the heart, not the face." For Paul, what was important is what is written in the heart by God's Spirit, for in the heart are the distinctives of the new covenant (cf. 3:3, 6; Jeremiah 31:33; Ezekiel 36:26, 27).

Marcus Dods, turn-of-the-century pastor and principal of New College Edinburgh, makes a pointed application:

> The ironical tone in this is unmistakable, yet it is not merely ironical. From the beginning of Christianity to this day, Churches have gathered round men, and made their boast in them. Too often it has been a boast "in face," and not "in heart"—in gifts, accomplishments, and distinctions, which may have given an outward splendour to the individual, but which were entirely irrelevant to the possession of the Christian spirit. . . . The same thing is seen every day, on a smaller scale, in congregations. People are proud of their minister, not for what he is in heart, but because

> he is more learned, more eloquent, more naturally capable, than other preachers in the same town.[6]

Dods, of course, wrote before the advent of the media pastor and the megachurch, before this true-life introduction: *Spotlight! Dramatic drum roll!* And then a booming bass introduction: "And now, ladies and gentlemen, may I introduce tonight's speaker, that humble servant of God, ________________!" Roaring applause as the "humble" preacher takes center stage, his *face* radiating in the spotlights.

Ever wary and attuned to his enemies in Corinth, Paul concludes his thoughts: "For if we are beside ourselves, it is for God; if we are in our right mind, it is for you" (v. 13). Whereas Paul's critics gave great credence to ecstatic experience as validating ministry, Paul did not. In point of fact Paul could boast that he had been caught up into the third heaven and "heard things that cannot be told, which man may not utter" (12:4). And, in fact, Paul earlier told the Corinthians, "I thank God that I speak in tongues more than all of you" (1 Corinthians 14:18). But he immediately dismissed it: "Nevertheless, in church I would rather speak five words with my mind in order to instruct others, than ten thousand words in a tongue" (1 Corinthians 14:19). *Glossalalia* was for God, but its use in public was "speaking into the air" (1 Corinthians 14:9). So for Paul, the mark of authentic ministry was not ecstatic experience but public ministry in his "right mind" (2 Corinthians 5:13)—in essence the passionate, sober, Biblical style with which he persuaded others.

Paul's healthy fear of the judgment seat of Christ induced him to place the public persuasion of people far above the pursuit of personal ecstasies. Knowing the fear of the Lord, Paul's consuming passion was to persuade others through the Scriptures about the truth of the gospel and the authenticity of his ministry, as they were inseparable. He did not need to persuade God, as God knew his heart and, likewise, the Corinthians would know it if they listened to their consciences. Paul argued his case so that the Corinthians would have a basis to boast about his apostolic heart.

"Therefore, knowing the fear of the Lord" (v. 11)—the focus of Paul's life was not inner-directed but outward as he labored in his right mind to "persuade others" of the truth of the gospel.

Love of Christ (vv. 14, 15)

The opposing side of the paradoxical power of Paul's revolutionary life is now introduced. Whereas verse 11 introduced the *fear* factor ("Therefore, knowing the fear of the Lord"), verse 14 introduces the *love* factor: "For the love of Christ controls us." Fear of Christ had motivated Paul, and now Christ's love for Paul completes the motivation.

We died in Christ. We're not left to wonder what the love of Christ is because it is demonstrated in his death—"because we have concluded this: that one has died for all, therefore all have died" (v. 14b). To uninformed ears, this may sound strange—"one has died for all, therefore all have died." Curious logic? A seemingly more reasonable expression would be, "One died for all, therefore all did not die." Or "One died for all, therefore all lived." The spiritual math of both these equations makes easy sums. But the mystic calculus of "one has died for all, therefore all have died"—how does that compute?

However, if you are familiar with the Bible, the math is rigorously logical and sublime because it sums up Christ's *representative* death for his children. As Gresham Machen, the great defender of the faith, explains:

> "Christ died for all, therefore all died" . . . is so because Christ was the representative of all when He died. The death that He died on the cross was in itself the death of all. Since Christ was the representative of all, therefore all may have been said to have died there on the cross outside the walls of Jerusalem when Christ died.[7]

Christ died our death, so we died! What unmitigated love!

Here Paul speaks of Christ's love as a controlling force. Love controls us—that is to say, it holds us within bounds[8] or hems us in. Just as our fear of Christ controls us, so likewise the unspeakable love of Christ positively controls us. The overpowering love of Christ, demonstrated when he died on the cross for us, controls us and calls forth a mighty response. This is what so mightily drove Paul in his epic missionary endeavors.

We live for Christ. "All have died," argues Paul, because Christ died as our representative on the cross. He died our death. And it is this unfathomable love that controls us. How does it control us? The answer follows in no uncertain terms: "he died for all, that those who live might no longer live for themselves but for him who for their sake died and was raised" (v. 15).

Hemmed in by Christ's love, Paul and those who walk in his revolutionary footsteps "no longer live for themselves." A thousand things that work to draw us into ourselves are attached parasite-like to our possessions and passions and appetites—all freighted with implosion, all laden with the potential to make us very small and useless. The fact that Christ in love died *our* death keeps us from living for ourselves, just as it did Paul, so that we are graciously hemmed in by Christ's love.

But gloriously, we're not hemmed in so that we can do nothing at all, but rather so we can do things that are more worthwhile. We are kept from doing evil things so that we might do good things. We are kept from doing things that bring death so that we might do things that bring life.[9] The utter positiveness of this lies in the mounting force of Paul's words: "and he died for all, that those who live might no longer live for themselves but for him who for their sake died and was raised" (v. 15). There is nothing constricted here. This is freedom. What good thing will be denied those who follow the living resurrected Christ (cf. Romans 8:32)? Indeed, it is the path to new freedoms and unfolding joys.

The energy cell in Paul's revolutionary heart was charged with a negative and a positive—the fear of Christ and the love of Christ. The combination was explosive. Paul was a *real* revolutionary.

After Mikhail Borodin's concession regarding the Apostle Paul, there was another long silence. But as the correspondent tells it:

> Then suddenly Borodin whirled, his face contorted with fury as he shook his fist in my face.
>
> "But where do you find him today?" he shouted. "Answer me that, Mr. Roots. Where do you find him? Where? Where? Where?"
>
> Then furiously, triumphantly: "You can't answer me!"
>
> Unnerved by this outburst, I sat speechless, then quickly changed the subject.
>
> Later that week he brought up the matter again. This time he was very quiet.
>
> "You must understand, Mr. Roots," he explained, "that with a revolutionary, his life is not his own. That is our pride. That is our strength. And because our opponents cannot match our sacrifice or our faith, they are powerless to stop our advance. For this reason Communism will win."[10]

Borodin's proud assertion rested upon ignorance of the essence of Christianity, ignorance of the radical commitment of gospel-committed missionaries, and his faith in the dialectical progress of metaphysical materialism. There were hundreds of missionaries in China living out the gospel in the dynamic paradox of fear and love. Their weapons were not brutality and the sword. Their courage and tenacity far exceeded that of Borodin and his train. Yet for a time Communism prevailed.

But today, as Borodin's sad ashes rest in a niche in the wall of the Novodedichi Cemetery outside Moscow with the other old revolutionaries who didn't quite rate the more prestigious Kremlin Wall, while Communism is morphing in China, Christianity is growing at an unparalleled rate.[11]

Paul's principles will prevail wherever men and women are galvanized by the *fear* of Christ and the *love* of Christ. May it be so for us. May we know the fear of Christ and his controlling love.

May we raise up an army of young men and women who are controlled by the paradox that fueled Paul's missionary heart.

15

Gospel Regard

2 CORINTHIANS 5:16, 17

AT ONE TIME PAUL, AS AN ARCH-PHARISEE, had judged Jesus Christ according to the flesh and found him to be wanting. To him, Jesus was a messianic pretender who pushed too far and got what was coming to him when he was condemned by the Sanhedrin and crucified by the Romans. In fact, Jesus' crucifixion proved to Paul that Jesus was cursed by God because the Law in Deuteronomy 21:23 categorically states that "a hanged man is cursed by God" (cf. Galatians 3:13). Jesus' suffering on the cross was therefore an emphatic and deserved rejection of Jesus' messianic pretensions.

The personal irony now for Paul in Corinth is that he himself had come to suffer the same disregard and rejection by some in the Corinthian church. They observed that he was weak in appearance and speech—and he was. But more, Paul's perpetual suffering (as he described it: "afflicted in every way . . . perplexed . . . persecuted . . . struck down," 4:8; cf. 11:23ff.) plus his daily dying proved to them that he was a phony. This was bitter irony: Jesus had been despised and rejected by Paul through fleshly regard, and now Paul himself suffered from the same fleshly evaluation and rejection. So now Paul, ever so subtly, is going to put his critics back on their heels by the famous statements of 2 Corinthians 5:16, 17.

Paul himself had come to be forever cured of regarding Christ and others according to the flesh when, on the way to Damascus, the risen Christ (whom Paul regarded as crucified and thus cursed) confronted him in the splendor of his glory, and the cross that Paul had so despised became the center of his life.[1] What Paul suddenly understood on the Damascus road is capsulized in verse 14 where he says, "we have concluded this: that one has died for all, therefore all have died." When Paul saw this, all fleshly regard ceased to have significance for him. The death Christ died on the cross was in itself the death of all, so that the old life died with all its fleshly surface distinctions regarding people.[2]

Gospel Disregard (v. 16)

So we have Paul's piercing declaration of *gospel disregard* (that is, the disregard of superficial evaluation that stems from our death in Christ on the cross): "From now on, therefore, we regard no one according to the flesh. Even though we once regarded Christ according to the flesh, we regard him thus no longer" (v. 16). Because of the gospel, Paul and all believers are to be done with their shallow, external, carnal regard of Christ and others—and especially those who are of the household of faith. Literally, "Therefore, from now on, *we know no one* according to the flesh." Gospel disregard!

Paul's declaration collides with the spirit of our age, a spirit that revels in superficial, fleshly regard. If I am to judge by the reading material available in most barber shops and doctors' offices, *People Magazine* is the devotional literature of our day, and it is read with an adoration and reverence that amounts to a religious longing. Looks, externals, dominate our existence.

How we look has been elevated to a moral virtue. For example, whereas in the past good girls were defined in terms of traditional moral categories, today good girls are categorized as to how they take care of their bodies. Good girls eat one apple a day. Bad girls eat hamburgers. Good girls work out. Bad girls don't.

The right look is everything. "It's all about image" is a cliché but a true capsulization of our culture. In a recent presidential election the Democrats and Republicans both employed their most powerful negotiators to format the presidential debates, and their contentions went far beyond substance—even lighting and camera angles were hotly debated. Image is everything, we're told. People evaluate one another externally according to their wealth, their position, their connectedness, and their fame or infamy (either of which is to be coveted). It makes no difference how it is attained, it is said—whether as a porn star or as a moral crusader. The little town in which I live and pastor has its own social registry based on family, education, and wealth. Yours probably does too.

As Christians we must be done with such carnal distinctions. If we aren't, we in effect deny that when Christ died for all, all died in him, and we revive distinctions that were put away in Christ's death.[3]

But there is an upside to regarding no one according to the flesh. Those who live out Paul's example grace everyone around. Robert Seelye, the most effective personal evangelist I have ever known, is like this. His great heart sees everyone through the eyes of Christ's love. All, whether senators or parking attendants, receive the same engagement. And what a varied multitude have come to God through his ministry. Because he regards no one according to the flesh, he sees the least likely of new converts as having immense potential. I can think of no one who has indelibly marked more souls than this man. He keeps in personal correspondence with hundreds around the world who follow Christ because of his ministry. This is even more remarkable because he isn't a professional evangelist or preacher but an insurance salesman. How Pauline, how Christlike, how Christian, how loving, how liberating, how empowering, how potent it is when "we regard no one according to the flesh."

Gospel Regard (v. 17)

Paul has urged on us the proper disregard that flows from the gospel due to the Christian's death in Christ. Now he declares how we ought to regard those who have died in Christ.[4] Here is *gospel regard*: "Therefore, if anyone is in Christ, he is a new creation. The old has passed away; behold, the new has come" (v. 17). This is the biography of *every* Christian! It is my biography. Though I was just a boy, God's Word became so alive to me that I could never get enough of it. Truly, old things had passed away, and new things had come. My burden of sin was gone. My guilt was gone. My sense of alienation from God and lostness and loneliness were gone.

Wondrous new things filled my life. New truths continued to rock my soul. I recall a year later, as a high school student, discovering Romans 12:1, 2: "I beseech you therefore, brethren, by the mercies of God, that ye present your bodies a living sacrifice, holy, acceptable unto God, which is your reasonable service. And be not conformed to this world: but be ye transformed by the renewing of your mind, that ye may prove what is that good, and acceptable, and perfect, will of God" (KJV). The logics of that great text sunk into my soul, and I pursued them to the best of my ability. I read Harry Ironside on the text in an attempt to understand it better. I purchased a red Bible and carried it to classes on top of my books because I wanted everyone to know what I now knew.

My Christian friends held a magnetism and were invitingly mysterious. I now know that came from our mutual sharing in the Body of Christ. I couldn't wait to get to our then tiny church and worship with the rest of the sixty-five members! It wasn't the youth group (all three of us!) that attracted me. It was gathered worship with loving adults.

Missions enthralled me. Missionaries seemed to me to live at an unattainable level of spirituality. I was sure they knew mysteries I would never know. Sometimes I prayed over an open map of the world.

Most of all, I loved Jesus. William Featherstone's old hymn (written when he was sixteen!) still expresses my soul as it did then.

My Jesus, I love Thee,
I know Thou art mine;
For Thee all the follies of sin I resign.
My gracious Redeemer,
My Savior art Thou;
If ever I loved Thee,
My Jesus, 'tis now.

William Featherstone, 1864

How good it is for us to return to the light of our conversion—our genesis. Every life will write it differently and originally, but "if anyone is in Christ, he is a new creation. The old has passed away; behold, the new has come" (v. 17) is the biography of every Christian. Philip Hughes comments on the phrase "if anyone is in Christ":

> The expression "in Christ" sums up as briefly and as profoundly as possible the inexhaustible significance of man's redemption. It speaks of security *in Him* who has Himself borne in his own body the judgment of God against our sin; it speaks of acceptance *in Him* with whom alone God is well pleased; it speaks of assurance for the future *in Him* who is the Resurrection and the Life; it speaks of the inheritance of glory *in Him* who, as the only-begotten Son, is the sole heir of God; it speaks of participation in the divine nature *in Him* who is the everlasting Word; it speaks of knowing the truth, and being free in that truth, *in Him* who Himself is the Truth. All this, and very much more than can ever be expressed in human language, is meant by being "in Christ."[5] (emphasis added)

"In Christ" describes the most intimate union possible. And when we are in Christ, there is a detonation. In fact, the Greek is explosive, "Therefore, if anyone in Christ (*boom!*) new creation." Sometimes the detonation is a bang, other times it is a long, rolling thunder, but the outcome is the same—"new creation." Just as with the creation in Genesis, God's Word (his will) does it. As Paul said in 4:6, "For God, who said, 'Let light shine out of darkness,' has shone in our hearts to give the light of the knowledge of the glory of God in the face of Jesus Christ." We became "his workmanship, created in Christ Jesus for good works, which God prepared beforehand, that we should walk in them" (Ephesians 2:10). God's finger sculpted us (so to speak) and then carved out a life for us to serve him.

The final phrase in 5:17 joyfully sums up our new creation in Christ: "The old has passed away; behold [look!], the new has come." The jubilation flows from the fact that the old has passed away permanently and that the new has come to stay[6] and will continue to be new because "the newness of God's new creation is not a newness that in the course of time palls and grows old and outmoded; it is a newness that is everlastingly new" (Hughes).[7] Therefore we have the abiding joy of the new creation.

The passing of the *old* and the coming of the *new* is meant by Paul to call to mind the old and new covenants that Paul described earlier in 3:6, where he says that we have been made "ministers of a new covenant, not of the letter but of the Spirit. For the letter kills, but the Spirit gives life." The new that has come therefore rides on the new-covenant blessings of Jeremiah 31—namely, a new *obedience*, the Law written on their hearts, a new *relationship*, God would be their God and they his people, a new *knowledge*, they would all know him, and a new *forgiveness*, for God would remember their sins no more (cf. vv. 31–34).

At the same time *old* and *new* recalls the coming second exodus and the deliverance of God's people from bondage. Isaiah 43 references the old and new as it proclaims the deliverance of God's people: "Remember not the former things, nor consider the things of old. Behold, I am doing a new thing; now it springs forth, do you not perceive it? I will make a way in the wilderness and rivers in the desert" (vv. 18, 19). So the passing of the old and the coming of the new means both complete deliverance from bondage and the dynamic blessings of the new covenant. And more, this newness is everlastingly new!

That is why we no longer regard Christ or his people according to the flesh, but rather with *gospel regard*. Believers are new creations in Christ. They have been brought forth in the exodus from bondage. They obey the Lord. They are his people. They know him. They are forgiven. Again, this is the biography of every Christian.

Christian, you are in Christ. You are a new creation. The old has passed out of existence. The eternally new has come. The law has been written on your heart. You're delivered. What then is required of you? Gospel regard for Christ as the crucified, risen, reigning, glorious Savior. And gospel regard for your brothers and sisters in Christ as new creations in Christ, liberated from the bondage of sin and living out the glories of the new covenant.

16

God's Reconciliation

2 CORINTHIANS 5:18—6:2

WHEN ADAM SINNED HE SINNED WILLFULLY, eyes wide open. His sin was freighted with rebellion and self-interest. Adam had watched Eve take the fruit, and nothing happened to her. So when he took the fruit from her, he sinned willfully against God, assuming there would be no consequences. The rebellion turned everything upside down. Eve followed the snake, Adam followed Eve, and no one followed God. Cosmic rebellion!

Adam and Eve plummeted from the pinnacle of innocence and intimacy into the pit of guilt and estrangement—"Then the eyes of both were opened, and they knew that they were naked. And they sewed fig leaves together and made themselves loincloths" (Genesis 3:7). There the first couple were, in their ridiculous fig leaves, slouching fearfully around paradise. In an instant the original couple had passed from life to death, from sinlessness to sin, from intimacy to alienation.

Adam's rebellion has been the lot and practice of the entire human race apart from the grace of God. Like Adam's, our rebellion is not a question of some minor misunderstanding that would easily be taken care of. Our rebellion is radical and incessant. And because of our sin, our rebellion is not the only factor in the alienation between God and man—our rebellion has been countered and matched by the wrath of God against sin. Thus Paul writes in Romans, "For the wrath of God is revealed from heaven against all ungodliness and unrighteousness of men, who by their unrighteousness suppress the truth" (1:18).

This fearful reality of universal alienation lies behind and frames 2 Corinthians 5:18—6:2. This is *the* great text on reconciliation, as evidenced by the forms of "reconcile" or "reconciliation" five times in brief succession.

Reconciliation Is All of God (5:18–20)

The other thing that catches our attention here is that reconciliation is God's unassisted work. Here God is shown to be the creator of the *messenger*, the *ministry*, and the *message* of reconciliation. This text is wholly God-centered. God is the mover of every mention of reconciliation in these verses.

The ministry of reconciliation as it is described in verse 19 is that "in Christ God was reconciling the world to himself, not counting their trespasses against them." Clearly then, reconciliation is not something we do—it is something God has accomplished. The ministry of reconciliation is not telling people to make peace with God, but telling them that God has made peace with the world. "At bottom, the gospel is not good advice, but good news" (Denney)[1]—"that is, in Christ God was reconciling the world to himself." Or, as Paul puts it in Romans:

> For if while we were enemies we were reconciled to God by the death of his Son, much more, now that we are reconciled, shall we be saved by his life. More than that, we also rejoice in God through our Lord Jesus Christ, through whom we have now received reconciliation. (5:10, 11)

We are not called to make peace with God—that is God's work! The method of reconciliation is reckoning, God "not counting their trespasses against them" (5:19, which will be explained in v. 21). There is a reckoning of sins. But they are reckoned not to the sinner but to Christ.

Aside from your own personal experience of reconciliation, if you have ever observed someone comprehend his or her own for the first time, you will never forget it. Though it has been thirty years, I can still see the faces of our young letter carrier and her seven-year-old son as her tears fell upon the pages of her Bible open to 1 Peter 2:24 as she read, inserting her own name, "He himself bore Bobbi's sins in his body on the tree, that Bobbi might die to sin and live to righteousness. By his wounds Bobbi has been healed." She understood that on the cross Christ took her sins, not counting her sins against her—"in Christ God was reconciling the world to himself" (5:19). And for the first time in her life she had peace—a peace, by the way, that has extended across the decades to her son's children.

Here the Apostle Paul (having been entrusted with the ministry and message of reconciliation) employs a bold analogy to describe his ministry, that of the ancient ambassador, an imperial legate in the Roman Empire, a man of immense authority.[2] As such, he did not speak in his own name or act on his own authority. Nor did his message originate in him, but from above. He stood in his Sovereign's stead and authority. So the actual truth was that as Paul spoke, God spoke. The ambassador analogy was not chosen because it approximated Paul's authority, but because it was reality. God really did make his appeal through him.

As the Apostle Paul made his ambassadorial appeal, it throbbed with divine conviction. The passion that welled in God's heart rose in Paul's heart—"We implore you on behalf of Christ, be reconciled to God" (v. 20). We must not miss the thrust of his passionate plea because it is not "reconcile yourselves to God" but "be reconciled" (passive)—that is, be reconciled *by* God.[3] Receive God's offer of reconciliation! This is a passionate offer of peace because peace with God is the result of reconciliation. The atoning, substitutionary death of Christ brings reconciliation and peace with God (cf. Romans 5:1–11). Beautifully, the promise of this peace was made long ago by the prophet Isaiah: "But he was pierced for our transgressions; he was crushed for our iniquities; upon him was the chastisement that brought us peace, and with his wounds we are healed" (53:5).

The gospel is not "reconcile yourselves." The gospel is "be reconciled." Receive reconciliation from God.

How God Reconciles (5:21)

Now we come to the heart of the atonement, the how of reconciliation: "For our sake he made him to be sin who knew no sin, so that in him we might become the righteousness of God" (5:21). These fifteen words in the original Greek, given in two parallel, mutually defining clauses, take us into the mystery of our reconciliation. James Denney says of this text:

> It is not the puzzle of the New Testament, but the ultimate solution of all puzzles; it is not an irrational quantity that has to be eliminated or explained away, but the key-stone of the whole system of apostolic thought. It is not a blank obscurity in revelation, a spot of impenetrable blackness; it is the focus in which the reconciling love of God burns with the purest and intensest flame; it is the fountain light of all day, the master light of all seeing, in the Christian revelation.[4]

Christ made sin. The first clause, "For our sake he made him to be sin who knew no sin" rides on the fact of Christ's sinlessness and is the most explicit statement of it in Scripture. Jesus Christ knew no sin. Other Scriptures, of course, also reference Christ's sinlessness, such as 1 Peter 2:22: "He committed no sin, neither was deceit found in his mouth" (also see Hebrews 4:15; 7:26; 1 John 3:5; cf. Romans 5:19; 8:3). The significance of Christ's sinlessness is that this is what he was as a *human being*. As a person, through every stage of his thirty-three years, he knew no sin. This awareness of sinlessness was part of his human consciousness (cf. John 8:46).[5] And we must realize that Jesus remained sinless when he became sin for us.

As to how God made him to be sin, we must first understand that it does *not* say that God made him to be a "sinner." This would do away with the ground of redemption. So then, how did God make Jesus, who never ceased being sinless, sin? Some would suggest that Jesus' being made sin means a "sin offering," which, of course, he was as the Lamb of God who fulfilled the Old Testament's vast promises. But I think that Dr. Murray Harris gets to the true depth of Christ's being made sin, as he explains:

> It seems Paul's intent to say more than that Christ was made a sin offering and yet less than he became a sinner. So complete was the identification of the sinless Christ with the sin of the sinner, including its dire guilt and its dread consequences of separation from God, that Paul could say profoundly, "God made him . . . to be sin for us."[6]

Thus Christ became sin while remaining inwardly and outwardly impeccable. He became sin as our substitute and sacrifice.

This is what happened during those three dark hours on Good Friday. Though all analogies or explanations of what happened fall short, they provide a glimpse. For example, think of Christ's heart as a sea hemmed in by the mountains of our festering sin. Then imagine our sins coursing down the mountains into his heart until all the mountains of evil slide into the sea. Or think back to the magnifying glass you played with as a child. If held under the sun's rays, it could start a fire. Remember how if you focused the white spot of its concentrated light on a leaf or a bug (only boys did this!), it would begin to burn. Our sins were focused on Christ on the cross, and he suffered the fiery wrath of God. On the cross Christ was robed in all that is heinous and hateful as the mass of our corruption poured over him. Wave after wave of our sin was poured over Christ's sinless soul. Again and again during those three hours his soul recoiled and convulsed as all our lies, hatreds, jealousies, and pride were poured upon his purity. "Christ redeemed us from the curse of the law by becoming a curse for us—for it is written, 'Cursed is everyone who is hanged on a tree'" (Galatians 3:13). Jesus was cursed as he became sin for us! Can you see him writhing like a serpent in the gloom (cf. John 3:14, 15)? Jesus in full, lucid consciousness took on your sins and mine and bore them with a unity of understanding and pain that none can fathom. And he did it willingly.

Sinners made righteous. The reason that Christ did this is given in the second clause of verse 21, "so that in him we might become the righteousness of God." There in the darkness our sins were imputed to Christ, and his righteousness was imputed to us who believe. All our sins were credited to Christ, and the spotless perfection of his righteousness was credited to us. Therefore, we are declared to have his righteousness.

Yet this is more than a legal declaration. On the one hand it was a legal forensic declaration by which the righteousness of God is given to us. On the other hand, the righteousness of God describes a new way of living. We live righteously because God has declared us righteous.[7]

Living out the righteousness of God was a burning concern to Paul. In terms of Paul's concern in this chapter it means to live our lives in the reality of the coming resurrection when we will stand before the judgment seat of Christ (cf. 5:10). It means serving God motivated by both the fear of God and the love of Christ (cf. 5:11–15). It means being done with fleshly regard of Christ and others (cf. 5:16, 17). It means, instead, regarding our brothers and sisters as new creations in Christ. It means living in the Spirit-directed freedoms of the new covenant, as people who have made the exodus from bondage (cf. 5:17). It means embracing the ministry and message of reconciliation and preaching its astonishing mystery—"For our sake he made him to be sin who knew no sin, so that in him we might become the righteousness of God" (5:21).

Plea for Reconciliation (6:1, 2)

Fittingly Paul closes his explanation of reconciliation with a plea: "Working together with him, then, we appeal to you not to receive the grace of God in vain. For he says, 'In a favorable time I listened to you, and in a day of salvation I have helped you.' Behold, now is the favorable time; behold, now is the day of salvation" (vv. 1, 2).

The logic of this appeal is drawn from Isaiah 49:8 (49:9, LXX, verbatim), where God speaks to his servant Isaiah in a text that prophesies the restoration of Israel and coincides with Paul's emphasis on the new creation in Christ. Paul says, in effect, that Isaiah's day of salvation has arrived in the reconciliation of the cross. Therefore, the Corinthians must not miss this long-awaited opportunity for salvation. The day of salvation is here. How unthinkable that they might "receive the grace of God in vain." How tragic is the thought that they might at one time have given apparent assent to Paul's proclamation, but now through unbelief and disobedience the wonders of the new covenant (with the new creation in Christ and the ultimate exodus from bondage) were being nullified. Paul was saying, you have been assenting to God's saving purposes; do not let it be in vain.

The urgency with which Paul feels this is indicated by his twin repetitions of "behold" or "look." Earlier he had said, "Therefore, if anyone is in Christ, he is a new creation. The old has passed away; behold the new has come" (5:17). Here he passionately declares, "Behold, now is the favorable time; behold, now is the day of salvation." In other words, don't receive the grace of God in vain! Don't put it off! I implore you on behalf of Christ.

The force of Paul's argument and the example of his great heart for his people has given me much to reflect upon as to what my heart must be for my people and has brought to mind the example of Charles Simeon.

Simeon was the man who almost single-handedly brought the evangelical resurgence to the Church of England. Fellow of King's College Cambridge, he had secured the pulpit of Holy Trinity, Cambridge, where he preached for over fifty years. For the first ten years of his ministry, his unhappy parishioners chained their pews closed, so that all listeners had to sit in the aisles! But Simeon persevered. His twenty-one volumes of sermons—*Horae Homilaticae* (*Hours of Homilies*)—set the standard for preaching in the following generations. His Friday night tea was used to disciple a generation of preachers and missionaries, including Henry Martyn.

He not only prevailed but three times gave the university lectures. When you visit Cambridge, you can view his artifacts at his church: the black Wedgwood teapot from which he served students at his Friday night study group, his umbrella (the very first in Cambridge), and his twenty-one volumes of sermons. And today, if you visit the National Gallery in London, you can see a famous set of silhouettes depicting Simeon in various homiletical postures as he implores his people from the pulpit of Holy Trinity.

I say all of this because Simeon was a passionate preacher of the Word with a heart for his people. When Simeon died, one of his obituaries carried this remembrance of calling his hearers to faith:

> And after having urged all his hearers to accept the proffered mercy, he reminded them that there were those present to whom he had preached Christ for more than thirty years, but they continued indifferent to the Saviour's love; and pursuing this train of expostulation for some time, he at length became quite overpowered by his feeling, and he sank down in the pulpit and burst into a flood of tears.[8]

Pulpit tears are not my normal custom, and I suspect they were not Simeon's. But they revealed the right emotion considering the unending tragedy of receiving the grace of God in vain.

At times in the moments after an infant dedication when I have held a beautiful baby in my arms and dedicated the child to God and have led the loving parents in solemn vows to raise their son or daughter in "the nurture and admonition of the Lord," I reflect on the sad events that have followed similar occasions in the past. The proud parents loved their child and prayed for him or her, however imperfectly. No parents are perfect, but they did raise that little soul in a godly home. The child grew up in the church through awkward junior high years and then high school and went off to university and a career but at present has never come to know Christ. The grace of God (the prayers, the preaching, the love of the Body of Christ) has been until now in vain. And some appear as if they will continue through life without ever truly responding to the Word. Such a waste. Such unmitigated sorrow. I pray that the grace of God will not be in vain.

So I appeal to you on behalf of Christ, do not receive the grace of God in vain. Look! Now is the day of salvation.

17

Ministry That Commends

2 CORINTHIANS 6:3–13

PAUL'S LYRICAL DEFENSE OF HIS MINISTRY in this section flows directly from his compelling plea that the Corinthians be reconciled to God. He had just explained how reconciliation with God is the work of God alone (5:18–20). So we must understand that people are never called to make their peace with God. It is all his work. Then (in what is, by consensus, one of the most crucial texts in the New Testament), the apostle explained how such reconciliation takes place: "For our sake he made him to be sin who knew no sin, so that in him we might become the righteousness of God" (5:21). This is what happened in those three dark hours on the cross on Good Friday—our sins were imputed to him and his righteousness to us. This is the stunning grace of God, which births Paul's passionate plea, "Working together with him, then, we appeal to you not to receive the grace of God in vain. . . . Behold, now is the favorable time; behold, now is the day of salvation" (6:1, 2). Don't put it off. Be reconciled to God. Receive his reconciliation.

Paul knew that most of the Corinthians had been reconciled to God. But he knew that some were still rejecting him (Paul), and by rejecting him as the messenger of reconciliation, they were rejecting the message of reconciliation. And Paul knew why they were rejecting him. It was because they could not believe that he could be a true apostle and be subject to such weaknesses and extraordinary sufferings (cf. 1:3–11; 7:4, 5). God's blessing, they reasoned, would be evidenced by peace and well-being. To their mind, his incessant troubles and miseries were *prima fascia* evidence of God's displeasure. They could not accept Paul!

So now comes Paul's eloquent defense, in which he shows that his endurance through multiple troubles proves his authenticity and is reason for the Corinthians to open their hearts to his message: "We put no obstacle in anyone's way, so that no fault may be found with our ministry, but as servants of God we commend ourselves in every way: by great endurance . . ." (vv. 3, 4a). Paul's heading the list that follows in verses 4–10 with the singular "endurance" and qualifying it as "great" in contrast to the unqualified plural descriptives that follow indicates that "great endurance" is the heading for all that follows.[1]

Endurance amidst adversities is the overarching quality of authentic ministry. This is because the natural inclination is to flee the conflicts of ministry. Timothy Dudley-Smith's biography of the great preacher John Stott, now in his mid-eighties, lifts the curtain as to how Stott has sometimes felt: "Well, the first temptation (to which I'm more exposed . . . I think) is to run away; not to give in, but to—what is the word?—to leave. I sometimes say my favourite text is from Psalm 55: 'O for the wings of a dove, that I may flee away and be at rest.' So I've found this constant controversy, this constant battling for the truth, very wearing."[2]

In my own small universe I've experienced the same inclinations for a place where there is no conflict. Hey, never play baseball, and you'll never strike out. Never lead and you'll never be criticized. Never preach and you'll never bore anyone. Never confront and conflicts will be minimized. The temptation is universal—and I've contemplated it many times over my forty years of ministry. How I thank God for the teaching of Paul—and for the examples of endurance by men like John Stott.

So now as we take up Paul's lyrical record of endurance in its structure and rising intensity, we must note that it consists of twenty-eight descriptives (in the original Greek), of which the first eighteen are introduced by the word "in," the next three by the word "through," and the final seven by the word "as." Here is how verses 4–10 read literally, with these twenty-eight little Greek words in place (note italics):

> . . . but as servants of God we commend ourselves in every way: in great endurance, in afflictions, in hardships, in calamities, in beatings, in imprisonments, in riots, in labors, in sleepless nights, in hunger; in purity, in knowledge, in patience, in kindness, in the Holy Spirit, in genuine love; in truthful speech, in the power of God; through the weapons of righteousness for the right hand and for the left; through honor and dishonor; through slander and praise. We are treated as impostors, and yet are true; as unknown, and yet well known; as dying, and behold, we live; as punished, and yet not killed; as sorrowful, yet always rejoicing; as poor, yet making many rich; as having nothing, yet possessing everything.

Great Endurance in Multiple Troubles (vv. 4b, 5)

St. Chrysostom termed the opening list as a "blizzard of troubles," and it is certainly that as troubles shower in triplets, from all angles. First, there is a trio of *general troubles*: "in afflictions, hardships, calamities" (v. 4b). Jesus told his disciples, "In the world you will have tribulation" (John 16:33). When Paul met Christ, the Holy Spirit informed him that afflictions awaited him (Acts 20:23). And Paul would tell his converts that "through many tribulations we must enter the kingdom of God" (Acts 14:22). The apostolic way was fraught with hardships and calamities that left Paul literally with no way out. All this went with the apostolic territory.

The second trio of troubles was *troubles from others*: "beatings, imprisonments, riots." Elsewhere Paul refers to his countless beatings and then lists only some of the worst: "Five times I received at the hands of the Jews the forty lashes less one. Three times I was beaten with rods" (11:24, 25a). Eight excruciating beatings! As to imprisonments, the Bible only records one—in Philippi where, beaten and in stocks, he and Silas brought down the house with their singing (cf. Acts 16). But this was just one of many humiliating nights in jail. Paul experienced riots in Pisidian Antioch, Iconium, Lystra, Philippi, Thessalonica, Corinth, Ephesus, and Jerusalem (cf. Acts 13:50; 14:5, 19; 16:22; 18:12; 19:23; 21:27). Paul stands alone in history in his record of long abuse from others. There is no one like him.

Add to this the trio of his *self-inflicted troubles*: "labors, sleepless nights, hunger"—troubles that came to him voluntarily as he willingly worked to exhaustion and went without sleep and skipped meals to do gospel work. Put this triple trio of troubles all together and we have the picture of Paul's life.

It was truly a blizzard of troubles from every perspective, and Paul's response was "great endurance"—more exactly, patient endurance, fortitude, and great persistence under persecution. Clement of Rome believed this to be Paul's distinctive and said so in his eulogy for the apostle:

> Paul by his example pointed out the prize of patient endurance. After he had been seven times in bonds, had been driven into exile, had been stoned, had preached in the East and in the West, he won the noble renown which was the reward of his faith, having taught righteousness unto the whole world and having reached the farthest bounds of the West; and when he had borne this testimony before the rulers, so he departed from the world and went unto the holy place, having been found a notable pattern of patient endurance.[3]

What a man Paul was—perpetually in the dust of the arena, beaten, bloody, mocked by the crowds, sweating, exhausted, hungry, sleepless—but always enduring.

In point of fact, Paul's sufferings did not disqualify him. Rather, they proved the authenticity of his faith and commitment. The fact that he didn't quit or curse God for his miseries as so many have done but endured testified to his genuine faith. In effect, his endurance declared that the gospel is true and that Jesus is worth it.

So often our words are ignored by others, including our nearest and dearest. But when they observe endurance for Christ in the midst of showers of troubles, they cannot deny the reality of our faith in Christ.

Great Endurance by Spirit-Given Graces (vv. 6, 7a)

Having described the troubles he endured through the three sets of triple-troubles, Paul next references the inner graces from which he derived his great endurance: "by purity, knowledge, patience, kindness, the Holy Spirit, genuine love; by truthful speech, and the power of God" (vv. 6, 7a). There is a surprise here because in the middle of these inner graces lies not a grace but the person of the Holy Spirit. So we must understand that these graces are not natural virtues, but gifts of the Holy Spirit.

Paul wants us to see that his great endurance in ministry is not an angry, tight-jawed, "I'll show you" endurance, but rather his endurance rests in his purity of motive and life, in Spirit-given knowledge of Christ himself, in a Spirit-imbued patience that is not provoked to anger, in a genuine, unhypocritical love, in truthful speech, and in the power of God. Paul's great endurance thus had a Spirit-endowed sweetness. It is possible to endure in this life but to do it in a self-righteous, resentful survivor-spirit that is self-pitying and angry at those who do not shoulder the burden with you while being inwardly proud of your grit. Instead of the fruit of the Spirit, there is bitterness and joylessness. In truth, God may not consider this kind of life to be one of endurance, and certainly not one of "great endurance" (v. 4). Paul endured with the inner graces of the Spirit. Sweet endurance is what the Scripture here enjoins.

Admittedly, there are ungodly people who exhibit remarkable endurance in difficulty. There are, no doubt, revolutionaries and terrorists who will endure beatings and imprisonments and even death for their causes, but none of them do it in the sweet endurance of the inner graces of the Holy Spirit. Sweet in-Spirited endurance testifies to the reality of Christ and that he is worth our trust and service.

Great Endurance Through Righteousness (vv. 7b, 8a)

Next we see that at the heart of Paul's great endurance is righteousness: "with [literally *through*] the weapons of righteousness for the right hand and for the left" (v. 7b). "Righteousness" here is most certainly righteous living, a holy life. As we saw in the great statement of 5:21, "For our sake he made him to be sin who knew no sin, so that in him we might become the righteousness of God." The righteousness of God is both a declared status and a way of life—the way a righteous person lives. Moreover, the immediate context in verses 6, 7 emphasizes that it is a righteous life.[4]

So Paul's endurance rides on his righteous living, his holiness. Paul employs "the weapons of righteousness for the right hand and for the left," meaning that righteousness thoroughly equips him to meet an attack from any quarter. In frankest terms the ministry is a character profession—righteous living must be at its heart. Those who lead God's people bear an immense responsibility by virtue of their calling and knowledge of the Scriptures. Paul began by saying, "We put no obstacle in anyone's way, so that no fault may be found with our ministry, but as servants of God we commend ourselves in every way" (vv. 3, 4a). Nothing will provide a greater stumbling block than moral/ethical failure.

Because of this, when we are looking for additions to the pastoral staff of the church I pastor, we ask them direct personal questions in front of the elders regarding their personal, moral conduct in every area. I have been known to gather my colleagues together and ask them individually about their moral lives. And then I've prayed, "If anyone is lying, take him home. It's better to die than disgrace God's name." Righteousness in ministry is more important than life. Of course, sensuality is just one issue when it comes to righteous living. The call is comprehensive and dynamic.

Great endurance rides on righteous living. Here we see in the following context that it will sustain Paul "through honor and dishonor, through slander and praise" (v. 8a). "Honor and dishonor" refers to personal treatment of Paul; "slander and praise" refers to what is said about him—especially behind his back.[5] Righteous conduct effects a clear conscience and the power to withstand such things, and as Paul would tell Timothy, a good conscience is essential for fighting the good fight (cf. 1 Timothy 1:18, 19).

Righteousness is at the heart of gospel endurance. That is how Christ endured the cross. And when it remains firm amidst the afflictions that shower upon God's servants, Christ is exalted. Righteousness for the right hand and the left, for all of life, is a chief means of declaring the reality of Christ.

Great Endurance in Triumphant Paradoxes (vv. 8b, 10)

Paul concludes with a mounting song of triumphant endurance that rides on the down-up rhythm of paradox. The first half of each of the seven paradoxes, read together, is like a dirge: "as imposters . . . as unknown . . . as dying . . . as punished . . . as sorrowful . . . as poor . . . as having nothing." But the second half is a dance. Each of the seven paradoxes of endurance ends in triumph.

• "We are treated as imposters, and yet are true."

Despite his critics' dishonor and slander, Paul knows before God that his apostolic call and ministry are from God and are true.

• ". . . as unknown and yet well known . . ."

This Pharisee of the Pharisees had become a nonentity. As he said earlier, "We have become, and are still, like the scum of the world, the refuse of all things" (1 Corinthians 4:13). However, though unacknowledged by the world, he is fully known by God.

• ". . . as dying, and behold, we live . . ."

Paul was slowly dying through his repeated beatings and illnesses and stresses and dangers. But look, he is alive! He was filled with life indeed—vital, animated, eternal, overflowing.

• ". . . as punished, and yet not killed . . ."

Paul had undergone at times the remedial, chastening of God, but it hadn't killed him. In fact, it had elevated his life.

• ". . . as sorrowful, yet always rejoicing . . ."

Friends had failed him, converts had turned upon him, and his works were threatened by wicked men. "But," as Philip Hughes explains, "no sorrow, no disappointment, however severe, could ever interrupt, let alone extinguish, the joy of his salvation with its vision of unclouded glory to come, for this joy was founded upon the sovereign supremacy of God, who overrules all things and causes them to work together for good to those He has called" (cf. Romans. 8:18, 28).[6]

• ". . . as poor, yet making many rich . . ."

Everyone could see the ragged man he was, a figure to be pitied, they thought. But that is not how he thought of himself. He was rich toward God (cf. Luke 12:21) and heir of all things (cf. Romans 8:17), and he spent his time bestowing riches.

• ". . . as having nothing, yet possessing everything."

Earlier he had told the Corinthians, "For all things are yours . . . all are yours, and you are Christ's, and Christ is God's" (1 Corinthians 3:21b, 22). He knew he was the heir of all things. Paul was true, well-known, alive and not dead, always rejoicing, making many rich, possessing everything. He endured triumphantly. That is why his endurance was great!

Paul's great endurance substantiated his ministry. He was the real thing, as seen by his endurance through a blizzard of troubles, by his endurance in the Spirit-given graces, by his endurance through righteousness, and by his endurance in triumph.

And now in his conclusion we see Paul abandon his apostolic plural and speak in the first person from his heart: "We have spoken freely to you, Corinthians; our heart is wide open. You are not restricted by us, but you are restricted in your own affections. In return (I speak as to children) widen your hearts also" (vv. 11–13). As Scott Hafemann has pointed out, Paul is not addressing the Corinthians as one whose feelings have been hurt, he is not trying to recover his ego, he has no need to bolster his self-esteem.[7] Paul has spoken from his heart—that is, he has opened before them what makes him tick, his inner motives for ministry.

His heart is seen in the depth of his endurance for the gospel. And here he is not attempting to get the Corinthians to like him but is calling them to respond to the heart-evidence before them. They must now understand that his endurance in suffering proves that his ministry is the real thing.[8] His endurance amidst suffering has shown him to be living out the life of Christ in him.

It is the same for us today. We commend the gospel to our families and the church and the world by our faithful endurance. The call to follow Christ is a call to endure in sufferings, by the graces of the Spirit, through righteousness, riding the triumphant, exultant paradoxes of Christ, thereby demonstrating that our faith in Christ is real and that he is worth our full allegiance.

18

Bringing Holiness to Completion

2 CORINTHIANS 6:14—7:1

IT IS OF UTMOST IMPORTANCE that we understand and believe that the greatest danger to the church is not from without but from within. This is a truth that has been repeatedly demonstrated in church history. Perhaps its most dramatic demonstration was in the German Protestant church in the last century. German Biblical criticism had so undermined confidence in the Bible that few pastors saw it as the infallible Word of God. Liberal theology was in the driver's seat—and pulpits catered to the cultured despisers. There were remarkable exceptions, of course, like the courageous pastor Martin Niemoller, who in 1933 preached on the occasion of Martin Luther's four hundred and fiftieth birthday about how tragic it would be if the devil filled German minds with the delusion that what they needed was not the grace of God but the courage of Martin Luther. Niemoller said, "There is absolutely no sense in talking of Luther and celebrating his memory in the Protestant church if we do not stop at Luther's image and look at Him to whom Luther pointed"—to a Jew, a rabbi of Nazareth.[1]

The next evening, in eerie fulfillment of Pastor Niemoller's words, 20,000 Christians under the umbrella of the German Evangelical Church, led by bishops and church officials in full regalia, gathered in the new Berlin Sports Palace. After a fanfare of trumpets and the singing of "Now Thank We All Our God," a Berlin pastor, Joachim Hossenfelder, announced that he was implementing the infamous Aryan paragraph in his diocese that dismissed all Christian Jews from church office, effective immediately. During the evening it was also announced among other things that Niemoller was suspended, that the Bible was to be reexamined for all its non-German elements (i.e., de-Semiticized), and that a proud, heroic Jesus must replace the model of the suffering servant. The speech was interrupted again and again by applause. Pathetically, not one of the bedecked bishops or church leaders stood up to disagree.[2] Clearly, the state church had imploded from within.

Forty years ago liberal theologian Langdon Gilkey gave this assessment of his church in America, an assessment that could describe much of the evangelical church today:

> All around us we see the church well acclimated to culture: successful, respected, wealthy, full, and growing. But are the transcendent and the holy there? In the area of belief we find widespread indifference to the Bible and ignorance of its contents—and strong resentment if a biblical word of judgment is brought to bear on the life of the congregation. In worship we find notably lacking any sense of the holy presence of God and of what worship is for. . . . In ethics we find the cultural ideals of friendliness and fellowship more evident than the difficult standards of the New Testament or historic Christendom.[3]

Hearing this today, who can deny that biblical ignorance, an absence of holiness in worship, and ethical accommodation have become widespread among evangelicals? As Joe Bayly, author and editor, wrote, "The evangelical church is sick—so sick that people are crowding in to join us. We're a big flock, big enough to permit remarriage of divorced people (beyond the exceptions of the Word of God), big enough to permit practicing homosexuals to pursue their lifestyle, big enough to tolerate almost anything pagans do. We're no longer narrow; it's a wide road of popular acceptance for us."[4]

Just as throughout history, the evangelical church's greatest danger is from within. And this is where the opening command of our text intersects our lives: "Do not be unequally yoked with unbelievers." The command is not (as is commonly thought) an injunction against marrying unbelievers or entering into contracted relationships with non-Christians (though both actions are un-Biblical), but rather a command not to be yoked together with those in the church who oppose the truth—unbelievers in the church.

The reason that we must understand "unbelievers" as opponents within the church is that in Paul's long argument that precedes and follows this command he repeatedly references his opponents in the Corinthian church as to their slanderous attacks on his apostleship (cf., e.g., 2:17; 5:12) as well as their bogus devotion in worshiping health and wealth and in preaching another kind of Jesus (cf. 11:1–4, 13–15, 20). In effect, they are unbelievers because they dis the gospel! Thus, those Corinthians who persist in siding with Paul's opponents will in effect renounce their own salvation, because it was through Paul that they received the message of grace and reconciliation. Therefore to be yoked together in the unbelieving viewpoint of Paul's opponents is in effect to reject the gospel of reconciliation and deny their own authenticity.

Paul was concerned about the enemy within—the unbelieving in the church. And his warning command echoes down the centuries to us: "Do not be unequally yoked with unbelievers"—that is, do not be allied with unbelievers as to their teaching or way of life or false worship. This is not a call to split theological hairs, seeing those who disagree with you as "unbelievers." Church history is tragically full of this. Neither is this a command to bar unbelievers from the fellowship of the assembled church. Church is the best place for unbelievers, because there they can hear the Word and be loved by the Body of Christ.

But in the context here, we are to disassociate ourselves from complicity with those who would attempt to propagate a false gospel within the church. Specifically, it means to sever the yoke with those who insinuate that reconciliation is not all of God and that we can make peace with God, that the substitutionary death of Christ on the cross in which God "made him to be sin who knew no sin, so that in him we might become the righteousness of God" (5:21) is not enough, but rather there are rituals and experiences and works that will make our salvation secure. Today it means to reject liberal, moralizing theories of the atonement. It means to reject a bootstrap sentimentality that if we do our best we will make it and that good people will find a way. And within the church, it demands that we never allow those who hold such doctrines to be yoked with us in ministry.

This is a call not to give those who would presume to lead and teach the church a pass because they are nice or theologically educated or gifted or related to us or have grown up in the church. Countless churches have fallen from within because godly leaderships have yoked themselves and their congregation with an unbelieving pastor. Often it has been the pastor's son or a favorite son of the church returned fresh from a prominent theological institution where he quietly discarded his faith but retained his religious vocabulary (redefined for his own purposes) and has learned ecclesiastical craftsmanship. He is pious, disarming, smiling, but unbelieving. Weimar Germany was full of pastors like this. And they sat on their hands while the church plunged into apostasy.

Today as we sing majestic hymns and affirm the Apostle's Creed, we mustn't imagine that we are immune. We and our churches can decline quickly if we yoke ourselves to unbelieving people who would aspire to lead us.

The structure of Paul's argument is easy to see and ever so powerful. The command "Do not be unequally yoked with unbelievers" is reiterated again in the middle of his argument in verse 17: "Therefore go out from their midst, and be separate from them, says the Lord, and touch no unclean thing." And then again it is stated as a general principle in the conclusion: "Since we have these promises, beloved, let us cleanse ourselves from every defilement of body and spirit, bringing holiness to completion in the fear of God" (7:1). The call to unyoke ourselves from unbelieving aspirants reverberates with passionate nuance.

Questions That Drive Home the Theology of Separation (vv. 14–16c)

The first line of Paul's argument supporting his command that the Corinthians sever their yoke with those opposing him is a series of five questions based on five astonishing facets that spring from their being new-covenant believers in Christ. The fivefold wonder is that:

1. *They are "righteousness" in that they have become "the righteousness of God" (5:21) in Christ.* Their sin has been credited to Christ, and in turn Christ's righteousness was credited to them. But more, having been declared righteous, they also have been bequeathed with a righteous way of life in him (cf. 6:7b).

2. *They also have become "light."* As Paul earlier said, "God, who said, 'Let light shine out of darkness,' has shone in our hearts to give the light of the knowledge of the glory of God in the face of Jesus Christ" (4:6). In John Donne's famous words:

> I am thy sonne, made with thy selfe to shine.
>
> *Holy Sonnets*, II, line 5

They have the light of Christ (cf. John 8:12), which will mean that in eternity they will need no lamp (cf. Revelation 22:5).

3. *They have Christ/Messiah.* As Paul has just said, "if anyone is in Christ [Messiah] . . . new creation" (5:17). They are in Messiah, and Messiah, the apotheosis of all biblical prophecy, is in them. They are Messiah-possessed, indwelt, new creations!

4. *They are designated as "believers"*—those who follow in the train of those who rested their trust in God—Abel and Enoch and Noah and Abram and Isaac and Jacob and Joseph and Moses and Gideon and Barak and Samson and Jephthah and David and Samuel and the prophets.

5. Lastly, *they are "temples."* Whereas God dwelt in the tabernacle and then the temple, Jesus displaced the temple, and now those in Christ become temples in which God dwells. So now the church, both in regard to individual members and to its life together, is the place of God's presence in the world.

How the five facets of the new covenant (righteousness, light, Christ, believer, temple) flash with glory! The new-covenant people (the church) are astonishing!

Thus Paul's fivefold rhetorical questions hammer the point home:

> Do not be unequally yoked with unbelievers. For what partnership has righteousness with lawlessness? Or what fellowship has light with darkness? What accord has Christ with Belial? Or what portion does a believer share with an unbeliever? What agreement has the temple of God with idols? For we are the temple of the living God. (vv. 14–16)

The spheres are mutually exclusive, and that is why Christians must never allow themselves to be yoked to and co-opted by would-be leaders who oppose the gospel within the church—those who accommodate culture, misuse the Bible, abuse divine worship, and front for the ethics of popular culture.

Scriptures That Undergird the Call to Separation and Holiness (vv. 16d-18)

Next, in order to further encourage the Corinthian church to separate from those who oppose Paul, Paul emphasizes two promises that were made as part of Israel's promised deliverance from bondage (or their second exodus). The two promises were a promise of personal *intimacy* and a promise of personal *adoption*. These promises (the first in verse 16 and the second in verse 18) are bookends and reinforce Paul's call to separation in verse 17.[5] What looks like a single quotation in verses 16–18 really consists of six single, mutually interpreting Old Testament quotations that are too complex to explain in an exposition.

But what we need to understand is what Dr. Greg Beale so convincingly argues in his 1989 article published in *New Testament Studies*: "Almost without exception, the six generally agreed upon Old Testament references refer in their respective contexts to God's promise to restore exiled Israel to their land."[6] Further, he demonstrates that while Paul would allow that this restoration began its fulfillment with the nation's return from Babylon, the escalated fulfillment occurred at Christ's death and resurrection.[7] The point is: The Corinthians were full beneficiaries of the new covenant's deliverance and restoration. And as such, they should pursue separation and holiness.

Restored to intimacy. In verse 16 Paul argues that the original covenant promise of intimacy with God is now being fulfilled in the Corinthian church: "as God said, 'I will make my dwelling among them and walk among them, and I will be their God, and they shall be my people.'" This promise is made up of two promises of intimacy, one from Leviticus 26:11, 12 (the Sinai covenant of the first exodus) and one from Ezekiel 37:27 (the new covenant of the second exodus).[8] Thus the Corinthians were direct beneficiaries of intimacy with God that converged on them from the flood of biblical history. The realization of their incredible blessings as heirs of the covenant formula ("I will make my dwelling among them and walk among them, and I will be their God, and they shall be my people") was meant to drive them to separation from sin and to holiness.

Restored by adoption. The promise of personal adoption in verses 17d, 18 ("then I will welcome you, and I will be a father to you, and you shall be sons and daughters to me, says the Lord Almighty") is composed of four separate Old Testament snippets from 2 Samuel 7:14, Isaiah 52:11, Ezekiel 20:34, and Isaiah 43:6—all of which come from contexts freighted with the promise of restoration.[9] Hafemann remarks:

> Indeed, "I will be a Father to you, and you will be my sons and daughters," is the "adoption" formula that is used in Scripture to indicate the covenant relationship between God and his people. In using this formula, Paul is reflecting the Jewish expectation that God's people would one day be "adopted" as his children by virtue of their allegiance to and incorporation in God's "adopted son," the Messiah.[10]

The point is crystal-clear: The Corinthians, having been adopted, are heirs of all the promises of the covenant and as such must separate themselves from impurity. As God's children they must separate from those ostensibly yoked to them within the covenant who actually do not belong and are making it unclean.

Thus the fact that the Corinthians have been graced with the fulfillment of the covenantal promises of personal *intimacy* with God and personal *adoption* by God demands full threefold separation prophetically voiced in the restoration text of Isaiah 52:11: "'Therefore go out from their midst, and be separate from them, says the Lord, and touch no unclean thing'" (v. 17).

Now having hammered the Corinthians both by the logic of the opening rhetorical questions and then with the covenantal promises of Scripture, Paul drives home his demand: "Since we have these promises, beloved, let us cleanse ourselves from every defilement of body and spirit, bringing holiness to completion in the fear of God" (7:1). His demand is personal and comprehensive. "Body and spirit" means everything that impacts the believer's life. The demand is also moral—for progressive moral transformation—"bringing holiness to completion." The great tragedy for so many is that as they get older, they do not get any holier. Time has been the enemy. They left their moral apex in junior high school. They were better boys than they are men. Holiness is farther from completion. The demand for holiness is fearful, "in the fear of God." We will all stand "before the judgment seat of Christ, so that each one may receive what is due for what he has done in the body, whether good or evil" (5:10). Knowing this fear, we must work at "bringing holiness to completion."

Paul's opening command to refuse to be yoked to unbelievers who would lead the church, along with his closing stress upon holiness, comes because he knew that the greatest danger to the church is from within. This is so for me personally. It is not the stresses that endanger me—it is my own heart if untended. I must live out the realities of the new covenant as to *righteousness*, as to being *light*, as to being *in Christ*, as to being a *believer*, and as to being *God's temple*.

Corporately, for the church, the great danger remains from within. To imagine otherwise is to arrogate ourselves above the lessons of church history. We are certainly no better than those who were seduced by errant leaders. We must never imagine that the professing church as we know it could not fall to the ignominies of the church in Weimar Germany if similar political conditions prevailed.

We must be perpetually vigilant. We must never allow those who oppose the gospel to ascend to leadership. We must yoke ourselves to the truth and the love of God. "For the love of Christ controls us, because we have concluded this: that one has died for all, therefore all have died; and he died for all, that those who live might no longer live for themselves but for him who for their sake died and was raised" (5:14, 15).

19

Comfort and Joy for a Caring Heart

2 CORINTHIANS 7:2–16

ON A NOTABLE SUNDAY MORNING IN 1866, the famous Victorian preacher C. H. Spurgeon shocked his five thousand listeners when from the pulpit of London's Metropolitan Tabernacle he announced, "I am the subject of depressions of spirit so fearful that I hope none of you ever gets to such extremes of wretchedness as I go to." For some of his audience it was incomprehensible that the world's greatest preacher could know the valley of despair. Yet it was a regular part of his life because twenty-one years later in 1887 he said from the same pulpit, "Personally I have often passed through this dark valley."

John Henry Jowett, the renowned pastor of Fifth Avenue Presbyterian in New York City, and later Westminster Chapel in London, wrote to a friend in 1920, "You seem to imagine I have no ups and downs but just a level and lofty stretch of spiritual attainment with unbroken joy and equanimity. By no means! I am often perfectly wretched and everything appears most murky."

Writing of Alexander Whyte, perhaps Scotland's greatest preacher since John Knox, G. F. Barbour said, "Resolute as was Dr. Whyte's character, he had seasons of deep depression regarding the results of his work in the pulpit or among his people."[1]

Martin Luther was subject to such fits of darkness that he would hide himself away for days, and his family would remove all dangerous implements from the house for fear he would harm himself. In the midst of one of these times, his indomitable wife, Katharina, entered his room dressed in mourning clothes. Startled, Luther asked who had died. She replied that no one had, but from the way he was acting, she thought God had died!

The reality is that godly believers sometimes get depressed. Those who have set their minds on "the things above, where Christ is seated at the right hand of God" (Colossians 3:1) have not been exempted from down times. Those who have gone for it all, who have scaled heights we may never attain, sometimes were subject to depression and despair—the "damp of hell" as John Donne called it.[2] Depression has been called the common cold of the soul, for sooner or later most people catch it. And God's servants are not immune.

Depression actually has apostolic precedent—in the experience of the Apostle Paul. Paul's self-description says that he was "downcast" (cf. v. 6), or as the NASB has it, "depressed"—a sense commended both by the context and the psychological import of Paul's description.[3] Paul is perfectly clear as to why he was down: "For even when we came into Macedonia, our bodies had no rest, but we were afflicted at every turn—fighting without and fear within" (note: "fighting" and "fear" are plural in the Greek) (v. 5).

This Macedonian misery was the culmination of Paul's excruciating anxiety over the Corinthian church to which he had written a harsh letter after suffering rejection in Corinth. So concerned was Paul with how the Corinthians would respond, he sent Titus to Corinth to find out and then report to him at an agreed-upon rendezvous in Troas. This plan only served to increase his stress because Titus didn't show. So Paul left Troas and traveled to Macedonia, fearing that something had happened to Titus (cf. 2:12, 13). But at first all he found there was the Macedonian mess. There in Macedonia Paul suffered exhaustion due to constant affliction as he was pressured externally and internally. The "fighting[s] without" refer to heated disputes with either unbelievers or believers, and likely both.[4] He was immersed in a maelstrom of quarreling. Paul could not escape. Every turn brought him face to face with conflict.

Along with this, he experienced "fear[s] within." These were not fears for his own life. We have too much evidence to the contrary to think that (cf. Philippians 1:21–24). His inner fears were about what might happen to his work, for he often spoke of this. For example, he told the Galatians, "I am afraid I may have labored over you in vain" (Galatians 4:11); and he wrote to the Thessalonians, "For this reason, when I could bear it no longer, I sent to learn about your faith, for fear that somehow the tempter had tempted you and our labor would be in vain" (1 Thessalonians 3:5); and then, to the Corinthians, he will say, "There is the daily pressure on me of my anxiety for all the churches. Who is weak, and I am not weak? Who is made to fall, and I am not indignant?" (2 Corinthians 11:28, 29).

These ministerial fears weighed heavily on Paul. He was always fearful for some troubled soul in one of the churches who was falling away. There was never a time when someone was not unhappy with him and maligning him. Ecclesiastic conflicts were his daily fare, and he was constantly writing to calm the waters and set things straight. Such depressing fears were recurrent for Paul, and the aggregate sometimes got him down.

Phillips Brooks, the peerless preacher and one-time bishop of Boston, said:

> To be a true minister to men is always to accept new happiness and new distress. . . . The man who gives himself to other men can never be a wholly sad man; but no more can he be a man of unclouded gladness. To him shall come with every deeper consecration a before untasted joy, but in the same cup shall be mixed a sorrow that it was beyond his power to feel before.[5]

The reason Paul was sorrowing and downcast was his other-directed love, here to Titus and to the church in Corinth. All his present fears and all his present fightings were grounded in his concern for others. This other-directedness was the basis of his depression and also, as we shall see, the springboard for his comfort and joy.

This text is about how God brings comfort and joy to a ministering heart.

Comfort and Joy Through Titus (vv. 6, 7)

How would you comfort Paul? Send him a tract? Remind him of theological realities? Probably not. After all, he wrote the realities.

Titus's coming. The divine antidote to Paul's depression was this: "But God, who comforts the downcast, comforted us by the coming of Titus" (v. 6). Without warning, Titus showed up! What a rush came over Paul. Titus was alive and safe. They joyously embraced. "Titus, what a sight you are for these weary old eyes! Why didn't you show in Troas? Well, no matter, you're here!" Paul's spirits began to lift. Even if Titus would deliver a bad report, Paul's joy welled.

Always the theologian, Paul put Titus's coming in theological perspective with his opening two words: "*But God*, who comforts the downcast, comforted us by the coming of Titus." God had come through Titus's arrival.

There is a beautiful passage from a now-forgotten old novel in which the care of God flows through a consecrated personality. Elisa, a poor woman, had just lost her son and was in the depth of grief. Her godly friend, Anna, joined her, and they knelt in prayer by the bedside. As they prayed, Anna suggested that Elisa ask God to lay his hand on her head. When Elisa made the request, Anna softly laid her hand on Elisa's head.

"He's done it! Glory to God!" cried Elisa.

Her friend coaxed her to tell about it, and Elisa replied, "There was a wonderful feeling that went down through me, and the hand was just like yours."

"The hand was mine," replied Anna gently, "but it was God's hand too."[6]

So it was with the coming of Titus, for in it God visited Paul.

The truth of this is substantiated by Paul's phrase, "God, who comforts the downcast," an allusion to Isaiah 49:13 (LXX) which speaks of God having "comforted the downcast of his people." Thus Paul saw his own relief at the coming of Titus as evidence of God's comfort of his people in the end-time.[7] "God, who comforts the downcast" speaks of God's grace to his people under the new covenant.[8] This is what God does for his people. All the comfort Paul received was from God regardless of the human source or instrumentality. By this, Paul teaches us how we ought to view the comforts that come our way. "The words of comfort were your words but the voice of God too. The hand was your hand, but also the comforting hand of God. All glory to God!"

Titus's comfort. As wonderful as Paul's joy was at Titus's return, it was exceeded by the news of Titus having been comforted by the Corinthians due to their positive re-embrace of Paul: "and not only by his coming but also by the comfort with which he was comforted by you, as he told us of your longing, your mourning, your zeal for me, so that I rejoiced still more" (v. 7). The other-directedness of Paul's life shines here. Initially he was downcast not for himself but for the uncertain fate of Titus and the looming apostasy of the Corinthians. But now his joy surges at Titus's comfort at the Corinthian turnabout evidenced in their longing and mourning and zeal for Paul, so that he "rejoiced still more." Again Paul has emphasized that the source of all this comfort is God alone. And Paul has received it fully because he is so God-focused and other-person focused. The comfort and joy of Titus and the Corinthians effected the comfort of his other-directed soul.

From here in verse 8 to the end of this section of thought in verse 16, Paul reiterates how his joy and comfort have been established in the well-being of others—namely, the Corinthians' repentance and Titus's refreshment.

Comfort and Joy Through News of the Corinthians' Repentance (vv. 8–13a)

At times a father has to deal severely with his children, disciplining them for their own good. A good father never enjoys this, but he does it. In the same way Paul's penning the severe letter to the Corinthians, his second epistle to them, was a distasteful but necessary task. As Paul earlier described it in 2:4, "For I wrote to you out of much affliction and anguish of heart and with many tears." The object of that letter was to bring about grief and repentance among the Corinthians.

Godly grief. Here Paul gives his retrospect in light of the Corinthians' repentance:

> For even if I made you grieve with my letter, I do not regret it—though I did regret it, for I see that that letter grieved you, though only for a while. As it is, I rejoice, not because you were grieved, but because you were grieved into repenting. For you felt a godly grief, so that you suffered no loss through us. For godly grief produces a repentance that leads to salvation without regret, whereas worldly grief produces death. (vv. 8–10)

There is a worldly grief that can be very bitter and intense, like that of Esau who grieved with many tears over the loss of his birthright but found no place for repentance (cf. Hebrews 12:16, 17). Worldly grief is deficient because it is not distinct from sin; rather it is redolent of the very essence of sin and self.[9] This is because self is the center point of sin. As Archbishop William Temple so memorably put it, "I am the centre of the world I see; where the horizon is depends on where I stand."[10] Therefore, "worldly grief" is a grief for oneself, centered on self, not grief for sin against God. It grieves over consequences. It aches with embarrassment. It focuses on its own hurt. It is self-pitying.

On the other hand, "godly grief" is a grief that comes from knowing that your actions are unpleasing to God. This is what the Lord commends in the second Beatitude: "Blessed are those who mourn"; that is, they mourn over their sins before God. And such grief is "blessed" because it drives us to God and to repentance. As parents we have learned that godly grief in our children is necessary for salvation and ongoing spiritual health. Sorrow is not enough. A child must own that his or her sin is against God and must be repentant before God. We must never be fooled by tears because they often are tears of self-pity or anger: "For godly grief produces a repentance that leads to salvation without regret, whereas worldly grief produces death" (v. 10). Here, in respect to the Corinthians, Paul rejoices because they have experienced godly grief and the requisite repentance.

Good grief! "Godly grief" is then good grief, which Paul describes with a sevenfold rhetorical intensification: "For see what earnestness this godly grief has produced in you, but also what eagerness to clear yourselves, what indignation, what fear, what longing, what zeal, what punishment! At every point you have proved yourselves innocent in the matter" (v. 11). Their repentance was verified in seven ways:

- "what earnestness" as the repentant sinner rejects indifference and becomes intentionally serious about the way he lives.

• "what eagerness to clear yourselves." Whereas before, the Corinthians had been apathetic as to their complicity against Paul, they now strove to prove their loyalty to Paul.

• "what indignation" against the offender and against themselves for supporting him.

• "what fear" of God's judgment as they had sinned against a holy God.

• "what longing" to make things right with Paul.

• "what zeal" to honor Paul and to do things right.

• "what punishment" demonstrated in their willingness to see Paul's offender properly dealt with.

And finally, having described their sevenfold repentance, Paul says in exultation, "At every point you have proved yourselves innocent in the matter" (v. 11b). Godly grief has worked a dynamic repentance. Good grief indeed!

It was the Corinthians' godly grief and repentance that expanded Paul's joy as he concluded, "So although I wrote to you, it was not for the sake of the one who did the wrong, nor for the sake of the one who suffered the wrong, but in order that your earnestness for us might be revealed to you in the sight of God. Therefore we are comforted" (vv. 12, 13a). The downcast gloom that had shrouded Paul's soul had lifted with the coming of Titus and now further dissipated with news of the Corinthians' repentance.

Paul was experiencing a particular comfort that can only be known by caring, other-directed hearts. It is a comfort that joyously wells up when others spiritually prosper. That is what Paul had hoped for when he wrote the painful letter, as he explained earlier: "And I wrote as I did, so that when I came I might not suffer pain from those who should have made me rejoice, for I felt sure of all of you, that my joy would be the joy of you all" (2:3).

This other-sourced joy was a distinctive of Paul's ministry. He called the Philippians "my joy and crown" (4:1). Similarly, he asked the Thessalonians, "For what is our hope or joy or crown of boasting before our Lord Jesus at his coming? Is it not you? For you are our glory and joy" (1 Thessalonians 2:19, 20). And later in the same letter, "For what thanksgiving can we return to God for you, for all the joy that we feel for your sake before our God?" (3:9). This joy derived from others' well-being was evidently an apostolic characteristic because the Apostle John said the same thing, and so beautifully: "I have no greater joy than to hear that my children are walking in the truth" (3 John 4).

Self-focused, inner-directed, selfish, "I am the center of the world" hearts can never benefit from the comfort that Paul experienced because they are incapable of finding joy in another's prosperity—especially spiritual prosperity. Shriveled, imploded hearts can only conceive of comfort and joy in terms of the enhancement of their own situation.

Comfort and Joy Through News of Titus's Refreshment (vv. 13b-16)

Returning to Paul's train of thought, he was lifted from his downcast state by the coming of Titus and then further by news of the Corinthians' repentance.

And now the cloud is completely lifted by news of Titus's refreshment: "And besides our own comfort, we rejoiced still more at the joy of Titus, because his spirit has been refreshed by you all" (v. 13b). Understandably, Titus would have been uneasy in delivering Paul's severe letter to the Corinthians. We have a proverb for it: "If you don't like the message, kill the messenger." But any of Titus's worries quickly turned to joy. In reality, his visit turned into a mutual love-fest.

> For whatever boasts I made to him about you, I was not put to shame. But just as everything we said to you was true, so also our boasting before Titus has proved true. And his affection for you is even greater, as he remembers the obedience of you all, how you received him with fear and trembling. I rejoice, because I have perfect confidence in you. (vv. 14–16)

Deep, mutually appreciative friendships developed between Titus and the Corinthians. They came to revere him, treating him "with fear and trembling" as a messenger of God himself.[11] It was a refreshed, energized, buoyant Titus who embraced this depressed mentor, Paul in Macedonia.

Thus we see how Paul was comforted and elevated to joy. First, there was the "Titus Touch" as Paul so eloquently explained: "But God, who comforts the downcast, comforted us by the coming of Titus, and not only by his coming but also by the comfort with which he was comforted by you, as he told us of your longing, your mourning, your zeal for me, so that I rejoiced still more" (vv. 6, 7). Secondly, he was encouraged by news of the Corinthians' repentance, and, thirdly, by Titus's joy.

As we reflect on this, we see that Paul's threefold comfort was all of God. God arranged the coming of Titus just at the right time. God effected the Corinthians' godly grief and repentance. God refreshed Titus. And Paul's great apostolic, other-directed heart was lifted from gloom precisely because he so cared for others. God's comfort was effectual because Paul had the kind of heart that could receive it.

We also see from this account that God's comfort very often comes through the instrumentality of others. And more, we must be sensitive to God's Spirit so we can minister the golden touch—so some will sense that the hand was yours, but it was the hand of God—that the kindness was yours, but it was also the kindness of God—that the voice was yours, but it was the consolation of God.

Depression sometimes visits the most godly believers, and often it is because they have willingly followed God into the fray so that their bodies have had no rest, and pressures have squeezed them as they are surrounded by fightings without and fears within. They need a loving touch.

Is there someone whom God is laying on your heart to encourage? Then be his instrument now.

20

The Grace of Giving

2 CORINTHIANS 8:1–15

FOLLOWING JESUS' INVITING HIMSELF to the home of Zacchaeus, to the crowd's amazement, off strode Jesus with the kingpin of the Jericho tax machine hurrying before him on busy legs. Jesus would spend the night there according to Hebrew custom. And sometime during that stay, probably after much discussion and prayer, a little big man would formally stand and declare for all Jericho to hear, "Behold, Lord, the half of my goods I give to the poor. And if I have defrauded anyone of anything, I restore it fourfold" (Luke 19:8).

What an enormous reversal! For starters, Zacchaeus gave away 50 percent of his wealth to the poor. And then, from the remaining 50 percent he pledged to make restitution of four times the amount of what he had extorted. He had apparently cheated many people—and thus now placed his entire fortune in jeopardy. In effect, he lived out the command that had caused the rich young ruler so much grief: "Sell all that you have and distribute to the poor, and you will have treasure in heaven; and come, follow me" (Luke 18:22). Zacchaeus was walking through the eye of a needle—and living to tell about it.

By grace, the little man had become immense. Acceptance by God had given the tax collector what he had vainly sought in the accumulation of wealth—wholeness and satisfaction. He went in mastered by the passion to get; he left mastered by the passion to give. Something had happened inside that house with Jesus.

We don't have to guess, because Jesus declared, "Today salvation has come to this house, since he also is a son of Abraham. For the Son of Man came to seek and to save the lost" (Luke 19:9, 10). The liberating joy of salvation was coursing through Zacchaeus' soul. He was a new man. That is why his grip was loosed from his earthly fortunes.

This is a crucial theological point in Luke's writing because verse 10 is by consensus the theme verse of this Gospel. So we understand, theologically, that authentic salvation changes our orientation to wealth. If our professed salvation has not loosed our grip on material things so that we have become giving people, we are not saved, despite our protestations.

And here in 2 Corinthians this same theological point informs Paul's advice to the Corinthians when, seemingly out of the blue, he challenges the Corinthians to give. Actually, however, Paul's challenge is integral to the rehabilitation of the Corinthians. You may recall that originally, at Paul's encouragement, the Corinthians had begun a collection of an offering for the poor in Jerusalem (cf. 1 Corinthians 16:1–4). But that had been thwarted by the Corinthians' falling out with Paul. However, now, with the return of Titus and his good news of the Corinthians' repentance, Paul reasserts the call to give, to contribute generously to the poverty-stricken church in Jerusalem.

And like Luke's record of Zacchaeus, Paul's purpose is theological. First, for the Corinthians, their renewed giving was an evidence of their real faith and a means by which they would grow in grace. Second, for the church, it was a demonstration of fellowship that would express the unity between Christian Jews and Gentiles. As Scott Hafemann observes:

> As a result, the collection illustrates the significance of Paul's theology of grace both for the individual (having received from God, Christians give to others) and for the life of the church (having been accepted by God, Christians accept one another). Completing the collection would therefore be the theological capstone of Paul's apostolic service, bringing his ministry east of Rome to an end (Acts 19:21; Rom. 15:18–29; 1 Cor. 16:1–2, 6; Gal. 2:9).[1]

It is also important that we understand that this section of Scripture is not about tithing or even regular giving to the local church. It is about a one-time special gift to another church. It is about God's grace as it relates to giving. It is about the motivation behind giving. And it is intentionally motivational regarding giving.

The Macedonians' Example (vv. 1–7)

Here, as Paul addressed the matter of giving with the Corinthian church in his second biblical letter to them, he did so with model tact, by citing the remarkable giving of their little sister churches in Macedonia. His words were ever so gentle: "We want you to know, brothers, about the grace of God that has been given among the churches of Macedonia" (v. 1). The "grace of

God" Paul was referring to was, as the context makes so clear, *the grace of giving* (the gracious inclination to give) that had fallen upon the Macedonian churches. This grace flowed from the primary source of grace, which is Christ's reconciliation of sinners to himself (cf. 5:18—6:1). The riches of God's grace had been poured out on them, and then they in turn poured out what they had on others.

The grace of giving is what this section is all about. The word *charis* ("grace") occurs eight times in chapters 8—9. In fact, *charis* occurs five times in 8:1–9: in verse 1, "the grace," *ten charin*; verse 4, "the favor," *ten charin*; verse 6, "this act of grace," *ten charin*; verse 7, "this act of grace," *ten chariti*; and verse 9, "the grace," *ten charin*. Paul's teaching on giving is a sermon on grace from beginning to end.

Concerning the grace among the Macedonians, "We want you to know, brothers, about the grace of God that has been given among the churches of Macedonia, for in a severe test of affliction, their abundance of joy and their extreme poverty have overflowed in a wealth of generosity on their part" (vv. 1, 2).

Poor. The Macedonians (namely, the churches of Philippi, Thessalonica, and Berea) were poor. The word Paul uses for "their extreme poverty" is the word from which we derive the English word *bathysphere*—the ship we use to probe the depths of the ocean—a Jacques Cousteau kind of word. They were in deep poverty. The great turn-of-the-century New Testament scholar Alfred Plummer translated it perfectly as "their down-to-the-depth poverty."[2] They were at the bottom—dirt-poor! For most of us, it is a major stretch to relate to deep poverty in an ancient setting. We fancy ourselves poor if we have to think about it before going out to dinner. As to credit cards, the Macedonians always left home without them. They had no cars, no designer wardrobes, no vacations, no TVs.

Afflicted. They were also "in a severe test of affliction" (v. 2). The literal idea is that they were being crushed by life. The surrounding culture kept squeezing them harder and harder because of the Macedonians' devotion to Christ. Immense pressure! They were poor and picked on. The grinding poverty and the crushing tribulation made life very difficult—impossible by our standards.

Giving. But out of their difficult situation they did what most of us would consider impossible—"their abundance of joy and their extreme poverty have overflowed in a wealth of generosity on their part" (v. 2). This is a truly incredible statement. In a parched existence, squalid little churches gushed forth with the joy of giving. The riches that welled over to others was not the small amount that the Macedonians could give but their joy in what God had done for them (cf. Philippians 4:4; 1 Thessalonians 1:6). It was the *grace of giving*. There is no other accounting for it.

And Paul went on to expand his thought: "For they gave according to their means, as I can testify, and beyond their means, of their own free will, begging us earnestly for the favor of taking part in the relief of the saints" (vv. 3, 4). They gave "beyond" (literally, "contrary to") their ability. St. Chrysostom marveled, "They did the begging, not Paul." The sense is that Paul, seeing their extreme poverty, was reticent to take their gifts because he knew it would deepen their deprivation and plight. But they wouldn't be denied. "Paul, we entreat you, don't deny us this honor."

Such is the grace of giving. It is not dictated by ability. It has nothing to do with being well-off. It is willing. It views giving as a privilege. It is joyously enthusiastic.

Self-giving. What is at the root of such grace-giving? The answer is given in verse 5: ". . . and this, not as we expected, but they gave themselves first to the Lord and then by the will of God to us." This is by far the most important thing about the Macedonians. Grace is first rooted in our response to God. It's all so basic: When we know that our lives are not our own, neither will we think that our possessions are our own. It's easy to surrender part when we've already given the whole. There is an implicit lesson here: It won't do any good to give our possessions to God unless we have given ourselves.

In fact, such "giving" will do us harm. The reasons are apparent. We will be tempted to imagine that giving of our substance is enough, that somehow this will make God pleased with us. External giving builds religious pride. Giving things instead of ourselves can easily become our religion, so that we never turn to Christ for salvation. It must be said that if you have not given your life to Christ, don't give your money. God doesn't need your money. Even more, he doesn't want you to delude yourself. This story about the Macedonians is told by Paul about believers, for believers, to instruct true believers—no one else!

> Now that my journey's just begun,
> My course so little trod;
> I'll stop before I further run,
> And give myself to God.
>
> Source unknown

What are the implications for the Corinthians, and for us? Paul is most clear: "Accordingly, we urged Titus that as he had started, so he should complete among you this act of grace. But as you excel in everything—in faith, in speech, in knowledge, in all earnestness, and in our love for you—see that you excel in this act of grace also" (vv. 6, 7). Earlier Paul had encouraged Titus to try to bring the Corinthians to completion/maturity in this area of giving. The Corinthians were a gifted group—many had "faith" or "speech" or "knowledge" or "earnestness" or "love," but they did not "excel in this act of grace"—giving. Despite all their good qualities, they were incomplete, and Paul wanted them to grow.

Which brings us to the major implication: There is no way to grow to spiritual maturity without committing your finances to the Lord. Jesus can have our money and not have our hearts, but he cannot have our hearts without our money.

Money is so entwined with one's soul. Some say that the average American spends 50 percent of his or her time thinking about money—how to get it, how to spend it. Whether the statistic is accurate or not, it is generally true. And it is also true that our handling of money defines our affections, the things we truly treasure, how tightly we are bound to the world, and so on.

In this, I would not be true to God's Word or to you if I did not say that some of you may have reached sticking spots in your spiritual growth because you have not begun to give as the Scriptures and conscience are directing you. I've heard all the "reasons" why one can't give. It's too hard. You have so many obligations. You'll begin when you get a full-time job. You'll begin when the car is paid for. You'll begin when the children are done with school. You'll begin when you can really give something. You'll begin with the next promotion. But God's Word says to excel in this act of grace now.

Jesus' Example (vv. 8–10)

Paul didn't have a command from the lips of Christ about the collection, but he did have the example of the Macedonians' earnestness in giving, as well as the ultimate example of Christ giving himself. The Corinthians could prove their authenticity by seeing how it compared with "the earnestness of others," namely, the Macedonians.

But, of course, Jesus was and is the great example and motivation for giving. So the apostle reaches for the highest example and the ultimate motivation: "For you know the grace of our Lord Jesus Christ, that though he was rich, yet for your sake he became poor, so that you by his poverty might become rich" (v. 9). Though Christ, in his preexistence with the Father, could hold a white-hot star in the palm of his hand, he emptied himself of his riches and became one of us and then died for us—such was his poverty. That was Heaven's stewardship program—the genesis of *the grace of giving*—and it is the pattern for us.

The Macedonians had not been induced into giving by gimmicks or fear. Rather it was the heavenly example of giving ("the grace of our Lord Jesus Christ") that brought about the grace of giving in their lives. This is the ultimate motivation for giving. There is no greater! And there must be no other. "For from his fullness we have all received, grace upon grace" (John 1:16).

Giving is a matter of grace from beginning to end. Christ gave himself for us. We receive his grace, and then we give ourselves to him and to others in his name. This response to grace includes giving what we have. That is how the Macedonians gave out of their poverty with great liberality. And that is how we give out of our affluence. It is the same.

Having called to mind the great example of Christ, Paul wisely comments, "And in this matter I give my judgment: this benefits you, who a year ago started not only to do this work but also to desire to do it" (v. 10). A year earlier, the Corinthians' initial giving to help the Jerusalem church was an encouraging sign to Paul that they had been truly converted. Thus, if again they now went back to taking an offering for the Jerusalem church, it would confirm that they were for real. However, if the Corinthians refused to complete their commitment, it would demonstrate that they were not part of God's people. The implicit warning is: Past performance doesn't count if there is no desire to be generous in the present. "You cannot serve God and money" (Luke 16:13b).

Paul's Directives (vv. 11–15)

The only command in Paul's teaching on giving in the whole of chapters 8—9 is in the imperative that introduces verses 11, 12: "So now finish doing it as well, so that your readiness in desiring it may be matched by your completing it out of what you have. For if the readiness is there, it is acceptable according to what a person has, not according to what he does not have."

Proportionate giving. Paul notes their "readiness" approvingly, because such readiness is an indication of the Corinthians' hearts being volitionally generous. During a Scottish worship service in Edinburgh, it is reported that one member of the congregation accidentally put in a crown piece instead of a penny, winced in the realization of what he'd done, and quietly asked for it back.

But the usher was Scottish too and answered, "In once, in forever." "Oh well," groaned the giver, "I'll get credit for it in Heaven." "No," said the usher, "you'll get credit for only a penny!"[3]

How right he was, because God's focus is on the heart. And God desires willing hearts that eagerly give "according to what a person has, not according to what he does not have"—in a word, proportionate giving. We are to give according to what we have, which means that both rich and poor can give great gifts to God—when they give according to what they have, from the heart.

Reciprocal giving. Paul envisioned that the proportionate giving among believers would effect a beautiful reciprocity.

> I do not mean that others should be eased and you burdened, but that as a matter of fairness your abundance at the present time should supply their need, so that their abundance may supply your need, that there may be fairness. As it is written, "Whoever gathered much had nothing left over, and whoever gathered little had no lack." (vv. 13–15)

It is doubtful that Paul is referring to an exact *quid pro quo* because the impoverished Jerusalem church would likely never be able to pay back the Corinthians. But on the other hand, through Paul the Jerusalem church had given the Corinthians the riches of the new covenant—the far greater gift.

The final line of our text with its quotation of Exodus 16:18 underscores the effect of such giving as it describes how equality and reciprocity were maintained under the old covenant when the Israelites went out to gather manna. There the reciprocity was maintained by a miracle of the manna. Now, under the new covenant, it is maintained by normal, gracious giving.[4] The miracle is what God has wrought in the hearts of his children. And that is why Paul's message was not a Sermon on the Amount. Paul leaves the amount of the gift up to the Corinthians, because he is convinced that "the quantity of their giving will match the quality of their changed hearts" (Hafemann).[5]

Like me, you're probably weary of the pop-Christian motivations for giving—like "give and God will prosper you," misapplying Malachi 3:10 as is so often done by modern preachers. One preacher sent out an appeals letter that stated, "You can't outgive God. We have figured out that if everyone who hears our program sends $67.00, we'll have all the money we need, and God will give it back to you five times over." An astute listener wrote back, "I believe you can't outgive God. So here's my deal: you send me $67.00 and I'll have the money I need, and then God will give it back to you five times over." Predictably, that was the last appeal he received.

On the other hand, we're told that by giving we will store up treasure in Heaven. And no doubt godly heart-giving will do so. But if we are fixated on getting credit for it in Heaven, remember the voice of the Scottish usher.

Some say we should give because it's fun! That's a proper hedonism. But one day giving may not be pleasurable or comfortable—but it will still be right.

What Paul teaches here is simply what Zacchaeus experienced when he came to Christ. Those who truly experience the saving grace of Christ give. In fact, giving itself is a grace. The *grace* of God was given to the

Macedonians, who then earnestly begged for the *grace* of taking part in the relief of the saints. Upon their example, the Corinthians were urged to complete the *grace* of God in their lives. But most of all it was and is the *grace* of Christ: "For you know the grace of our Lord Jesus Christ, that though he was rich, yet for your sake he became poor, so that you by his poverty might become rich" (v. 9). God's people give joyfully according to what they have. Let us all be God's people.

21

Integrity and Giving

2 CORINTHIANS 8:16–24

LUKE TEACHES IN HIS GOSPEL that salvation and the love of money are mutually exclusive. He quotes Jesus as saying, "But woe to you who are rich, for you have received your consolation" (6:24). Jesus pronounced a woe on the rich because in their self-sufficiency they are the opposite of those to whom he came to preach the gospel, as he affirmed at the onset of his ministry in Luke 4: "The Spirit of the Lord is upon me, because he has anointed me to proclaim good news to the poor" (v. 18), meaning poor in spirit or humble. Concerning those who trust in riches, Luke records these solemn words to the rich man in chapter 12: "But God said to him, 'Fool! This night your soul is required of you, and the things you have prepared, whose will they be? So is the one who lays up treasure for himself and is not rich toward God'" (vv. 20, 21). Later Luke recalls Jesus' famed axiom, "No servant can serve two masters, for either he will hate the one and love the other, or he will be devoted to the one and despise the other. You cannot serve God and money" (16:13). And finally Jesus looked sadly at the rich young ruler and said, "How difficult it is for those who have wealth to enter the kingdom of God! For it is easier for a camel to go through the eye of a needle than for a rich person to enter the kingdom of God" (18:24, 25).

So Luke records Jesus as saying over and over that it is useless to talk about loving him and trusting him and having the sweet assurance of forgiveness and the glorious hope of Heaven unless it makes a difference in our material attachments. Strong emotions, deep sweet feelings, and confidence in forgiveness are valid only if they open our hands.

For purposes of understanding 2 Corinthians 8—9, we must understand that Paul and Luke shared the same theology, as does the rest of the New Testament. Chapters 8—9 of 2 Corinthians contain Paul's extended motivational plea to the Corinthians to get on with the grace of giving because their failure to do so would reveal their repentance to be vain and their salvation a delusion. The flow of Paul's thought was logically powerful and motivating. Nevertheless, he was not at all sure that the Corinthians would complete their offering for the poor in Jerusalem. One of the reasons was very personal—namely, his enemies in Corinth had accused him of financial abuse, suggesting that the reason he didn't accept payment for his services was that he had other ways of fleecing the flock (see 12:14–18; cf. 2:17; 7:2; 11:7–12). So now Paul based his motivation to give on his own integrity and the integrity of the process of taking the offering from the Corinthians to Jerusalem. Paul put forth his financial probity and his adherence to the highest principles as reason for the Corinthians to complete their offering for the Jerusalem church.

Here we must pause to say that though Paul was beyond reproach, this is not always the case with those in public ministry. It is said that Thomas Aquinas once called on the Pope while the Pope was counting a large sum of money. "You see, Thomas," said the Pontiff, "the church can no longer say, 'Silver and gold have I none.'" "True, Holy Father," said Thomas, "and neither can she now say, 'Arise and walk.'"

Perhaps you've heard about the old miser who called his doctor, lawyer, and minister to his deathbed. "They say that you can't take it with you," said the dying man, "but I'm going to. I have three envelopes with $100,000 in cash in each one. I want each of you to take an envelope, and just before they close the casket, I want each of you to slip your envelope into my casket." They all promised to do so. And at the end of the funeral they did it! On the way home, the conscience-stricken doctor confided, "I'm building a clinic, so I took $50,000 and put the rest in the coffin." Then the lawyer confessed, "I kept $75,000 for a legal defense fund and put $25,000 in." At this, the preacher said, "Gentlemen, I'm ashamed of you. I put in a check for the full amount!" Ah yes, ministerial integrity.

In the spirit of this, my son Carey and his high school friends were talking about how much their dads made, and Carey said, "My dad beats yours. All he does is get up and say a few words and offer a prayer, and it takes eight people to carry the money away!"

Actually, as you know, money and ministry is a very serious matter. I once was approached by a friend who pastored a small church. He shared privately that his meager salary was inadequate and that he could not continue in the ministry without financial help. I wrote him a personal check for $2,000—only to learn later that he had scammed at least $50,000 from others with the same story. You've never really been taken until you've been taken by a "brother"—and a minister, to boot! Some preachers pay more attention to the fleece than to the flock.

Paul understood the problem well and had likely witnessed financial abuse. So he took great care with the Corinthian offering and thus provided wisdom for the church down through the ages.

The Brothers Three (vv. 16–22)

The first thing we should observe is that Paul distanced himself from the actual gathering of the offering from the Corinthians. By doing this, his enemies could not accuse him of extortion through placing undue personal pressure on the Corinthians or by his force of personality. Neither could they accuse him of having his hand in the till.

So in this section Paul penned a letter of commendation for three brothers who would collect the offering from the Corinthians—apart from him. They included his soul brother, the famous brother, and the earnest brother.

His soul brother. Paul's soul brother was, of course, Titus, of whom he said, "But thanks be to God, who put into the heart of Titus the same earnest care I have for you. For he not only accepted our appeal, but being himself very earnest he is going to you of his own accord" (vv. 16, 17). Titus was Paul's soul brother in that he had a heart for the same earnest care for the Corinthians that Paul had.

It hadn't always been this way. Titus had been uneasy when Paul gave him the unenviable task of delivering his severe letter to the Corinthians. As a result, when Titus missed a planned rendezvous, Paul was so worried about him that he left a flourishing ministry in Troas to find him. And what a relief to discover that Titus was not only refreshed by the Corinthians, but that a deep bond of affection had developed between them (cf. 7:7, 13–16). The experience of Titus in Corinth had made him just as earnest as Paul in his care and concern for the Corinthians.

We see the same thing at work today when we send our short-term teams to visit missionaries and find that a bond develops with them as the short-termers become very earnest in their care for their new friends. Paul said here that God had done that to Titus: "But thanks be to God, who put into the heart of Titus the same earnest care I have for you" (v. 16). God had made his heart and soul like Paul's other-directed heart. He shared Paul's special love for the Corinthians. And the earnestness of Titus for the Corinthians was the same as Paul's—specifically that they should excel in the grace of giving (cf. v. 7)—thus demonstrating the validity of their faith and salvation. Titus was so earnest about this that he was virtually on his way "of his own accord," before Paul asked.

Paul was brilliant here. Paul's heart was virtually cloned in that of Titus. And Titus, as the only emissary here named, would assume leadership of the trio.

The famous brother. The second brother of the three was anonymous, though ironically he was *famous* among the churches and *appointed* by the churches:

> With him we are sending the brother who is famous among all the churches for his preaching of the gospel. And not only that, but he has been appointed by the churches to travel with us as we carry out this act of grace that is being ministered by us, for the glory of the Lord himself and to show our good will. (vv. 18, 19)

The phrase "the brother who is famous among all the churches" is literally "the brother whose praise in the gospel is among the churches."

From earlier centuries this description was thought to refer to Luke. In fact the Prayer Book's collect for St. Luke's Day assumes that it is Luke: "Almighty God, who calledst Luke the Physician, whose praise is in the gospel, to be an Evangelist and Physician of the soul; may it please Thee that by the wholesome medicines of the doctrine delivered by him, all the diseases of our souls may be healed." But there is no solid evidence for Luke's identification as this brother. Others have guessed that the famous brother was Barnabas or Silas or Timothy or Aristarchus or Sopater or Secundus or Trophimus or Tychicus.[1] But whoever it was, Paul could think of no higher commendation than this man's gospel fame, and therefore someday this anonymous brother's name will be recognized before the Throne in the only fame that counts.

But while the second brother's fame tells us little, the fact that he was "appointed by the churches" tells us that he was elected by a show of hands, as the Greek indicates. Thus it could not be said that he was Paul's personal envoy, but only the elected representative of the Macedonian churches. No one could say that the messengers were Paul's hand-picked lot.

This was very astute on Paul's part. And here, before moving on to identify the third envoy, Paul was very candid about his reason for using an elected courier: "We take this course so that no one should blame us about this generous gift that is being administered by us, for we aim at what is honorable not only in the Lord's sight but also in the sight of man" (vv. 20, 21). Unless Paul was exaggerating or being ironic, the gift was a very large amount. And considering the distance and danger of the journey by land and sea, putting the offering in great peril, he was deeply sensitive to criticisms, as his enemies gave him no quarter. Later in chapter 11 he said indignantly:

> Or did I commit a sin in humbling myself so that you might be exalted, because I preached God's gospel to you free of charge? I robbed other churches by accepting support from them in order to serve you. And when

> I was with you and was in need, I did not burden anyone, for the brothers who came from Macedonia supplied my need. So I refrained and will refrain from burdening you in any way. (vv. 7–9)

Paul knew that few things would destroy his ministry as much as doubts cast upon his integrity in matters of money. So in verse 21 he further emphasized the extreme care taken: "for we aim at what is honorable not only in the Lord's sight but also in the sight of man." These words echo Proverbs 3:4 and show that while Paul was careful to do what was right in the Lord's sight, his driving interest was doing what was honorable in the sight of man, both friend and foe.[2] As Calvin said, "there is nothing that so leaves a man open to sinister insinuation as the management of public funds."[3] And again, "Thus the higher the position we occupy, the greater our need to imitate carefully Paul's circumspection and modesty."[4] In the same vein, perhaps cued by Calvin, William Barclay writes, "It is a most interesting thing to note that this same Paul who could write like a lyric poet and think like a theologian could, when it was necessary, act with the meticulous accuracy and care of a chartered accountant. Paul was a big enough man to do the little things and the practical things supremely well."[5]

There is a tendency among some churches and Christian organizations to be lax in financial matters. This may stem from a pious, indiscriminate application of the new covenant that Paul so powerfully expounded in 2:14–17. Some lazily assert, "We're new-covenant believers through Christ. We all know the Lord, the Spirit has written the Law on our hearts, God is our God, and we are his people (cf. Jeremiah 31:31–34 and Ezekiel 11:19, 20; 36:26, 27). There's no need for such vigilance. We need simply to pray and trust our brothers and sisters."

Whatever the origin of this casual approach to financial matters, I know of a large church that sends the Sunday offerings to the home of an elder to be counted. I also have a pastor friend who involved the police in a sting to catch an usher who had been stealing $200 a week for years. And yet there are organizations and churches that are dismissive of the need for audits.

What folly and what disdain for the name of Christ. We too readily trust ourselves. We have too much faith in our own honesty. Many have ruined themselves by too much trust in their own integrity.[6] The unsullied reputation of Billy Graham ought to inform us. No one has undergone greater public scrutiny than Billy. His secret? As his ministry began to grow, he formed a board of Christian businessmen to handle all money. They put everyone in his organization on a salary, and the organization's books and Billy's personal finances were audited annually and the records made public. And the result is that amidst the wrecks of ministerial scandal, Graham and his organization are world-renowned as models of integrity.[7]

The earnest brother. Paul now names a third unknown soldier whom we will call the earnest brother: "And with them we are sending our brother whom we have often tested and found earnest in many matters, but who is now more earnest than ever because of his great confidence in you" (v. 22). Because Paul mentioned him last, we surmise that he was of lesser seniority. But Paul's calling him "our brother" suggests that Paul knew him well. It is not clear whether he was appointed by Paul or elected by the churches. That Paul knew him suggests he was chosen by the apostle. But verse 23 calls both anonymous men "messengers [literally, "apostles"] of the churches," which argues that they were sent out by the churches. However, the thing that Paul wanted us to see was that this unnamed brother was "earnest," that he had a God-given zeal and energy to get the job done—especially as to completing the collection. And more, he was confident that the Corinthians would do it. He believed in them! Such a positive, energetic spirit could not help but cause the Corinthians to do the right thing.

The three brothers, then, were quite a trio. They were led by Paul's super-earnest soul brother, Titus, who book-ended with the other earnest brother, and in between was the brother who was famous for his gospel commitment.

Summary Call (vv. 23, 24)

Paul summarized all three in verse 23: "As for Titus, he is my partner and fellow worker for your benefit. And as for our brothers, they are messengers of the churches, the glory of Christ." Titus had been Paul's colleague at least since the Council of Jerusalem (cf. Galatians 2:1). He had sailed rough seas with Paul. He was his soul brother. In fact the designation "my partner" (*koinonos*) is the only place Paul used this word of a colleague.[8] He was his earnest, intimate associate[9]—his buddy. The unnamed brothers were "messengers of the churches" (i.e., the poor, giving churches of Macedonia). And as such they were "the glory of Christ"—manifestations of Christ's life-changing glory.[10]

James Denney expands on the grandeur of Paul's anonymous envoys:

> What an idealist Paul was! What an appreciation of Christian character he had when he described these nameless believers as reflections of the splendour of Christ! To common eyes they might be commonplace men; but when Paul looked at them he saw the dawning of that brightness in which the Lord appeared to him by the way.[11]

Finally, closing his comments about these anonymous messengers of the grace-giving Macedonian churches who radiated the glory of Christ in going to the Corinthians to help them complete their gift of grace, Paul sealed his argument: "So [literally, "therefore"] give proof before the churches [of

Macedonia] of your love and of our boasting about you to these men" (v. 24). O Corinthians, prove it—give! Show that you have not received the grace of God in vain.

This was a life-and-death matter to Paul. He had gone to the extremes of probity to ensure that the Corinthians would not miss their opportunity. He had demonstrated his own integrity and the integrity of the process of completing the offering of the poor in Jerusalem. The importance of the offering extended beyond the Corinthians into eternity. 1) It would prove the validity of their faith—that it was not in vain. 2) It would help the impoverished church in Jerusalem survive. 3) It would demonstrate the miracle of the new covenant—Jews and Gentiles are actually one in Christ. 4) It would declare the glory of the Lord to the church and to the world.

For parallel reasons, what we do with our money is of significance now and in the world to come. It will declare whether or not salvation has come to our house, and thereby whether or not we are sons of God. When the Corinthians did generously give, it demonstrated that the impossible had happened as wealthy Corinthians walked through the eye of the needle, for "what is impossible with men is possible with God" (Luke 18:26b).

A personal pastoral epilogue. When I began the ministry, my pastor/mentor gave me some advice by example because he distanced himself from the handling of money and access to church giving records. So from the beginning and over more than forty years I have never touched an offering plate except to give; and I have never inquired as to how much any person gives. Thus I do not know if a family gives or no longer gives or if their giving is requisite with their income. I perhaps can surmise who the generous souls are, but I have no certain knowledge.

This means that I am not tempted to defer to the givers and that I treat all people the same. How liberating this has been! And it has freed me to preach God's Word about giving with powerful abandon.

22

Ready, Willing, Generous Giving

2 CORINTHIANS 9:1–15

WHEN PAUL ASSEMBLED THE TRIO OF ENVOYS to go to Corinth to collect the Corinthians' offering for the church in Jerusalem, it was not to persuade the Corinthians to give but rather to assist them in bringing to generous completion their already declared readiness to give. In a word, Paul wished to ensure ready, willing, generous giving from the Corinthians.

Orchestration of Ready, Willing, Generous Giving (vv. 1–5)

So in the opening verses of chapter 9, Paul acknowledges the Corinthians' readiness: "Now it is superfluous for me to write to you about the ministry for the saints, for I know your readiness, of which I boast about you to the people of Macedonia, saying that Achaia has been ready since last year. And your zeal has stirred up most of them" (vv. 1, 2). It was, in fact, Paul's boasting about Achaia's readiness to give (i.e., the Corinthians' readiness to give—Corinth was the capital of Achaia)—a year prior that had stirred the impoverished Macedonians' amazing overflow of generosity. Indeed, it would be redundant and superfluous to write to the Corinthians about giving because they had already received Paul's directive (cf. 1 Corinthians 16:1–3) with self-proclaimed readiness.

Readiness ensured. However, it was not superfluous for Paul to ensure that their readiness materialized. Thus he explains about the envoys:

> But I am sending the brothers so that our boasting about you may not prove vain in this matter, so that you may be ready, as I said you would

> be. Otherwise, if some Macedonians come with me and find that you are not ready, we would be humiliated—to say nothing of you—for being so confident. (vv. 3, 4)

Imagine the potential for humiliation. The poverty-stricken Macedonian church, upon hearing of the rich Corinthians' readiness to give, had reached down in their affliction and poverty and overflowed in a wealth of generosity, giving beyond their means, begging Paul for the honor of relieving the saints (cf. 8:1–6). Picture a ragged party of Macedonians appearing in Corinth and finding the wealthy Corinthians unprepared. Infamous, unremitting humiliation!

But there was a far more ominous possibility that Paul carefully states—namely, that his boasting in the Corinthians might prove "vain." It is the same word used in 6:1 to describe receiving the grace of God "in vain." Thus their claim to repentance and salvation would be shown to be false. This means that the authenticity of the Corinthians will soon be decided. The three envoys are actually agents of grace—insurance agents.

Willingness insured. Paul not only sent the threesome to ensure the Corinthians' readiness but their willing generosity: "So I thought it necessary to urge the brothers to go on ahead to you and arrange in advance for the gift you have promised, so that it may be ready as a willing gift, not as an exaction" (v. 5). To grasp what Paul is saying, we must understand that the word "gift" used twice in this verse is literally "blessing" (*eulogian*). So the verse could well read, "So I thought it necessary to urge the brothers to go on ahead to you and arrange in advance for the blessing you have promised, so that it may be ready as a willing blessing, not as an exaction from a grudging spirit."[1] Paul's hope is that his envoys' arrival well in advance of him would provide time for the Corinthians to spiritually rise to the level of the blessed, graced giving of the Macedonians—so their giving would not be grudging from stingy hearts, but a blessing from graced, willing, generous hearts.

Again, Paul was concerned with their souls. His agents were sent to insure (so to speak) the Corinthians' readiness and willingness to generously give—and thus to confirm the salvation of their souls (cf. Luke 19:8–10). Mere giving itself is no sign of grace or redemption. It will save no one's soul. The giving of the redeemed is a response to the grace of our Lord Jesus Christ: "For you know the grace of our Lord Jesus Christ, that though he was rich, yet for your sake he became poor, so that you by his poverty might become rich" (8:9). Those who receive such grace give.

The Nature of Ready, Willing, Generous Giving (vv. 6, 7)

Having described his careful orchestration of giving through his envoys, Paul now shows us what willing, generous giving is like.

Bountiful generosity. Paul does this with an easily understood proverb: "The point is this: whoever sows sparingly will also reap sparingly, and whoever sows bountifully will also reap bountifully" (v. 6). There are two ways to sow. One is to carefully place each seed in a furrow as if one were placing the Star of India in a vault. "Let's see, here's a seed for this one, and here's one for this one. One must be careful with one's seeds." This harvest will not be much! The other is that of the sower, striding long steps across the earth, reaching into his abundance, and sowing with generous swings of his arm. At springtime the earth will sprout accordingly, so that when fall comes, the harvest will be untold.

But there is even more here because the proverb employs the Greek word sometimes translated "blessing" (it is used in the previous verse). Here our text renders it "bountifully." Thus, supplying the literal sense of "blessing," the proverb literally reads "Whoever sows sparingly will also reap sparingly, and whoever sows with blessings will also reap with blessings." This goes back to the giver's heart and God's grace and the manner of giving. "God gives back 'blessings' to those who give as a matter of 'blessing'" (Hafemann).[2] So it is not how much we give but rather that we give as generously as possible with an attitude of the joy of blessing.

Going back to the basic agricultural image of this proverb, O. E. Rölvaag's *Giants in the Earth*, a novel about Midwest pioneers, describes an old farmer's joyous energy at the potential of what he is about to sow.

> With what zest he broke the tough-fibered prairie sod, which had never been broken before since the beginning of time. . . . And with what reverence he held up the beautiful seed which he was to sow on his own ground. The plump kernels appeared to glow with some inner golden light as the warm rays of the sun struck full across them, and they seemed to be squirming in the hand that grasped them as if they were charged with a life, suddenly roused from slumber, that was seeking release there.[3]

The old farmer would sow generously in glad anticipation of reaping a great harvest. But it is even more so with respect to the spiritual realities that Paul intends here, because whoever sows with blessing will also reap blessing. Such sowing is charged with life. Great generosity births exponential blessing. Here is the bottom line: We are to be a generous people. What we give, though material, glows with the golden light of eternity. Generosity unleashes that light. To be generous is divine.

Cheerful willingness. The logical conclusion of this proverb is Paul's advice that immediately follows: "Each one must give as he has made up his mind, not reluctantly or under compulsion, for God loves a cheerful giver" (v. 7). The force of the call to cheerful giving has its origin in

Deuteronomy 15:10, 11, which admonishes God's people under the old covenant, saying:

> You shall give to him freely, and your heart shall not be grudging when you give to him, because for this the LORD your God will bless you in all your work and in all that you undertake. For there will never cease to be poor in the land. Therefore I command you, "You shall open wide your hand to your brother, to the needy and to the poor, in your land."

This call to cheerful, ungrudging giving had special reference to the Sabbatical year of remission in which every seven years Israel was to forgive all debts (cf. vv. 1, 2). But now, under the new covenant, those in Christ are to make such cheerful generosity their *daily* practice.[4]

Today's culture is more like that pictured in a Victorian cartoon of two men sitting in a London club. One is holding a book in his hand and explains, "It's a new story by that Dickens fellow—about a worthy banker named Scrooge, who finally degenerates into a sentimental weakling."

Know any Christian Scrooges? Think twice. The terms are mutually exclusive. It is impossible to be a Christian and a Scrooge. Paul taught that the religion of the Corinthian Scrooges was vain, empty (cf. 8:8, 24; 9:3). New-covenant believers, Christians, are to be generous people who find giving a merry venture.

The Benefits of Ready, Willing, Generous Giving (vv. 8–15)

Having described the nature and theology of Christian giving in verses 6, 7, Paul now turns to the benefits of generous giving.

Personal benefits. He begins with personal benefits, the first of which is *sufficiency*: "And God is able to make all grace abound to you, so that having all sufficiency in all things at all times, you may abound in every good work" (v. 8). The simple truth is, God will give us what we need to give to others—we will always be rich enough to be generous. Do we doubt this? Then we doubt his grace, the grace with which this verse begins: "And God is able to make all grace abound to you . . ." We also forget that this mention of "grace" refers to the grace given to the poor Macedonian churches: "We want you to know, brothers, about the grace of God that has been given among the churches of Macedonia, for in a severe test of affliction, their abundance of joy and their extreme poverty have overflowed in a wealth of generosity on their part" (8:1, 2). This mention of grace here in 9:8 is the seventh of the eight references to grace in chapters 8—9.

The point is that grace has been given to us (as it had been given to the Corinthians) so that right now we (like the Macedonians and the

Corinthians) have what we need to give and minister to others. God's grace is sufficient for every good work he calls us to do. The challenge for us is not our wealth or lack of it, but belief and obedience. The generous, giving heart will live in this grace—"so that having all sufficiency in all things at all times, you may abound in every good work." There will always be enough to be generous.

The other personal benefit to the generous heart is *righteousness.*

> "He has distributed freely, he has given to the poor;
> his righteousness endures forever."
>
> He who supplies seed to the sower and bread for food will supply and multiply your seed for sowing and increase the harvest of your righteousness" (vv. 9, 10).

As you can see, verse 9 quotes a poetic line from Psalm 112:9. The righteousness of the man in this Psalm is proved by his care for the poor. Since it is genuine, it endures forever.

Paul continues this idea of righteousness in verse 10 by citing Isaiah 55:10 almost word for word from the LXX: "He who supplies seed to the sower and bread for food . . ." Then Paul alludes to Hosea 10:12, telling his readers that God who supplies seed to the sower will multiply their seed (i.e., material resources) and thus increase the harvest of their righteous deeds. The harvest of the Corinthians' righteousness will increase personally and then will spread to the church in thanksgiving and glory to God as described in the remaining verses of this text.[5]

What spectacular benefits go to the generous giver. First, sufficiency for any generous deed to which God calls us: "And God is able to make all grace abound to you, so that having all sufficiency in all things at all times, you may abound in every good work" (v. 8). And second, a righteousness that endures forever, demonstrated by willing, generous giving that then is followed by a personal harvest of righteousness that extends to the church at large.

Willing, generous, giving people enjoy sufficiency and a harvest of righteousness that goes far beyond themselves.

Church-wide benefits. The church-wide benefits of such giving are threefold.

First, *thanksgiving to God*: "You will be enriched in every way for all your generosity, which through us will produce thanksgiving to God. For the ministry of this service is not only supplying the needs of the saints, but is also overflowing in many thanksgivings to God" (vv. 11, 12). The Corinthians' enrichment through giving was not material prosperity. Their financial condition would wax and wane, like that of others, but they would be enriched by God himself. The overarching benefit was that the wider church poured out thanksgiving to God.

The second and parallel benefit is *glory to God*: "By their approval of this service, they will glorify God because of your submission flowing from your confession of the gospel of Christ, and the generosity of your contribution for them and for all others" (v. 13). The Corinthians' embrace of the gospel would be proved not only by their confession of belief but by their submission to the grace of giving and their generous contribution to the poor church in Jerusalem. And there in the city of Jerusalem, the Jewish church would praise God for the demonstration of God's righteousness among the Corinthians. The Jewish church would know for sure that the Gentile church was for real and that through the new covenant they were all brothers and sisters.

The third benefit, perhaps unanticipated, was *affection for the Corinthians themselves*: "while they long for you and pray for you, because of the surpassing grace of God upon you" (v. 14). This is the eighth and final mention of grace in this exhortation that began in 8:1 with the first mention of grace, the grace of giving. As Paul anticipates that "the surpassing grace of God" will produce a generous offering, he knows that the Jewish believers will long for the Gentiles and make them a focus of their prayer, enhancing the wider unity of the church.

The church-wide benefits of ready, willing, generous giving, then and now, are remarkable: thanksgiving to God, glory to God, and a bond of affection within the church.

As Paul caps his exhortation to give, he can scarcely contain himself: "Thanks be to God for his inexpressible gift!" (v. 15). He was giving thanks, of course, for the gift of Christ (cf. 8:9).

This is the first time the Greek word translated "inexpressible" appears anywhere in the Greek language. Paul could find no word to express the ineffable character of God's gift, so he made one up—a word that says, in effect, that the gift can't be described.

What we must understand from this is that Paul's call to ready, willing, generous giving is not a call to reach down deep within our beings and rise to the best that is within us. Rather, it is a call to authentically come to Christ in true belief and repentance. It is a call to contemplate Christ's giving as the example for our giving—his embrace of poverty that we might become rich. It is not a call to legalistic observance but to grace, as Paul's repeated mentions of grace emphasize: "the grace of God"—"the favor [literally, "grace"] of taking part in the relief"—"complete among you this act of grace"—"excel in this act of grace"—"for you know the grace"—"as we carry out this act of grace"—"God is able to make all grace abound to you"—"the surpassing grace of God." It is a call to rise to *his* best within us. It is not a call to save ourselves but to demonstrate by our giving that our faith is not in vain.

There is no such thing as a Christian Scrooge. Christians give. Generous giving is the province of a regenerate heart.

This is a call to be ready.

This is a call to be willing.

This is a call to be generous.

This is a call to merriment.

23

Call to Church Discipline

2 CORINTHIANS 10:1–6

AS CHRISTIANS, we live in both the now and the not yet of the kingdom. Christ's death, resurrection, ascension, and exaltation have introduced the kingdom. Those of us who trust in Christ as the messianic King are in him and are members of the kingdom. Being in Christ, we are seated with God "in the heavenly places in Christ Jesus" (Ephesians 2:6). And God has "blessed us in Christ with every spiritual blessing in the heavenly places" (Ephesians 1:3). Both the seating and blessing are now, in the present, though the full realization will happen at Christ's return.

This creates an ongoing tension in the now of today. As Christians we presently have eternal life, the indwelling of the Holy Spirit, forgiveness of sins, fellowship in the Body of Christ, and the blessed hope of Christ's return. At the same time, we do not have all the blessings that will come. We do not have new bodies or a new heaven or a new earth. We have not seen the face of God. Perfect love and holiness and fellowship are not ours. We still experience sin, pain, and death. As God's children we are called to balance the realities of now and not yet.

Overemphasis on the not yet of the future kingdom can lead to a speculative mind-set, date-setting eschatology, and a minimizing of the graces that we already have. On the other hand, an overemphasis on the now of the kingdom can lead to a loss of focus on Christ's return and the delusion that promises reserved for future fulfillment are ours in the present. The heretics Hymenaeus and Philetus fell to an extreme form of this as they preached that the resurrection had already taken place and therefore the blessings of the future state were already here. This teaching brought shipwreck to many (cf. 2 Timothy 2:17, 18; cf. 1 Timothy 1:19, 20).

Though the Corinthian detractors may not have succumbed to such extremes, they were prone to imagining that the promised blessings of the future kingdom are now, even applying this to such areas as spiritual gifts (cf. 1 Corinthians 12—14). To them, fleshly displays of giftedness proved how spiritual a person was and that such a person was appropriating the blessings that Christ had already provided. This thinking is what had produced so much ego-pumping division in Corinth. As D. A. Carson explains:

> In short, the Corinthians were quick to seize every emphasis in Christianity that spoke (or seemed to speak) of spiritual power, of exaltation with Christ, of freedom, of triumph, of victorious Christian living, of leadership, of religious success; but they neglected or suppressed those accents in Christianity that stressed meekness, servanthood, obedience, humility, and the need to follow Christ in his suffering if one is to follow him in his crown. They glimpsed what Christ had done, yet failed to contemplate what remains to be done; they understood that D-day had arrived, but mistook it for V-day. They loved Christian triumphalism, but they did not know how to live under the sign of the cross.[1]

At present a small unrepentant minority of such detractors and interlopers opposed Paul in Corinth. Guided by their inverted values, they judged Paul's ministry to be fleshly. His unimpressive persona, his lack of rhetorical skills, his meek and humble demeanor, his poverty, his working with his hands, the absence of ecstatic experiences and visions, his incessant trials and difficulties (rather than "success") were, to his opponents, incontrovertible evidence that his ministry was of the flesh and not of the Spirit.

The inverted values of Paul's opponents plus their rejection of Paul's apostolate meant that nothing less than the gospel was at stake, and ultimately the salvation of their souls. So now in chapter 10 Paul calls the faithful in the Corinthian church to obedience in joining him in disciplining his unrepentant opponents.

It is here that 2 Corinthians takes an ominous turn. Whereas chapters 1—9 were directed to the repentant majority in Corinth, chapters 10—13 focus on the unrepentant minority. Paul now goes to war against rebellion!

Paul's Ironic Appeal (vv. 1, 2)

Irony. The apostle begins with an appeal to the faithful Corinthian majority couched in brilliantly measured irony: "I, Paul, myself entreat you, by the meekness and gentleness of Christ—I who am humble when face to face with you, but bold toward you when I am away!" (v. 1). Paul knew what his enemies were saying about him—and part of it was true. He certainly had been humble when he was with them. That was his characteristic day-to-day demeanor. Paul also had written them a bold, scorching letter after his surprise painful visit (cf. 2:1–3). However, his detractors were woefully wrong in imagining that he was a cringing and obsequious little man who could only be bold when he was away penning his paper bullets.

Paul's enemies obviously suffered from a values deficit because they regarded humility not as a grace but as a weakness. Apparently, they were influenced by the classical Greek tradition that regarded great men as anything but humble. In fact, classic literature couples meekness and humility with servility, which stands opposite to nobility and dignity.[2] Thus Paul's arrogant detractors were living their lives in profound dissonance with the values of the Bible and of Christ himself. And when we see this, we can see and even feel the laser point of Paul's irony in the preceding clause: "I, Paul, myself entreat you by the meekness and gentleness of Christ" (v. 1a). Jesus Christ described himself as gentle and humble at heart (cf. Matthew 11:29). Thus Paul, by identifying himself with Christ, demolishes the accusation that his own meekness and gentleness are signs of weakness or a lack of power and authority.[3]

Brilliant! And even more so when we take note that far-away-Paul has penned not a paper bullet but this gentle plea. Paul's subtle irony has taken the wind out of his detractors' sails and demonstrates that their values are eternally different from those of Christ.

Appeal. Though Paul's irony was powerful, it is lovingly gentle as he extends his plea in verse 2: "I beg of you that when I am present I may not have to show boldness with such confidence as I count on showing against some who suspect us of walking according to the flesh." Here the apostle warns the faithful majority of the Corinthians to abandon any complicity with the minority—"some who suspect us of walking according to the flesh"—lest they too suffer his bold judgment. As to who the ill-fated "some" are, they are probably not the Corinthians themselves but outsiders. The so-called "super-apostles" were no doubt part of them, and perhaps these "false apostles" were their leaders (cf. 11:5, 13–15). These interlopers doubtless fancied themselves as superior and cosmically gifted—masters of rhetoric, knowledgeable of mysteries, recipients of visions and ecstasies.

The irony was that while they charged Paul with "walking according to the flesh," it was they who were fleshly. Their values were world-centered. Their walk was a death-walk—"according to the flesh."

Again Paul's plea is ever so gentle. He begs the Corinthian majority to respond in obedience so he will not have to show boldness to any of them, and so the minority who will be subjected to judgment will be minimized, even reduced.

Paul's Unique Warfare (vv. 3, 4a)

Unconventional warfare. But notwithstanding his gentle, peace-loving nature, Paul, like Christ, will wage warfare if necessary, as he goes on to explain: "For though we walk in the flesh, we are not waging war according to the flesh" (v. 3). Conventional warfare, as conducted by the false apostles, would be fought with dazzling flourishes of rhetoric voiced by imposing men whose esoteric preaching was laced with personal accounts of their visions and ecstatic experiences and spiritual exploits. The intended effect would be to overwhelm their listeners with their confident, charismatic, strutting carriage as supposed great men.

But Paul's method of warfare was utterly unconventional, "not . . . according to the flesh." This Paul had made memorably clear in his first letter to the Corinthians:

> And I, when I came to you, brothers, did not come proclaiming to you the testimony of God with lofty speech or wisdom. For I decided to know nothing among you except Jesus Christ and him crucified. And I was with you in weakness and in fear and much trembling, and my speech and my message were not in plausible words of wisdom, but in demonstration of the Spirit and of power, that your faith might not rest in the wisdom of men but in the power of God. (2:1–5)

Supernatural weapons. Looking again to our text, we see that Paul embraced supernatural weapons: "For the weapons of our warfare are not of the flesh" (v. 4a). Paul, of course, had long donned the soldier's armament for spiritual warfare: the helmet of salvation, the breastplate of righteousness, the shield of faith, and so on as he put on the whole armor of God (cf. Ephesians 6:10–20). But passages in 2 Corinthians suggest that the weapon Paul employed was the proclamation of the gospel. For example:

> But we have renounced disgraceful, underhanded ways. We refuse to practice cunning or to tamper with God's word, but by the open statement of the truth we would commend ourselves to everyone's conscience in the sight of God. And even if our gospel is veiled, it is veiled to those who are perishing. In their case the god of this world has blinded the minds of the unbelievers, to keep them from seeing the light of the gospel of the glory of Christ, who is the image of God. For what we proclaim is not ourselves, but Jesus Christ as Lord, with ourselves as your servants for Jesus' sake. For God, who said, "Let light shine out of darkness," has shone in our hearts to give the light of the knowledge of the glory of God in the face of Jesus Christ. (4:2–6; cf. Romans 1:16)

Paul's Effectual Warfare (vv. 4b, 5)

As Paul has revealed his unconventional warfare and supernatural weaponry, we now see that Paul continues to pile up military terms: verse 3, "waging war"; verse 4, "weapons," "warfare," "strongholds"; verse 5, "destroy arguments and every lofty opinion" (literally, "every high thing," i.e., tower); verse 6, "being ready to punish every disobedience" (i.e., court-martial).[4] By stacking these terms, Paul portrays his ministry as a mighty, conquering army that overcomes every opposing force.[5] Paul's arsenal of weapons has "divine power" (v. 4). Paul is not contrasting his weapons with spears and missiles but with the conventional weapons of his opponents: ingenuity, rhetoric, showmanship, splashiness, spiritual pretension, personal charisma—the kind of things Paul disavows. And because Paul avoids these things, they think he is inferior and despise him! But no matter—Paul's weapons nevertheless have "divine power."

First, they "have divine power to destroy strongholds" (v. 4b). Every fortified city had strongholds, bulwarks that were particularly impregnable. "Strongholds" references the central arguments that fortify his opponents' message.[6] Paul's gospel has "divine power" to demolish impregnable arguments.

Second, the military metaphor expands to destroying high towers and ramparts—"We destroy arguments and every lofty opinion raised against the knowledge of God" (v. 5a)—literally, "We destroy every high thing lifted up against the knowledge of God."[7] As Carson points out, Paul's language of destruction here is not merely about winning arguments or debates. "He means something far more: his weapons destroy the way people think, demolish their sinful thought patterns, the mental structures by which they live their lives in rebellion against God."[8] In Paul's own words, his spiritual weapons tear down "every high thing lifted up against the knowledge of God." Paul is referencing the citadels of sin in our lives—every high thing, every haughty thought, every action that forms a barrier to the knowledge of the living God.

Happily, the gospel regularly destroys the high things lifted up against the knowledge of God. Paul declared in Romans, "For I am not ashamed of the gospel, for it is the power of God for salvation to everyone who believes, to the Jew first and also to the Greek" (1:16). And he has already explained here in 2 Corinthians, "For God, who said, 'Let light shine out of darkness,' has shone in our hearts to give the light of the knowledge of the glory of God in the face of Jesus Christ" (4:6). The creation power of the first chapter of the Bible pulls down the high things raised up against God. When people come to believe, it is not because of their cleverness or charisma or the cut of their clothing or their clever cant, but because the gospel has cut down the high towers in their souls that were once set against the knowledge of God.

Third, in ancient warfare when strongholds were captured and towers pulled down, the defenders were taken into captivity. Here Paul extends the military language to thoughts—"and take every thought captive to obey Christ" (v. 5). The word "thought" refers more specifically to the mind as the intellectual center of our being.[9] The idea is that Christ does not simply help people to think holy thoughts, but that "their mental structures, the plans and schemes, are taken over and transformed as they come to a new allegiance" (Carson).[10]

Most Americans are materialistic, and many are metaphysical materialists as they functionally accord things with a religious "Diamonds are forever" weight. But Christ transforms such thought patterns and installs new paradigms. Likewise, a Buddhist's agnosticism and indifference is revolutionized when his thoughts are taken captive by the gospel of Christ.

Could anything be more wonderful than to have every thought experience captive obedience to Christ? Could we wish anything better for others? Could anything be more beautiful?

Paul's Punishment (v. 6)

The incredible military might of Paul's gospel warfare (the power to destroy strongholds of argument, to destroy high towers of rebellious thought, to take every thought captive to Christ) will be unleashed when Paul comes again to Corinth. But Paul does not want to do it alone because he knows that church discipline is most effective when the entire church willingly participates. So he concludes, "being ready to punish every disobedience, when your obedience is complete" (v. 6). Paul asks the Corinthians to disassociate themselves from his opponents and their fleshly version of Christianity. He hopes that the disassociation will bring some of them to repentance and protect the faithful majority of the Corinthians from their error.

Paul will be bold when he comes, he will be ready, and he will not shirk his responsibility. But how much better if he did not have to take such measures because the church had engaged in discipline.

Paul's message comes down the corridors of time to today's church as its people live in the not yet. The call is to flee the fleshly versions of Christianity with strutting preachers and splashy displays and prosperity dogmas and esoteric visions and promises of health—that will only come in the not yet.

The message is to embrace the apostolic gospel preached and modeled by Christ and his apostles—to fully enjoy the present blessings of salvation: eternal life, the indwelling of the Spirit, the forgiveness of sins, the fellowship of Christ's body, and the blessed hope of Jesus' return—to embrace "the meekness and gentleness of Christ" (v. 1)—to abandon conventional warfare that wages war "according to the flesh" (v. 2)—and to embrace our weakness as the ground and occasion for his power.

24

Boasting in the Lord

2 CORINTHIANS 10:7–18

THE HEALTH-AND-WEALTH, ENTERTAINMENT-FOCUSED CULTURE of neo-Corinth, the astonishing Greco-Roman boom town of A.D. 56, made the Corinthian church susceptible to what we have come to call "over-realized eschatology"—the false teaching that the future benefits promised to us at Christ's return are realized now in the present. In fact, Paul had sarcastically chided the Corinthians for succumbing to this thinking in his initial letter to them:

> Already you have all you want! Already you have become rich! Without us you have become kings! And would that you did reign, so that we might share the rule with you! . . . We are fools for Christ's sake, but you are wise in Christ. We are weak, but you are strong. You are held in honor, but we in disrepute. (1 Corinthians 4:8, 10)

They had all that they wanted. They were rich—kings—wise—strong—honored! And they had it in the already. The sad result was that some of the Corinthians had therefore come to believe that Paul's less-than-prosperous circumstances were due to his diminished spirituality. He needed faith and more of the Spirit.

This overemphasis on the already has reappeared throughout history in various experience-focused Holy Spirit movements and is represented today in the present *New York Times* number-one best-seller *Your Best Life Now* by television pastor Joel Osteen. Ironically, this kind of thinking invites the enfolding of the desires and values of present culture into the church. Many Christian leaders have been so taken with the styles of leadership they see in politics and the entertainment industry that they unthinkingly have transferred these secular ways into the church. In Paul's day, his enemies in

Corinth had so effectively read their Greco-Roman culture back into their Christianity that they interpreted the gospel in terms of their values. They boasted in the preacher's presence and bearing; they boasted in rhetorical eloquence; they flashed their resumés and endorsements and letters of commendation; they bragged of their large honoraria; they boasted of their connectedness that inferred greatness by association; and, they compared themselves with one another.

As a group, Paul's enemies had become boastful and dismissive of Paul's authority because Paul displayed none of the values that they so treasured. So here Paul answers them with a defense of his authority and a charge to embrace a ministry that boasts only in the Lord.

Paul's Authority: A Rational Boast (vv. 7–11)

Observe the obvious. As we engage Paul, we see that he is continuing in an aggressive, commanding vein: "Look at what is before your eyes" (v. 7a)—literally, "Look at the things before your face." Look at the facts—not at what these false teachers say, but at what all you Corinthians can plainly see.[1] The Corinthians must look carefully at Paul and his teaching. If they do, the truth will become apparent.

Specifically, Paul wanted them to observe what was before their eyes—namely, "If anyone is confident that he is Christ's, let him remind himself that just as he is Christ's, so also are we" (v. 7b). Paul's detractors' claims to be of Christ were not simply claims to be Christians; rather they were elitist assertions because they believed that they were of Christ in some special way.

Their claims bore a clubbish, inner-circle attitude. They saw themselves as the spiritually knowledgeable, the *cognoscenti*, and likely conveyed it with a smug tone of voice and corresponding tilt of the head and facial expression: "*we*—are—of Christ." To this Paul counsels, "let him remind himself [let him reckon, let him calculate again] that just as he is Christ's, so also are we." Their elitist argument cut two ways: they couldn't make that subjective claim, and they couldn't deny Paul the right to make the same claim.[2] Moreover, Paul's claim was freighted with apostolic precedence. Paul belonged to Christ long before any of the Corinthians, and likely before any of his detractors. If Paul had wanted, he could have argued that he was the elite of the elite because he had encountered Christ's glory on the Damascus road and later had been caught up into the third heaven, as he will reticently explain in 12:1–10. Corinthians, detractors, observe! "Look at what is before your eyes"—namely, authentic apostolic authority.

Observe the new covenant. The Apostle Paul had an innate aversion to giving even the slightest appearance of boasting about himself. Paul didn't want to do the sin that he criticized others of doing. However, because of what was at stake, Paul took the risk. Thus Paul carefully says, "For even if I boast a little too much of our authority, which the Lord gave for building you up and not for destroying you, I will not be ashamed" (v. 8). We must understand here that Paul's boast was in the authority of the new-covenant ministry that he had been expounding and celebrating from chapter 2 on. We know this because his words "for building you up" are from the introduction to Jeremiah's prophecy of the new covenant where Jeremiah says, "I will watch over them to build and to plant, declares the LORD'" (Jeremiah 31:28b).

Thus, as a minister of the new covenant of Christ, Paul pictured his ministry as building up the church. So if the Corinthians would think a little about it, they would remember that it was Paul who brought them the gospel, founded the church, and built them up in the faith. In fact, Paul uses the metaphor of building repeatedly in the New Testament as a pulsing image of all that his ministry entailed. As a minister of the new covenant in fulfillment of Jeremiah's promise, Paul will say, "It is in the sight of God that we have been speaking in Christ, and all for your upbuilding, beloved" (12:19b).

Paul's boasting was not the outworking of his pride but the overflow of his love and calling as a minister of the new covenant.[3] And here Paul confidently states that as a minister of the wondrous new covenant he will never ever be put to shame as a vain boaster. "Look at what is before your eyes."

Observe Paul's character. Among the descriptions of Paul that have come down to us, the only one that has any possibility of being based on early tradition is the famous paragraph from *The Acts of Paul and Thekla*, which the great classical scholar and archaeologist Sir William Ramsey assigned to the first century. The description in the Syriac version reads: "A man of middling size, and his hair was scanty, and his legs were a little crooked, and his knees were projecting (or far apart); and he had large eyes, and his eyebrows met, and his nose was somewhat long."[4]

This agrees with Paul's detractors' estimation of his bodily presence as "weak" (v. 10). By both estimates Paul in person cut a sorry figure and was far from the Greco-Roman ideal.[5] Paul was no Adonis. He was a before and definitely not an after!

As to Paul's speech, it appears that his performance varied. His eloquence seemed godlike to the dwellers of Lystra (cf. Acts 14:8–12). Nevertheless he was no match for Apollos's rhetorical style. And poor Eutychus fell asleep during one of Paul's discourses (cf. Acts 20:9).

As to Paul's letters, some were scorchers. Variously, Paul had threatened *destruction* to the destroyer of God's people (cf. 1 Corinthians 3:16, 17) and then *exclusion* from the Kingdom to those who continued in sin (cf. 1 Corinthians 6:9, 10). Paul had also three times called for *judgment* among God's people (cf. 1 Corinthians 5:1, 2 and 2 Corinthians 2:4–11). Therefore, we can be quite sure his tearful letter was a formidable, fiery missive (cf. 2 Corinthians 2:4; 7:8).

Of course, Paul knew all that was being said about his looks and his speech and his letters, as well as the negative connecting of the dots by his opponents leading to the conclusion that he was a spineless little phony. So Paul writes, "I do not want to appear to be frightening you with my letters. For they say, 'His letters are weighty and strong, but his bodily presence is weak, and his speech of no account'" (vv. 9, 10). This was a natural deduction for his detractors who "felt that true Christian leadership should be impressive, bold, visionary, triumphalistic, and characterized by signs of rhetoric."[6]

And because Paul knew what his enemies were saying, he put them on notice! "Let such a person understand [count this, compute this] that what we say by letter when absent, we do when present" (v. 11). There was no disjunction between Paul's words and deeds, and there never would be. His character was of one fabric. In truth, Paul's arrogant detractors ought to have been terrified!

The Corinthians, and especially Paul's critics (adrift in the Neverland of their over-realized, Corinthianized ethics), needed to look at what was before their eyes. They needed to observe the obvious: 1) Paul was preeminently of Christ; 2) he was *the* minister of the new covenant whose job it was to build them up; and 3) they needed to consider his unchanging apostolic character that allowed no separation between word and deed. The Corinthians needed to repent, acknowledge his authority, and make him their boast.

The problem was, they were far too full of their culture and themselves and their mutual admiration society. So Paul now goes on a withering offensive against his critics.

Paul's Authority: A Proper Boast (vv. 12–17)

Improper boasting. Recently as I flew from Los Angeles to Chicago, the jet took its typical route on a crystal-clear afternoon. It looped out over the Pacific, circling left until it crossed back over LAX and then rose slowly over Santa Monica, Westwood, and Hollywood, where I stared down on the famous city's streets and trademark sign aglow atop the Hollywood hills in the late-afternoon sun. Its unspectacular architecture and the restricted size of Hollywood are remarkable in themselves. It's not much of a place.

Second Corinthians 10:12–17 reminds me of Hollywood—how so many there seem to imagine that their town and (by association) they themselves are the center of the universe, not unlike Corinth in Paul's day. Consider:

- Hollywood's notorious groupthink.
- Hollywood's creation of its own value system.

• Hollywood's proliferation of self-congratulating societies such as The Academy of Motion Picture Arts and Sciences, which awards its favorite denizens provided they brook its values.

• A city of perpetual awards ceremonies.

• A city of illusion, bereft of understanding.

This was culture not unlike that which opposed Paul in Corinth.

And as Paul turns up the heat, he indulges in appropriate satirical irony: "Not that we dare to classify or compare ourselves with some of those who are commending themselves. But when they measure themselves by one another and compare themselves with one another, they are without understanding" (v. 12). Paul, assuming a mock humility, shows that he is so unlike those who criticize him from the pinnacle of assumed superiority. They say that he is a coward in person. Well, he has to admit that he does not rise to their awesome courage. He could never dare to place himself on the level of people who bravely sing their own praises and elevate themselves by the folly of mutual comparisons.[7]

The folly of the self-appointed apostles is that they had set up their own subjective standards of excellence (training in rhetoric, speaking fees, ecstatic experiences, commendations, awards, and so on) and then judged themselves by conformity to those standards! These false apostles had no desire to measure themselves by the objective criteria used by Paul—allegiance to the gospel, conformity to Christ's character, and participation in Christ's sufferings.[8]

Thus, as Paul clearly saw, to claim apostolic authority by self-created criteria was to be "without understanding." The false apostles of Corinth boasted in folly.

Proper boasting. Paul had effectively set up a contrast between improper boasting of the false apostles and proper apostolic boasting—the ground of Paul's boasting. For Paul there was a proper sphere for boasting—namely, the divinely given area of service:

> But we will not boast beyond limits, but will boast only with regard to the area of influence God assigned to us, to reach even to you. For we are not overextending ourselves, as though we did not reach you. We were the first to come all the way to you with the gospel of Christ. We do not boast beyond limit in the labors of others. (vv. 13–15a)

Paul confined his boasting to the geography of his own apostolic ministry, which, by the way, included Corinth! The place where he did his pioneer evangelism and church planting defined for Paul the "area of influence" that God had given him. Paul rejoiced when others built upon his apostolic foundation, as he explained in his initial letter to the Corinthians: "According to the grace of God given to me, like a skilled master builder I laid a foundation, and someone else is building upon it. Let each one take care how he builds upon it" (3:10).

However, the false apostles were not content to build on Paul's foundation. They boasted that any spiritual vitality in Corinth was due to *their* ministry, not Paul's. Carson aptly remarks, "Little men can be dangerous, especially when they position themselves in such a way as to capture some stolen glory from great men."[9] Paul, the great man, never raised his boast upon others' works, and his boast was never in himself, but in God's work in the God-ordained sphere of his calling.

Proper hope. The great apostle always had his eyes on the west, toward Rome's Seven Hills, to "castles rising in Spain," to "spires away on the world's rim," as poets have put it (cf. Romans 15:24). Thus he expressed his heart's hope: "But our hope is that as your faith increases, our area of influence among you may be greatly enlarged, so that we may preach the gospel in lands beyond you, without boasting of work already done in another's area of influence" (vv. 15b, 16). The apostle hoped that the Corinthians' growth in faith, evidenced by their rejection of his detractors (cf. 6:14—7:1) and their participation in the collection for the poor in Jerusalem (8—9), would allow him to go on westward with his mission to the Gentiles. He knew that he could not go until the faith of the Corinthians was stabilized. Again Paul said that he wanted to "preach the gospel in lands beyond . . . without boasting of work already done in another's area of influence." But note that this is not a repeat of his rebuke to the false apostles but is a declaration of his awesome vision.

Clearly, the only boasting that Paul was interested in was in God. He wanted to move on in the power of God across Europe, so that he might further boast of what God would do!

Proper principle. There is only one proper boast and principle for boasting: "Let the one who boasts, boast in the Lord" (v. 17). Paul had earlier referenced Jeremiah 31. But here he references a different text, Jeremiah 9:23, 24, which is a call to acknowledge God for all his gracious acts and providence. What is striking, though, is that Paul gives us a shorthand version that substitutes "in the Lord" for Jeremiah's list of what the Lord provides. This is because God is known for what he does.[10]

It is human to boast. We all do it very well. But to boast in the Lord is heavenly. "Let the one who boasts, boast in the Lord."

In a day when the desires and values of culture have been infused into the church, so that the styles and assumptions of politics and entertainment have walked uncritically into the pulpit, so that it is common to boast in show and personality and pretense and wealth and success—in such a day let us hear God's Word: "Let the one who boasts, boast in the Lord."

A glance at the opening chapters of the book of Revelation tells us that there will be no vain boasting in Heaven. Not one word of such boasting will ever be uttered in the eternal estate—ever! All will perpetually boast in the Lord.

> "Holy, holy, holy, is the Lord God Almighty,
> who was and is and is to come!" (Revelation 4:8b)
>
> "Worthy are you, our Lord and God,
> to receive glory and honor and power,
> for you created all things,
> and by your will they existed and were created." (Revelation 4:11)
>
> "Worthy are you to take the scroll
> and to open its seals,
> for you were slain, and by your blood you ransomed people for God
> from every tribe and language and people and nation,
> and you have made them a kingdom and priests to our God,
> and they shall reign on the earth." (Revelation 5:9, 10)
>
> After this I looked, and behold, a great multitude that no one could number, from every nation, from all tribes and peoples and languages, standing before the throne and before the Lamb, clothed in white robes, with palm branches in their hands, and crying out with a loud voice, "Salvation belongs to our God who sits on the throne, and to the Lamb!" (Revelation 7:9, 10)

In the Revelation there is no self-congratulation, only divine adulation!

What ultimately matters is God's approval: "For it is not the one who commends himself who is approved, but the one whom the Lord commends" (v. 18).

> Forbid it, Lord, that I should boast,
> Save in the death of Christ my God;
> All the vain things that charm me most,
> I sacrifice them to His blood.
>
> Isaac Watts

25

Apologia for Boasting

2 CORINTHIANS 11:1–15

MANY YEARS AGO a number of government officials in The Hague, who were more fashionable than religious, invited Van Courtonne, the famous court preacher of Paris who was of Dutch descent, to preach in their State Church chapel. But because Van Courtonne considered their interest more social than spiritual, more a curiosity than a zeal for truth, he declined to come. When the invitation was repeated several times, he agreed to accept—on the condition that all the government officials would be present. They agreed.

The famous Van Courtonne appeared and preached on "The Ethiopian" from Acts 8. His sermon had four points: 1) A government official who read his Bible—something rare. 2) A government official who acknowledged his ignorance—something rarer still. 3) A government official who asked a lesser person for instruction—something extremely rare. 4) A government official who was converted—the rarest thing of all! Van Courtonne never received a second invitation.[1]

Tough talk from a man who was evidently a tough preacher. But his toughness was not without precedent, even apostolic precedent. The Apostle Paul was a tough man, and as he was coming to his limit with his detractors in the Corinthian church, he would have some tough things to say, as we will see when we come to the end of this section.

Paul had just completed a hard-hitting defense of his apostolic authority in which he contrasted the *improper* boasting of the false apostles with *proper* apostolic boasting, which he then capped with this defining quotation from Jeremiah 9:23, 24: "'Let the one who boasts, boast in the Lord'" (10:17). Fleshly, man-centered boasting was anathema to Paul. Paul loathed human boasting, especially among professed believers. "'Let the one who boasts, boast in the Lord.' For it is not the one who commends himself who is approved, but the one whom the Lord commends" (vv. 17, 18).

However, now (unthinkably to Paul) he realizes that he must engage in the boasting he so abominates. The reason that Paul must indulge in boasting is that his opponents' boasting has made such deep inroads in the Corinthian church that their deadly teaching has gained a hearing. Thus Paul will be compelled to boast "as a fool"—"like a madman" as he will describe it (11: 21–23). But first he must prepare his readers for his stooping to such distasteful foolishness. So in verses 1–15 Paul lays out the justification for his participation in boasting. Paul's reticence is obvious in his opening request: "I wish you would bear with me in a little foolishness. Do bear with me!" (v. 1). "Bear with me as I play the fool so I can expose the foolishness of my opponents."

Boasting Justified Because They Are Being Led Astray (vv. 2–6)

Paul's paternal jealousy. Paul asks for the Corinthians' forbearance because he has a fatherly jealousy for them: "I feel a divine jealousy for you, for I betrothed you to one husband, to present you as a pure virgin to Christ" (v. 2). At their conversion the Corinthians were betrothed to Christ, and at their glorification they will be presented to Christ as his bride. Thus Paul pictures himself as the father of the bride whose ultimate purpose was to present her as a virgin to the Bridegroom at his appearance (cf. 4:14; Ephesians 5:27). And Paul was properly jealous about this. "Human jealousy is a vice, but to share divine jealousy is a virtue" (Harris).[2] Paul seethed with this virtue. And like the heroic Phinehas of the old covenant, Paul would do anything that was necessary to protect the church's purity (cf. Numbers 25:1–13)—even loathsome boasting.

Paul's fears. Paul's intense paternal zeal was fed by the true and present danger that the Corinthians might be led astray, and the bridal image just mentioned quite naturally brought to his mind the first human bride and how she was led astray by her deceiver.

> But I am afraid that as the serpent deceived Eve by his cunning, your thoughts will be led astray from a sincere and pure devotion to Christ. For if someone comes and proclaims another Jesus than the one we proclaimed, or if you receive a different spirit from the one you received, or if you accept a different gospel from the one you accepted, you put up with it readily enough. (vv. 3, 4)

This is the first of two mentions of Eve in the New Testament, and it is utterly intentional. Eve was completely deceived by Satan's cunning (cf.

1 Timothy 2:14). When Eve fell, it was not because she was beaten into submission by Satan, but by his encircling her soul with sequential coils of deception as he promised Eve things he could not deliver.

So it was with the betrothed Corinthian community as they were susceptible to Satan's cunning as he led them away from Christ into the promise of a more triumphant, victorious, prosperous Christianity—a Christianity that was dismissive of taking up the cross and weakness and suffering. Indeed, Satan was so cunning that he had convinced many of the Corinthians that it was Paul who was the cunning one (cf. 12:16).[3] D. A. Carson applies the text:

> From the time of the Fall to the present day, men and women have frequently succumbed to the deceptive devices of the devil. Christians are especially open to the kind of cunning deceit that combines the language of faith and religion with the content of self-interest and flattery. We like to be told how special we are, how wise, how blessed. . . . We like to have our Christianity shaped less by the cross than by triumphalism or rules or charismatic leaders or subjective experience. And if this shaping can be coated with assurances of orthodoxy, complete with cliché, we may not detect the presence of the arch-deceiver, nor see that we are being weaned away from "sincere and pure devotion to Christ" to a "different gospel."[4]

The wolves in the church that devour sheep do not howl and bare their teeth. They come in sheep's clothing, smiling, reciting Scripture, full of understanding, promising something more than Christ.

Paul feared that through satanic deception the Corinthians would fall to three delusions: "another Jesus," "a different spirit," and "a different gospel." In fact, he says sarcastically, "you put up with it readily enough" (v. 4b). The triplet of Jesus, spirit (the Holy Spirit), and gospel all suffered distortion at the hands of the false apostles who conflated the Judaizers' demands that the Gentiles keep the old covenant with a promise of more of the Spirit and the health and wealth and ecstasies of the heaven now of over-realized eschatology. "In terms of the imagery of our text, the opponents claimed to be married to Christ already, whereas Paul saw the church as betrothed but still waiting for her wedding day" (Hafemann).[5] Thus Paul's enemies were preaching another Jesus and a false understanding of the work of the Spirit—which meant a different gospel.

This was all first-century reality in Corinth just a handful of years after Paul had planted the church. Many really were beginning to follow a Jesus and a spirit and a gospel that did not exist. And that is still the real danger today. The mantra-like use of the name Jesus is used today by false apostles as well as by true. The question is, is this the Jesus of the Bible or the Jesus of another gospel?

Here in our passage, the intensity of Paul's fearful feelings, his jealousy to keep the church pure, to protect his people from Satan's cunning to keep them following the real Jesus and Spirit and gospel—all of these things were why Paul would condescend to boast in his ministry and why the Corinthians were asked to put up with such foolishness.

Paul's authority. A further reason why the Corinthian church had to bear with Paul's boasting was his apostolic authority: "I consider that I am not in the least inferior to these super-apostles. Even if I am unskilled in speaking, I am not so in knowledge; indeed, in every way we have made this plain to you in all things" (vv. 5, 6). "Super-apostles" on Paul's lips drips with sarcasm. His opponents called themselves "apostles," but Paul contemptuously called them "super-apostles" because they arrogated themselves over him, the Apostle to the Gentiles.

Though Paul granted that he was "unskilled in speaking" (according to the artificial, stylized standards of Greco-Roman rhetoric), he really conceded nothing because he defined the criteria for preaching, namely, *knowledge*—"I am not so [i.e., unskilled] in knowledge; indeed, in every way we have made this plain to you" (v. 6). Likely, Paul was a powerful, persuasive preacher who refused the synthetic style of the rhetorician.[6] And that was obvious to the Corinthians. This was a further reason to forbear the foolish boasting he was about to do.

Boasting Justified by Paul's No-Charge Ministry (vv. 7–12)

Today in the academic and business and political worlds speaking fees are determined by your status. Certain people, like ex-presidents and star CEOs, can garner as much as $100,000 for a single speaking engagement.

The practice is as old as Greece and Rome. And the church has not escaped. The advent of agents (an idea imported from the media and literary industries) has driven Christian speakers' fees to scandalous levels—sometimes $30,000 for a single event. What imprecations would Paul rain down today?

Traveling speakers and professional philosophers in Paul's day were accorded status by the fees they charged. In fact, a cheap fee was thought to imply that the message wasn't important. Therefore Paul's refusal to accept money for his ministry in Corinth was negatively interpreted to mean either 1) an admission that his teaching was of low caliber, 2) that his message wasn't worth much, 3) that he gave the gospel away because nobody would pay for it, or 4) that he was not really an apostle. Add to this the fact that the "super-apostles" charged for their renditions of the gospel and you have the picture.

Paul's free ministry. So Paul raised the prickly subject:

> Or did I commit a sin in humbling myself so that you might be exalted, because I preached God's gospel to you free of charge? I robbed other churches by accepting support from them in order to serve you. And when I was with you and was in need, I did not burden anyone, for the brothers who came from Macedonia supplied my need. So I refrained and will refrain from burdening you in any way. (vv. 7–9)

The fact is that while Paul would not presently take any support from the Corinthian church, he did accept support from other churches. In his first letter to the Corinthians he defended his right as an apostle to receive support from the churches (cf. 9:15–17). However, in Corinth, due to charges launched against his integrity, he refused any money from the prosperous church. Instead, so as not to burden the Corinthians, he "robbed" churches that were in abject poverty![7]

The Corinthians were meant to get the point of this ironic hyperbole—and they certainly did. But it was the false apostles who received the brunt of this because, notwithstanding the cultural expectations that they accept money for doing the gospel, Paul's rejection of pay called into question their motivation and integrity. And more, Paul's practice was in accord with that of Christ himself. His preaching for free was consistent with the free grace of God: "For you know the grace of our Lord Jesus Christ, that though he was rich, yet for your sake he became poor, so that you by his poverty might become rich" (8:9).

Obviously, Paul's raising the subject of money put his opponents back on their heels. They knew that Paul's example made them look shabby. In spite of their assertions that it was a mark of apostolic dignity to be supported by the congregation and that Paul refused support because he knew he did not match their apostolic level, they knew they were a burden to the Corinthians and he was not.[8]

Paul's oaths. Paul seals his commitment to take no money with two brief back-to-back oaths. First, "As the truth of Christ is in me, this boasting of mine will not be silenced in the regions of Achaia" (v. 10). The "super-apostles" saw his refusal to take money as an indication of his disqualification. But Paul sees it for what it is—as objective evidence that he is following Christ.

So he boasts in it. Paul would rather die than let anyone deprive him of the boast of giving up his apostolic rights to financial supply (cf. 1 Corinthians 9:15).

Second, because Paul senses that his refusal to accept honoraria from the Corinthians may be interpreted as spite, he resorts to another oath: "And why? Because I do not love you? God knows I do!" (v. 11). The Corinthian detractors were so far gone, so perverted in their indicting of Paul, that Paul called God as witness ("God knows I do!") to prove that he truly loved them. The Corinthians have missed altogether that Paul was simply following the example of Christ.

Small wonder that Paul now will conclude that his enemies are not Christian at all (cf. 2 Corinthians 13:5). So now Paul gears up for his offensive thrust as he asserts, "And what I do I will continue to do, in order to undermine the claim of those who would like to claim that in their boasted mission they work on the same terms as we do" (v. 12). There was no way that the money-loving "super-apostles" were on Paul's level. They did not come close to his ethics and, most of all, his love! So he will keep laboring at no cost to undermine their fraudulent claims of equality. Soon Paul will engage in his foolish boasting to prove his authenticity and their pretense. But first he will take off his gloves in an assault that makes that of Van Courtonne against the Dutch politicians look positively congenial.

Boasting Justified Because of False Apostles (vv. 13–15)

False apostles. So now, using some of his strongest language ever, he further explains why his opponents do not measure up: "for such men are false apostles, deceitful workmen, disguising themselves as apostles of Christ" (v. 13). The deceit of the false apostles was fully volitional; they disguised themselves or masqueraded as apostles of Christ. The term normally means physical transformation (cf. Philippians 3:21)—"to transform, to change the outward appearance of a person or thing, to disguise."[9] Thus Paul's opponents may have affected an apostolic dress, perhaps through ornamentation and vestments.[10] Their apostolic chic when compared to unimpressive bodily presence would have fooled many of the culture-bound Corinthians. However, it was the false apostles' deceit that was intentional and thoroughgoing.

This kind of deception has been the bane of the church. In the eighteenth century the New Testament scholar Reimarus publicly defended Christianity in his best-known book, *The Principle Teachings of the Christian Religion.*

But in private Reimarus had been, all along, working on a massive book entitled *Apologia for the Rational Work of God*, which Jaroslav Pelikan described as "a radical attack on most of those 'principle teachings of the Christian religion' in the name of a thoroughgoing rationalism and deism."[11] In Corinth, such conscious deceit was in full force and was taking its toll. Leaders were given full sway to "work against the gospel in the name of the gospel, seduce the people to another Jesus in the name of Jesus, and in the name of greater Christian maturity instill a deadly triumphalism."[12]

Going deeper still, Paul explains, "And no wonder, for even Satan disguises himself as an angel of light. So it is no surprise if his servants, also, disguise themselves as servants of righteousness" (vv. 14, 15a). This is the only time that Satan is described as "an angel of light," though the idea is certainly in the Old Testament (cf. Isaiah 14:12–15). The point is that he is the arch-deceiver. Jesus said of him, "When he lies, he speaks out of his own character, for he is a liar and the father of lies" (John 8:44). When Satan is at work we never smell sulfur or glance down at a cloven hoof; rather he is sweetness and a congenial, smiling light—until he has control. Remember Screwtape's diabolical counsel to Wormwood? "Indeed, the safest road to Hell is the gradual one—the gentle slope, soft underfoot, without sudden turnings, without milestones, without signposts."[13] The devil is the angel of light. Ronald Knox was so right when he said, "It is so stupid of modern civilization to have given up believing in the devil when he is the only explanation of it."[14]

Because Satan is an angel of light, Paul concludes with the pounding application, "So it is no surprise if his servants, also, disguise themselves as servants of righteousness" (v. 15a). The methodology of false apostles is that of servants of righteousness, not unrighteousness. The temptations that come from such teachers are tinted with the artificial light of pseudo-righteousness. Those under their sway rationalize their way into evil by seeing some kind of good in it, or by ignoring its evil. They cheat on their income tax because they tell themselves that the government takes too much, and there is so much government waste, and everyone is doing it. They gossip about their friends and neighbors and leaders because they reason that they are passing on truth and discernment. They nurse bitterness and hate because they are persuaded that their emotions are not evil but righteous.[15]

Their end. Paul concludes his point ominously: "Their end will correspond to their deeds" (v. 15b). The "super-apostles" were not Christians at all. They were of the devil—and diabolically wrong.[16] And a special wrath awaited them.

Paul has been so hard-hitting, but at the same time gracious. Just as Van Courtonne's message, if heeded, would have led to grace, so much more Paul's. In reality, Paul was making a last run at the false apostles' souls. His withering dissection of their deceitful hearts could be the beginning of grace. What a fearful indictment! But what grace could follow!

If the Corinthian church (and the false apostles) have at all engaged what Paul is saying, they will then engage his foolish boasting, which is meant to authenticate his apostleship and ultimately save their souls. Let us beware when some smiling, well-dressed preacher tells us "we can have it all now" without taking up the cross. Let us beware of another Jesus, a different spirit, and another gospel.

26

Paul's Boasting

2 CORINTHIANS 11:16–33

AS WE HAVE SEEN in chapters 10—11, the Apostle Paul abominated boasting. Most especially, he hated the boasting of those he derisively called the "super-apostles" because their self-boasting had gained them a hearing in the Corinthian church while diminishing his apostolic authority. The super-apostles' gains had been so substantial that Paul realized he would have to engage in the same foolishness. That is why the first part of chapter 11 is devoted to preparing his readers for the boasting he so loathes.

Now Paul is ready. But, fearing that some of his hearers might imagine that his boasting is anything but foolish, Paul restates his warning: "I repeat, let no one think me foolish. But even if you do, accept me as a fool, so that I too may boast a little. What I am saying with this boastful confidence, I say not with the Lord's authority but as a fool. Since many boast according to the flesh, I too will boast" (vv. 16–18). Paul reasons that though he doesn't want to be thought to be a fool, it's okay, if the Corinthians will then listen to his boasts. And he knows that though such boasting is not something Jesus himself would have done, it is a necessary foolishness.

Paul's loathing for what he is about to do is evident in his biting sarcasm as he ironically calls the Corinthians "wise" for their putting up with his enemies' boasting: "For you gladly bear with fools, being wise yourselves! For you bear it if someone makes slaves of you, or devours you, or takes advantage of you, or puts on airs, or strikes you in the face" (vv. 19, 20). In effect, Paul says, "You are so brilliant that you put up with fools while they exploit you." To which he adds with mock shame, "To my shame, I must say, we were too weak for that!" (v. 21a)—that is, "I was too weak to enslave you and devour your resources and ensnare you and lift myself up and abuse you. Shame on me!" The Apostle Paul knew how to make a point. Ouch!

Foolish Boasting (vv. 21b, 22)

So now, having qualified himself with appropriate sarcasm, the apostle begins his dreaded boasting in carefully arranged clauses: "But whatever anyone else dares to boast of—I am speaking as a fool—I also dare to boast of that. Are they Hebrews? So am I. Are they Israelites? So am I. Are they offspring of Abraham? So am I" (vv. 21b, 22).

Paul's threefold fleshly identity is impeccable. As a Hebrew he has pure *ethnic* identity. He was in fact "a Hebrew of the Hebrews" (Philippians 3:5), which meant that he was a full-blooded Jew, and more than that he was a Hebraic Jew who was fluent in Hebrew and Aramaic and thoroughly steeped in Hebrew culture.[1] As an Israelite, he had full *religious* identity with the people of God with all the rights and privileges thereof. As Paul explained to the Romans, "They are Israelites, and to them belong the adoption, the glory, the covenants, the giving of the law, the worship, and the promises. To them belong the patriarchs, and from their race, according to the flesh, is the Christ who is God over all, blessed forever. Amen" (Romans 9:4, 5)—an awesome religious identity. As the seed of Abraham he was of God's *covenant* people and a participant in the salvation-historical privileges of the elect people of God.[2]

So Paul had the pedigree. No one could gainsay his famous lineage and culture, and few could equal it. Later he would tell the Philippians:

> If anyone else thinks he has reason for confidence in the flesh, I have more: circumcised on the eighth day, of the people of Israel, of the tribe of Benjamin, a Hebrew of Hebrews; as to the law, a Pharisee; as to zeal, a persecutor of the church; as to righteousness, under the law blameless. (Philippians 3:4b-6)

Paul's fleshly superiority was incontrovertible. "Top this, you super-apostles! You can't."

It was true, but Paul could barely bring himself to voice it, because it countered the gospel of grace and the call to assume the humble character of Christ and take up the cross and follow him (cf. Matthew 16:24). This was foolish boasting indeed. And Paul could hardly do it. Therefore, as Paul poses the next question, "Are they servants of Christ?" and answers, "I am a better one," he reflexively adds, "I am talking like a madman" (v. 23).

And with that he switches from boasting in his fleshly strengths to boasting in his weaknesses. This was doubly foolish boasting because Paul's enemies rejected his weaknesses, viewing them as disqualifications. He boasts in his seeming disqualifications.

Doubly Foolish Boasting (vv. 23–29)

D. A. Carson suggests that Paul's detractors might have expected Paul to have said something like:

> I have established more churches; I have preached the gospel in more lands and to more ethnic groups; I have traveled more miles; I have won more converts; I have written more books; I have raised more money; I have dominated more councils; I have walked with God more fervently and seen more visions; I have commanded the greatest crowds and performed the most spectacular miracles.[3]

In truth, this kind of list was common in pagan culture. For example, Augustus Caesar wrote a eulogy in his own honor, listing his accomplishments, the famous *Res Gestae Divi Augusti* in which he numbered his accomplishments.[4] But here as Paul numbers his weaknesses—"Five times I received . . . forty lashes less one. Three times I was beaten with rods"—his boasting is a studied parody of the *Res Gestae*[5]—of Caesar's resumé.

Paul turns convention on its head and argues for the authenticity and superiority of his apostolic service from his weaknesses, not from his strengths. Double foolishness. Holy foolishness! The apostle begins with a generalized statement of his sufferings—"with far greater labors, far more imprisonments, with countless beatings, and often near death" (v. 23). He pictures a life overflowing with perpetual, incalculable sufferings.

This was Paul's claim to authenticity. Certainly, none of the super-apostles could match it, and more certainly, none cared to.

Specific sufferings. In conscious parody of Caesar's proud resumé, Paul lists his specific sufferings, giving explicit substance to what he has just summarized: "Five times I received at the hands of the Jews the forty lashes less one. Three times I was beaten with rods. Once I was stoned. Three times I was shipwrecked; a night and a day I was adrift at sea" (vv. 24, 25).

Beatings. The "forty lashes less one" was a unique Jewish punishment administered in the synagogue and was the most severe beating allowed by Scripture (cf. Deuteronomy 25:1–3). It was extremely painful and humiliating. No more than forty stripes could be administered at one beating, and that is why they were limited to thirty-nine—because if the executioner exceeded forty, he himself was liable to be flogged. Remarkably, not one of Paul's floggings is mentioned in Acts or any other source. Therefore, the five floggings all occurred early in Paul's ministry—and were likely followed by more!

Five floggings total 195 stripes. Imagine Paul's anguish as in full knowledge of the excruciating pain that was coming he awaited another beating. Even more, imagine his love for his people, the Jews. When Paul entered a town he went to the Jews first though in many cases that meant a thirty-nine stripe flogging in the synagogue for false teaching and blasphemy.

What astonishing love! It was proof of his declaration to the Jews in Rome: "For I could wish that I myself were accursed and cut off from Christ for the sake of my brothers, my kinsmen according to the flesh" (Romans 9:3). Paul's painful, heroic love remained perpetual and unflagging as he went to the Jews first. His credentials dripped with his own blood.

The rod, on the other hand, was the instrument of Roman and therefore Gentile punishment. Paul's only recorded beating with the rod in Scripture took place in Philippi as described in the beatings of Paul and Silas in Acts 16:22, 23. They were stripped naked and beaten until the magistrates were satisfied. In 2 Corinthians 11 Paul lists three such separate beatings with the rod. Surely, Paul experienced more in his extended missionary journeys. His body became a living monument to his suffering, as he would write at the conclusion of his letter to the Galatians: "From now on let no one cause me trouble, for I bear on my body the marks of Jesus" (6:17). They were marks of apostleship and evidence of his superior qualifications over the super-apostles. Most of all, they were scars of love.

Stoning. We have a full account of Paul's stoning at Lystra where his attackers left him apparently dead (cf. Acts 14:19). The physical trauma inflicted by such events is a matter of historical record. No doubt Paul's face also bore the marks of Jesus. The only reason Paul escaped alive at Lystra is that the stoning was the inefficient work of a Jewish mob. If it had been a judicial stoning as proscribed in the *Mishnah* (Sanhedrin 6:1–6), the outcome would have been otherwise.

Shipwreck. Maritime disasters were not unusual in the ancient world due to fragile vessels, poor navigation, misleading maps, and meteorological guesswork. Paul's three shipwrecks occurred before the famous shipwreck on the island of Malta described in Acts 27. So Paul was involved in at least four shipwrecks. And one of them was particularly miserable because it was mid-sea, so that Paul became flotsam for twenty-four hours in open sea.

The five synagogue floggings, the three Roman beatings, the stoning, and the three shipwrecks cited here total twelve "near death" occasions (cf. v. 23)—all this with more missionary work to go! To those caught up in the prosperity gospel of the super-apostles, these were hardly resumé enhancers, but foolish admissions. But to Paul, they were proof positive that he was a servant of Christ. Suffering, not success, authenticated Paul's ministry.

Specific dangers. Next Paul catalogs his perils with rhythmic specificity: "on frequent journeys, in danger from rivers, danger from robbers, danger from my own people, danger from Gentiles, danger in the city, danger in the wilderness, danger at sea, danger from false brothers" (v. 26).

Paul was no tourist! The dangers are all frequent-traveler perils and fall into two categories: *places* and *people*. Paul experienced danger everywhere he went—rivers, the city, the wilderness, at sea. But it was people rather than places that were the greatest dangers—"danger from robbers, danger from my own people, danger from Gentiles . . . danger from false brothers." Acts records six Jewish plots against Paul and three perilous encounters with Gentiles (cf. 9:23, 29; 13:45; 14:2–19; 15:26; 17:5ff.; 18:12; and 14:19, 20; 16:16–40; 19:23–41).

Most significantly, "danger from false brothers" is positioned at the conclusion of the dangers and is unpaired with a parallel danger, which gives "false brothers" preeminence over the other dangers.[6] These "false brothers" are the same as the "false apostles" of verse 13 who are trying to pass themselves off as "apostles of Christ" and "disguise themselves as servants of righteousness" (v. 15).[7] "Danger from false brothers" flashes like a blinking neon sign at the end of Paul's dangers, indicating both the pain that he has suffered and the peril to the Corinthian church. It is these who have posed and pose the greatest danger to Paul. Indeed, it was these very people who were denying Paul's credentials with their triumphalist, prosperity theology.

Volitional suffering. Paul summarizes the overall experience of his apostolic lifestyle as "in toil and hardship, through many a sleepless night, in hunger and thirst, often without food, in cold and exposure" (v. 27)—which recollects immense suffering over a period of years.[8] Obviously Paul had freely chosen to live out a counter-prosperity lifestyle. Paul labored night and day with his own hands to preach the gospel (cf. 1 Thessalonians 2:9). His sleepless nights were a voluntary insomnia because his manual labor and his prayers and his preaching often curtailed his sleep. He suffered hunger and thirst and cold and exposure because of his extreme travels for the sake of the gospel. Paul volitionally chose all of this. So we see that while the false apostles taught a prosperity-drenched gospel replete with large honoraria and the good life, Paul chose to live hand-to-mouth.

The contrast could not be greater. Paul's antagonists exulted in their ostensible strength, and he in his weakness. And they despised him for it.

Such sufferings! Certainly others have suffered worse pain in the moments of their martyrdom. But is there anyone in recorded history who has suffered so much over the course of years—the multiple near-death floggings, the gruesome stoning, the frequent shipwrecks, the dangers on the road from both places and people, the great suffering over an extended period of time? Is there an equal to Paul's suffering? I think not. The annals of the world's epic lives and journeys contain nothing to rival the courage and endurance—and love—of the Apostle Paul. Paul is not only the church's great hero, but the world's great hero.

Pastoral heartache. Nevertheless, for Paul the catalog of sufferings was not the sum of it. His greatest suffering rested in his pastoral heart: "And, apart from other things, there is the daily pressure on me of my anxiety for all the churches. Who is weak, and I am not weak? Who is made to fall, and I am not indignant?" (vv. 28, 29). Paul's opening, "And, apart from other things," indicates that his catalog of sufferings is illustrative and not complete.[9] Chrysostom believed that Paul had not told the half of it.[10] Certainly his anxiety over the churches was his greatest suffering of all. We saw it earlier in 2 Corinthians 7 when Paul was so anxious to discover how the Corinthians had responded to his tearful letter that he sent Titus on ahead to find out. And then when Titus didn't rendezvous with him in Troas, Paul went on to Macedonia where, he says, "our bodies had no rest, but we were afflicted at every turn—fighting without and fear within" (7:5b). He had such anxiety about their welfare. Similarly, Paul wrote to the Thessalonians, "when I could bear it no longer, I sent to learn about your faith, for fear that somehow the tempter had tempted you and our labor would be in vain" (1 Thessalonians 3:5).

Paul's great heart rose and fell with his people. His greatest pains were heart-pains over his people! This is driven home by his rhetorical questions, "Who is weak, and I am not weak? Who is made to fall, and I am not indignant?" (v. 29). Paul's becoming weak when his people were weak testifies to his empathy—he felt with his people. There was not an ounce of indifference in Paul's heart.

The fierce counterpart to Paul's empathy was his indignation over the thought of someone falling away from Christ. Literally, the question reads, "Who is entrapped into sin, and I do not burn?" His people's fallings set Paul's heart ablaze with pain. This is why Paul got so inflamed about Satan's servants in disguise, declaring, "Their end will correspond to their deeds" (v. 15b). One commentator writes, "Paul's greatest boast is his constant worry over their welfare"[11]–and I think he is right.

Paul's foolish boasting was confined to his threefold boast in his superior heritage and culture. And it was immediately subsumed by his doubly foolish boasting in his weakness. We say doubly foolish because while Paul felt the fool in boasting in his superiority, the false apostles could not comprehend the compound foolishness of boasting in weaknesses—boasting in his beatings and shipwrecks and dangers and deprivations. The crowning boast (which was incomprehensible to his detractors) was his anxiety for all his churches. His greatest suffering was his greatest boast. Paul's pastoral heart (his matching his weakness to his people's weakness, his burning pain at their fall) was the primary proof of his apostleship.

The apostle's parody of Caesar's resumé turned everything on its head. It was countercultural. Weakness is the singular apostolic qualification, not human strength. This, too, flies in the face of today's resumé-obsessed culture, which worships strength and beauty and intelligence and pedigree and success. This also counters much of church culture that is embarrassed by the weak and lowly.

At the same time verse 29 sets up the Corinthians for a "surprising insight into the relationship between suffering, weakness, and Paul's apostleship."[12]

Boasting in Weakness (vv. 30–33)

Paul introduces his concluding thoughts with a summary sentence: "If I must boast, I will boast of the things that show my weakness" (v. 30). The apostle does this by recounting a very low point in his life, when he was lowered in a basket from a window in the city wall to escape. The telling of this event would be so incredible to his triumphalist detractors that he uses an oath to assure them that it is true—"The God and Father of the Lord Jesus, he who is blessed forever, knows that I am not lying" (v. 31). This oath ensured that his detractors would listen. Why the oath? we wonder. The story is patently benign. "At Damascus, the governor under King Aretas was guarding the city of Damascus in order to seize me, but I was let down in a basket through a window in the wall and escaped his hands" (vv. 32, 33). How can this story merit an oath?

The key to the answer comes from the identification of the city as Damascus. It was to Damascus that Paul first went as a proud Pharisee to seek out and destroy the people called Christians. But it was on the road to that city that he met Christ and received his call. And when he left the city it was like a lowly criminal, "lowered like a catch of dead fish in a basket whose smelly cargo he had displaced."[13] In effect Paul views the incident in Damascus as a paradigm for his life. God's strength would be perfected in his weakness. Paul tells us by this story that weakness was at the heart of his calling from the very beginning of his apostleship.

Paul's parody in verses 23–27 struck hard at the thinking of the Corinthian church, which had imported the values of Corinth right into its midst. Caesar's *Res Gestae* was the cultural model for the false apostles whose self-promoting vitas read like this: "I have six letters from prominent people in Athens and Rome who extol my virtues. Three times I have spoken before imperial legates. Once I was received by Pompeii. Twice I have received honoraria beyond my peers. In every quarter I am esteemed." But Paul, instead of extolling his achievements, boasted in bearing the cross of Christ in suffering and weakness.

Today we too find it easier to interpret the gospel in terms of our received culture rather than interpreting the culture by the gospel. We need to be wary of our Christianity becoming a Christianized version of our own culture. We must not write our resumés after the example of Caesar but after that of Paul. As Christians we must avoid boasting about our education and training and successes and bank accounts and vacation homes and honors as if it is these things that give us our value. As Christians we must acknowledge and embrace our weaknesses, because as we give them to Christ, they become occasions for his strength and glory. To quote Paul again:

> Such is the confidence that we have through Christ toward God. Not that we are sufficient in ourselves to claim anything as coming from us, but our sufficiency is from God, who has made us sufficient to be ministers of a new covenant, not of the letter but of the Spirit. For the letter kills, but the Spirit gives life. (2 Corinthians 3:4–6)

Can we embrace our weaknesses? Will we embrace our weaknesses? The answer to that question has everything to do with the authenticity of the gospel and the church and its mission.

27

Paul's Greatest Boast

2 CORINTHIANS 12:1–10

THE BOASTING THAT THE APOSTLE PAUL WAS REQUIRED TO DO was a matter of painful awkwardness for him. When Paul's opponents, the super-apostles, boasted about their ethnic and religious pedigrees, Paul had reluctantly responded by reciting his own transcending pedigrees—which he quickly turned into an extended boast in his weaknesses.

Now we see the same hesitation as Paul is called to counter his opponents' boast in their ecstatic spiritual experiences by describing his own surpassing experience. You can sense Paul's discomfort and reticence in the opening verse of chapter 12: "I must go on boasting. Though there is nothing to be gained by it, I will go on to visions and revelations of the Lord" (v. 1). Though Paul is doubtful of what such sharing will accomplish, he fully understands the dangers of default, so he will again play the fool. Significantly, however, he will not waste his time telling of lesser phenomena but will cut straight to his vision and revelations of the risen Lord.[1] Not unsurprisingly, Paul's boast in the incredible revelation accorded him will be followed by an even greater boast in his weakness—Paul's greatest boast of all.

Paul's Rapture and Modest Boast (vv. 2–6)

Rapture. Paul opens with a bare-bones description of his personal rapture into the third heaven and paradise:

> I know a man in Christ who fourteen years ago was caught up to the third heaven—whether in the body or out of the body I do not know, God knows. And I know that this man was caught up into paradise—whether in the

> body or out of the body I do not know, God knows—and he heard things that cannot be told, which man may not utter. (vv. 2–4)

The apostle twice refers to himself in the third person with almost identical phrases, but there is no doubt that it is Paul himself, because in verse 7 he switches to the first person and identifies himself as the recipient of the surpassing revelations. Paul's use of the third person signals his discomfort and embarrassment in indulging in ecstatic biography, which he deems of little profit. The very fact that Paul had told no one about his rapture to paradise shows that he considered private experiences like this as unimportant to his gospel ministry. Fourteen years earlier would have been *circa* A.D. 42 when Paul was in Tarsus or Antioch before his first missionary journey.[2] Certainly, the rapture had been important in Paul's preparation for missionary service. But Paul believed that its subjective individual nature was of no profit to others; otherwise he would have shared it as he repeatedly did with the story of his conversion encounter with Christ on the Damascus road. Paul's experience of rapture here had been thoroughly ecstatic—so ecstatic that Paul didn't know whether he had been caught up bodily like Enoch or Elijah, or whether it was simply the out-of-the-body transport of his human spirit (cf. Genesis 5:24 and Hebrews 11:5; 2 Kings 2:11 and Mark 9:4). All Paul knew is that it happened, and he had been there!

Biblical cosmology views the heavens as threefold. The first heaven is the atmosphere. The second heaven is the place of the stars. And the third heaven is the abode of God.[3] The parallel designation "paradise" seals the locale of the third heaven as the very presence of God. The word "paradise" occurs in only two other places in the New Testament: Luke 23:43 where Christ says to the repentant thief, "Today you will be with me in Paradise," and Revelation 2:7 where the Spirit says, "To the one who conquers I will grant to eat of the tree of life, which is in the Paradise of God." Scholars such as Philip Hughes hold that these three mentions of paradise are mutually defining and that they refer to the presence of Christ throughout salvation history.[4] Hughes writes:

> The Apostle was caught up "*as far as* the third heaven": this specifies the "height" or "distance" of his rapture. Also, but not separately, he was caught up "*into* Paradise": this specifies the "depth" of his rapture, and is a more precise disclosure of the particular "part" or nature of the third heaven into which he was taken.[5]

There in the paradise of the third heaven Paul saw the resurrected Christ, and there he saw the souls of the redeemed "at home with the Lord" (5:8), awaiting the crowning consummation of their salvation, the bestowal of their glorious resurrection bodies as the new heaven and the new earth are inaugurated and all God's purposes are finally fulfilled.[6] There in paradise Paul "heard things that cannot be told, which man may not utter" (v. 4). What he heard was beyond utterance, not because they were unintelligible or because there was any deficiency in Paul, but because God had forbidden Paul to speak of them. They were private. They were given to Paul for his own personal benefit, not to pass on.

What an awesome transcendental experience had been granted to the Apostle Paul! Apart from the book of Revelation there is nothing in the New Testament to compare with it. His personal rapture was Mosaic in its grandeur. But why was it so awesome, we ask, if it was not to be shared? John Calvin supplies the answer: ". . . this thing happened for Paul's own sake, for a man who had awaiting him troubles hard enough to break a thousand hearts needed to be strengthened in a special way to keep him from giving way and to help him to persevere undaunted."[7] Paul was granted a greater view of the glory to come in order that it might sustain him in his epic beatings and shipwrecks and betrayals and heartaches that rose and fell with the fortunes of his churches. This epic experience sustained an epic heart.

Modest boast. Most people, had they been granted an ecstasy like Paul's wherein they actually had been raptured to paradise (to God, to his Son, to the Holy Spirit, to the souls of the departed, to the discourse of Heaven), would scarcely be able to contain themselves. Today they would write a bestseller—*My Rapture: A Personal Account of My Trip to Heaven and Back*. Seminars on "5 Steps to Your Own Rapture" would be sold out. The writer's words would be accorded the status of divine revelation. Why, you could build an entire denomination on it and even fund a college—"Rapture U." Paul, however, from the evidence of the text, would certainly have taken the story of his rapture to the grave were it not for the compelling necessity to boast in it for the sake of the Corinthian church.

And now, as he does reticently boast, it is modest and restrained as he continues in the self-effacing third person:

> On behalf of this man I will boast, but on my own behalf I will not boast, except of my weaknesses. Though if I should wish to boast, I would not be a fool, for I would be speaking the truth. But I refrain from it, so that no one may think more of me than he sees in me or hears from me. (vv. 5, 6)

Although Paul would be completely justified in boasting in his amazing experience, he forgoes doing so and boasts in his weaknesses instead. By doing this Paul ensured that authority in the church would not be based on ecstatic experience but on the actions and words of its leaders. Paul forbids any assessment of himself and his ministry by standards other than his actions and words. This provides essential wisdom for navigating the currents of the modern church. We must understand that regardless of how great a personal claim is made to visions and ecstasies, nothing can replace conduct and speech as indications of truly following Christ.

Paul's Thorn and His Greatest Boast (vv. 7–10)

Up to this point Paul has written obliquely of his rapture to paradise from the perspective of the third person, but now as he switches to the first person, he becomes crystal-clear.

Thorn. The essence of Paul's thought in verse 7 is that the revelation accorded him was so personally exalting that he needed a humbling thorn in his flesh: "So to keep me from being too elated by the surpassing greatness of the revelations, a thorn was given me in the flesh, a messenger of Satan to harass me, to keep me from being too elated." Note well that Paul's thorn "came to him *after* his 'surpassingly great revelations' and in consequence of them."[8] As to what the thorn was, we can only conjecture. Some have speculated that the thorn was opposition, perhaps the Judaizers or the super-apostles. Certainly the metaphor is used this way. Others have supposed a specific ailment, such as poor eyesight, noting that Galatians 6:11 mentions Paul writing with large handwriting. But there Paul seems to be writing large for dramatic effect.

The speculations run wild. And if you've suffered from maladies such as earaches, headaches, malaria, hysteria, hypochondria, gallstones, gout, rheumatism, sciatica, gastritis, leprosy, deafness, dental disease, or neurasthenia, a thorn seems an apt metaphor.[9] Whatever the reality, the fact was that Paul's thorn was debilitating and, likely, humiliating. Actually, the thorn's anonymity has proven a good thing, because it allows a broad application to the afflictions that God ordains for his children.

But the truth here about the thorn that we all should note is that while the thorn was Satan's work, it was God who allowed it. Just as God was the one who was responsible for the ecstasy of Paul's rapture to the third heaven, God was also responsible for the agony of his thorn.[10] Divine wisdom determined that the thorn was what Paul needed, because without it the apostle would have become conceited.

This turned the argument of Paul's critics on its head because Paul's loathsome thorn (the very thing his critics loathed in him and saw as evidence that God was not with him) was actually proof of the transcending superiority of his experience when raptured into the presence of God. What a stunning rebuke to the super-apostles who worshiped health and well-being and who viewed affliction and weakness as the absence of God's blessing.

This does not suggest, however, that Paul enjoyed his thorn in the flesh. He didn't, as evidenced by his prayer: "Three times I pleaded with the Lord about this, that it should leave me" (v. 8). Paul was no masochist, moaning,

"Afflict me, Lord! I like it." He would have no sympathy with those who later sought discomfort and destitution and affliction and martyrdom under the delusion that such seeking had apostolic precedent. What Paul sought was the removal of the thorn.

Here his trio of prayers refers to a singular event in which he pled passionately that the thorn would leave him. Significantly, Paul's three prayers parallel Jesus' threefold prayer to the Father in Gethsemane that the cup of suffering be removed, and which also culminated in assurance that the prayer had been answered, even though the cup, as with the thorn, was not taken away (cf. Mark 14:32–41).[11] In Gethsemane, Christ Jesus pled with his heavenly Father. Here Paul pleads with Christ Jesus risen from the dead. Paul's prayer was a passionate, heart-rending plea like that of Jesus in Gethsemane to his loving Father. And Jesus, like his Father, lovingly answered no to Paul. Thus, we must take this to heart: Whenever Christ says no to our desperate passionate pleadings, the no is freighted with his perfect, compassionate goodness and love. The Lord's answers to our prayers are never negative, except in a superficial sense, because ultimately they are fully positive, bringing God's unending blessing.[12] How good for us it is when our hearts embrace this.

Greatest boast. Jesus' no to Paul came in the form of an explanation and is the high point of the entire letter: "But he said to me, 'My grace is sufficient for you, for my power is made perfect in weakness'" (v. 9a). Scholars agree: "This is the summit of the epistle, the lofty peak from which the whole is viewed in true proportion."[13]

The grand theme, the melodic line, of 2 Corinthians is authentic ministry as Paul describes and defends the ministry of the new covenant. And the persistent motif of authentic ministry is *power in weakness*. At the onset of this letter Paul introduced his experience of weakness as being burdened beyond his strength:

> For we do not want you to be unaware, brothers, of the affliction we experienced in Asia. For we were so utterly burdened beyond our strength that we despaired of life itself. Indeed, we felt that we had received the sentence of death. But that was to make us rely not on ourselves but on God who raises the dead. (1:8, 9)

Paul's utter weakness was the platform for resurrection power.

Then in 2:14 Paul explains how his being led in weakness to death in a Roman triumphal procession effects the power of the gospel: "But thanks be to God, who in Christ always leads us in triumphal procession, and through us spreads the fragrance of the knowledge of him everywhere." Power in weakness. Paul's weakness wafted the aroma of Christ so redolent with saving power.

The most eloquent statement of the power in weakness motif is in 4:7–12:

> But we have this treasure in jars of clay, to show that the surpassing power belongs to God and not to us. We are afflicted in every way, but not crushed; perplexed, but not driven to despair; persecuted, but not forsaken; struck down, but not destroyed; always carrying in the body the death of Jesus, so that the life of Jesus may also be manifested in our bodies. For we who live are always being given over to death for Jesus' sake, so that the life of Jesus also may be manifested in our mortal flesh. So death is at work in us, but life in you.

The theme of power in weakness is seen also in the litany of Paul's endurance in 6:4–10:

> . . . but as servants of God we commend ourselves in every way: by great endurance, in afflictions, hardships, calamities, beatings, imprisonments, riots, labors, sleepless nights, hunger; by purity, knowledge, patience, kindness, the Holy Spirit, genuine love; by truthful speech, and the power of God; with the weapons of righteousness for the right hand and for the left; through honor and dishonor, through slander and praise. We are treated as impostors, and yet are true; as unknown, and yet well known; as dying, and behold, we live; as punished, and yet not killed; as sorrowful, yet always rejoicing; as poor, yet making many rich; as having nothing, yet possessing everything.

"'Power in weakness,' therefore, runs as a thread throughout the letter, reaching its most powerful expression here" (Barnett).[14] "But he said to me, 'My grace is sufficient for you, for my power is made perfect in weakness'" (12:9a). The massed force of Paul's repeated eloquent statements of power in weakness is meant to capture our souls and make it the motif of our lives.

But what we most need to see is that power in weakness is shorthand for the cross of Christ. In God's plan of redemption, there had to be weakness (crucifixion) before there was power (resurrection). And this power-in-weakness connection is what Paul reflected on when he contemplated Christ's praying three times amidst his weakness and powerlessness in Gethsemane before his death on the cross, which was followed by the power of the resurrection![15] Paul came to understand and embrace the fact that his thorn in the flesh was essential to his ongoing weakness and the experience of Christ's ongoing power.

With this we come to Paul's greatest boast ever: "Therefore I will boast all the more gladly of my weaknesses, so that the power of Christ may rest upon me" (v. 9b). Paul feels no reticence here in boasting, no sense of playing the fool. His shyness has evaporated. Paul boasts "all the more gladly," with total enthusiasm. He joyously boasts of his weaknesses—his thorn as well as his beatings and hardships and sleepless nights and hunger and thirst. Why? It is the *power-in-weakness* principle—"so that the power of Christ may rest upon me."

This is so beautiful, and we must not miss it. "Rest upon me" is the vocabulary of the tabernacle from the time when God pitched his tent with his people (cf. Exodus 40:34). It is also the language used of Jesus when "the Word became flesh and dwelt [literally, *pitched his tent*] among us" (John 1:14). So here in 2 Corinthians 12:9b, Paul employs the same awesome image to teach that the all-powerful Christ "pitches his tent" with his people in their weakness.[16]

Life is not as it appears to be. We are led by today's culture to imagine that God pitches his tent with the especially famous and powerful—those who can speak of ecstasies and miraculous power and who command large crowds as they jet from city to city and enjoy the spotlight of center stage—but it is not so. Christ pitches his tent with the weak and the unknown, the suffering shut-in, the anonymous pastor and missionary, the godly, quiet servants in the home and the marketplace.

Disposition. This brings us to Paul's disposition, the way he approached his life and ministry: "For the sake of Christ, then, I am content with weaknesses, insults, hardships, persecutions, and calamities. For when I am weak, then I am strong" (v. 10).

There is no value in the endurance of hardships and indignities in themselves. There is no virtue in suffering. Everything turns on the phrase "for the sake of Christ." Only a fanatic would find contentment in self-inflicted suffering and miseries. But a Christian will find a special contentment in sufferings endured "for the sake of Christ."

This is because such a believer understands and has taken to heart the *paradox of power*—"For when I am weak, then I am strong." The spiritual math is never, "my weakness plus his strength equals my power." Rather, it is, "my weakness plus his strength equals his power."

Henrietta Mears, who was used so mightily to strengthen the evangelical church through her discipleship and writing, suffered from childhood on with extreme myopia and general eye weakness and irritation. And she, like Paul, cried out for relief, but to no avail. In her maturity Miss Mears often remarked, "I believe my greatest spiritual asset throughout my entire life has been my failing sight, for it has kept me absolutely dependent upon God."[17] Henrietta Mears went on, still plagued by her increasing disability, to set the standard for Sunday schools in America. She founded Gospel Light and wrote the million-plus best-seller *What the Bible Is All About.* She was influential in shaping the ministries of Billy Graham in his beginning stages,

Bill Bright, founder of Campus Crusade for Christ, and Richard Halverson, Chaplain of the United States Senate, to name only a few!

The paradox of power is: "For when I am weak, then I am strong." God doesn't need our perceived strengths, if that is what we depend upon. He wants our weaknesses, our sufferings, our inadequacies, our disabilities, our failures, our fears. Even more, he wants us to boast of our weaknesses, so that Christ in his power will pitch his tent in us.

Christ in us! That is the reward of those who serve him with their weakness.

Forbid it, Lord, that I should boast,
Save in the death of Christ, my God;
All the vain things that charm me most,
I sacrifice them to his blood.

Isaac Watts

28

Authenticating Apostleship

2 CORINTHIANS 12:11–21

THE HIGH POINT OF THE APOSTLE PAUL'S SECOND LETTER to the Corinthians comes to us in the form of a direct statement from Jesus to him: "'My grace is sufficient for you, for my power is made perfect in weakness'" (v. 9a). The statement is what theologians call dominical, because it comes from the very lips of the Lord (Latin, *dominus*). Christ's words came as Paul pled three times that his thorn be removed (paralleling Christ's own plea in Gethsemane). We do not know how he heard Christ's reply, whether audibly as he did on the road to Damascus or perhaps in an inner voice. Regardless of the mode, Paul heard Jesus himself voice the grand paradox of true ministry: *strength in weakness*.

The logic of this dominical word sank deep into the apostle's heart, so deep that his weakness then became his greatest boast: "Therefore I will boast all the more gladly of my weaknesses, so that the power of Christ may rest upon me" (v. 9b). Paul rejoiced in his limitations because Christ in his power literally pitched his tent with him in his weakness. This said, Paul joyously extended the logic of his boast: "For the sake of Christ, then, I am content with weaknesses, insults, hardships, persecutions, and calamities. For when I am weak, then I am strong" (v. 10). There is no shyness here. In effect he gladly boasts, "I am weak." The paradox declares that Paul is awesomely strong. And in reality his boast was nothing more than a reassertion of what he has already twice said: "'Let the one who boasts, boast in the Lord'" (10:17; 1 Corinthians 1:31; cf. Jeremiah 9:23, 24).

As we have observed, boasting was not Paul's thing. He despised it. However, for the sake of the Corinthian church he had briefly boasted in his Hebrew pedigree and then shyly boasted in his rapture to paradise. But here he lets out all the stops as he boasts of his weaknesses (plural). In effect, this amounted to multiple glad boasts.

This is the practical and theological summit of this letter—astonishing, perplexing boasts in the context of received culture then and now! They were counterintuitive and effeminate to Greeks. They are irrational today, yet paradoxically and eternally true. *Keep on boasting, Paul!* And this he will continue to do—in the Lord.

Nevertheless, though this boasting is true and proper, his discomfort with boasting reasserts itself, and he declares, "I have been a fool! You forced me to it, for I ought to have been commended by you" (v. 11). And with this self-deprecation, he refocuses in his attempt to get his enemies in Corinth to recognize his authenticity.

Here Paul begins his final run at authenticating his apostleship. His heart's desire is that his enemies will accede to his authority before he makes his planned third visit to the church—for his sake and, most of all, for theirs.

Authentication by Apostolic Insignia (vv. 11, 12)

Paul's rebuke—"You forced me to it [boasting], for I ought to have been commended by you" (v. 11b)—is sharply ironic because earlier in the letter he had affectionately written, "You yourselves are our letter of recommendation, written on our hearts, to be known and read by all" (3:2). The Corinthians were his letter of commendation. The changed lives of the Corinthians had demonstrated beyond question that Paul's ministry was genuine. And proof positive of his loving affection for them was that they were permanently written on *his* heart, the epicenter of his being. And more, the Holy Spirit had written directly on *their* hearts, so that they had become letters from Christ delivered by Paul. Thus their failure to defend Paul was an inexcusable sin of silence. Rather they, as his letter of commendation, should have been commending and defending him.

Superior insignia. The Corinthian church should also have come to Paul's defense because he and his ministry were superior: "For I was not at all inferior to these super-apostles, even though I am nothing. The signs of a true apostle were performed among you with utmost patience, with signs and wonders and mighty works" (vv. 11b, 12). Paul's "I am nothing" implies derisively that the self-promoting super-apostles were themselves less than nothing.

In fact, Paul alone displayed the insignia of a true apostle. "Signs and wonders" is an Old Testament expression, often used in reference to what God did in the exodus in bringing about the deliverance and salvation of his people. "Mighty works" is used in the New Testament for miracles.[1] These three things together, "signs and wonders and mighty works," as used by Paul refer to the great spiritual exodus brought about by the death and resurrection of Jesus and made effectual by Paul's preaching of the gospel.[2] "Signs" authenticated the message, "wonders" evoked awe, and "mighty works" manifested divine power. Paul did all of these as he preached Jesus Christ crucified and risen from the dead—the new covenant's exodus from sin.

Of equal apostolic significance is that Paul performed these apostolic signs "with utmost patience" (or literally, "with all perseverance or endurance") amidst incessant beatings and shipwrecks and dangers and pastoral afflictions. Calvin comments, "Such heroic virtue is like a heavenly seal by which the Lord marks out his apostle."[3] It was not just the signs that proved his apostleship; it was that he did them under great stress with magnificent patience and perseverance. Astonishing apostolic fortitude!

The Corinthians' failure to stand with Paul was without excuse. They were his letters written by the Spirit and delivered by Christ. And his performance of the apostolic insignia with utmost patience was superior. But because of the Corinthians' silence, he had been reduced to the humiliation of boasting. Now the very least they can do is affirm his apostolic authenticity. Corinthians, step up!

Authentication by Apostolic Sacrifice (vv. 13–18)

Paul was not finished with his irony. In fact, he turns it up as he transitions to another proof of his authenticity—namely, his sacrifice for the Corinthians: "For in what were you less favored than the rest of the churches, except that I myself did not burden you? Forgive me this wrong!" (v. 13). The reproachful tone breathes frustration and hurt—"Forgive me for working to support myself so that I would not be a financial burden to you. Forgive me for attempting to do good to you. Forgive my selfless sacrifice." Paul's emotions were on the surface. He felt deeply.

Glad prospect. But Paul's tone was, as we know, the reproach of an aching heart, and the next lines switch from irony to tenderness:

> Here for the third time I am ready to come to you. And I will not be a burden, for I seek not what is yours but you. For children are not obligated to save up for their parents, but parents for their children. I will most gladly spend and be spent for your souls. If I love you more, am I to be loved less? (vv. 14, 15)

Paul's lines "I seek not what is yours but you" and "I will most gladly spend and be spent for your souls" are moving testaments of pastoral intent and set the standard for all true ministry.

The apostle's "I seek not what is yours but you" was said with a disapproving glance at his opponents who lived off the Corinthians (cf. 11:20). Far from their money, Paul wanted the whole of the Corinthians (their souls), so he could present them to Christ as a bride (cf. 11:2). In this, he identified his ministry with that of Christ who will present the church to himself (cf. Ephesians 5:27). As he was the Corinthians' spiritual father, selfless, other-directed sacrifice drove Paul's labors. He wanted nothing but them—their souls—for Christ. This is the hallmark of all true ministry at every level.

Paul's selfless sacrifice is restated and intensified by his parallel great statement, "I will most gladly spend and be spent for your souls." Again, this is exactly what Christ did as described by Paul in 8:9—"though he was rich, yet for your sake he became poor, so that you by his poverty might become rich." The apostle's spending of himself replicated the suffering of Christ who gave himself for his people. Unlike Christ's sufferings, Paul's sacrifices did not save the Corinthians but were in continuity with those of Christ.[4]

True ministry selflessly seeks the spiritual welfare of others, gladly spending and being spent. This is true whenever you serve, be it with believers or unbelievers or children or students or the ill or in the pulpit or in world missions. This is what is most needed if authentic ministry is to take place—joyously seeking the best for others and gladly spending self. This is Christlike, apostolic, true ministry.

Paul willingly spent everything for the Corinthians—all his material resources and all his energies. The price he paid was impoverishment, poor health, premature old age, and, as we know, a martyr's death.[5] It was the logic of this example that led the wealthy, privileged Victorian athlete and scholar C. T. Studd, upon graduation from Cambridge, to spend his life in the Congo with this motto: "If Jesus Christ be God, and died for me, then no sacrifice can be too great for me to make for him."

The Apostle Paul's ministry had been authenticated for the Corinthians by his glad spending of himself for them, exceeding that of parents for their own children. And thus he asked, "If I love you more, am I to be loved less?" (v. 15b). Paul is painfully incredulous: "My love for you exceeds that of parents for their children, so how can you love me less than a parent?"

Good question. This was heart-wrenching logic. Of course, Paul knew why his love had not been returned.

A clarifying retrospect. His enemies in the church had to concede that he had not burdened them by asking for support, but they argued, rather, that his self-support was a deceptive ploy: "But granting that I myself did not burden you, I was crafty, you say, and got the better of you by deceit" (v. 16). Some actually believed that Paul was a con man. They reasoned that his working with his hands and refusing support was done to make them believe that he was a man of integrity, with the result that when he asked them to give to the poor in Jerusalem they gave generously, and from their abundance Paul lined his own pockets. Paul's refusal of Corinthian support was nothing more than a clever psychological ploy to extort more money, they charged. Clearly, this was a case of projection if there ever was one! Paul's enemies imputed to him the very things they did when they had the chance. After all, as Paul had said earlier, his detractors were false apostles in the service of Satan (cf. 11:13–15).

So Paul here exposes the hollowness of their accusations with some pointed questions: "Did I take advantage of you through any of those whom I sent to you? I urged Titus to go, and sent the brother with him. Did Titus take advantage of you? Did we not act in the same spirit? Did we not take the same steps?" (vv. 17, 18). The absurdity of his enemies' accusations was embarrassingly clear to all. Titus's integrity, plus the great care with which Paul had earlier arranged to send Titus and a respected "brother" to Corinth to gather the offering for transport to Jerusalem, proved the emptiness of the charges (cf. 8:16–24).

Paul's apostolate and his ministry to the Corinthians was one of hard-working sacrifice from beginning to end. He had sought nothing but their spiritual well-being. In fact, he was spending everything he had for their souls. He was ministering like Christ, for Christ. Therefore, to reject the apostle was to reject Christ himself.

Authentication by Apostolic Fears (vv. 19–21)

The logic of Paul's intensely emotional argument so far has been that his ministry is authenticated, first, by his performance of the apostolic signs and, second, by his sacrifices. Now he adds that his fears are authenticating.

Paul knew that some of the Corinthians, and especially his enemies, would dismiss his letter as a defensive, self-serving epistle. So he asks, "Have you been thinking all along that we have been defending ourselves to you? It is in the sight of God that we have been speaking in Christ, and all for your upbuilding, beloved" (v. 19). Of course, Paul has been defending his ministry, but far from expressing a self-serving rant, he has been speaking literally "before God in Christ." He was not a man merely arguing on his own self-interests but was speaking in the presence of God who sees all and of Christ who is both his Savior and his Judge (cf. 5:10).[6] Therefore, an oath-like solemnity accompanies his insistence that it is "all for your upbuilding, beloved." Every part of the letter, including the defensive parts, are meant to build up his beloved Corinthian church.

And it is Paul's longing for their edification that makes his fears so authenticating:

> For I fear that perhaps when I come I may find you not as I wish, and that you may find me not as you wish—that perhaps there may be quarreling,

> jealousy, anger, hostility, slander, gossip, conceit, and disorder. I fear that when I come again my God may humble me before you, and I may have to mourn over many of those who sinned earlier and have not repented of the impurity, sexual immorality, and sensuality that they have practiced. (vv. 20, 21)

Paul's fears are wholly pastoral. Here the words of Phillips Brooks will again help us grasp Paul's heart:

> To be a true minister to men is always to accept new happiness and new distress. . . . The man who gives himself to other men can never be a wholly sad man; but no more can he be a man of unclouded gladness. To him shall come with every deeper consecration a before untasted joy, but in the same cup shall be mixed a sorrow that it was beyond his power to feel before.[7]

Because Paul fathered the Corinthian church, because he had been the presiding physician at the rebirth of souls, because he had worked night and day for them through multiple discomforts and dangers, because of his sacrifice and because of his desperately passionate love for them, he was a happy man. But his gladness was never immune to the fear that someone might fall to sin or unbelief. Paul had hitched his very life to the Corinthians, and he could not help riding with them through the highs and the lows.

It is the same today. Love the church, serve her, spend and be spent, seek souls, and your heart will know an index of fears unknown to the uncommitted heart. But you will also know joys that are unknown to the self-serving.

During his second visit to Corinth, Paul had encountered the list of vices catalogued in verse 20. And now he feared that on his third visit he would have to relive them. Even more, he feared that they would not find him as they wished because he would come with the rod of discipline. His fear is real and ominous. It is also a pastoral warning as it gives them time to repent.

Paul's parallel expression of fear, "I fear that when I come again my God may humble me before you," reveals even more about his heart's attachment to his people. The act of disciplining the errant Corinthians as, say, in publicly excluding them from the church, would be a great humiliation to Paul, even though it would authenticate his apostolic power. It is clear that the great apostle did not exercise his authority from an aloof plain high above the people, but as a loving pastor-father. Because he was such a man, gladness and sadness were the province of his soul.

The proofs of Paul's authenticity were there for all to see, curious and odd as they might seem both in Corinth and in today's world. There were his *apostolic insignia*: "signs and wonders and mighty works" wrought with the apostolic sign of "utmost patience" (v. 12)—endurance amidst immense trials. There were the *apostolic sacrifices* of a man who, unlike the false apostles, sought only the souls of the Corinthians, gladly spending and being spent for them, like Christ Jesus himself. And there were the authenticating *apostolic fears*, fears that only come to a heart that loves with an unremitting love.

These authenticating qualities were an oddity in the self-promoting culture of that day and are curiosities in the world culture in which we live. Nevertheless, they are indicators of the real thing.

And you will see them where God's servants are great boasters in their weaknesses, for when they are weak they are strong.

29

Final Warnings and Exhortations

2 CORINTHIANS 13:1–10

REBELLION AGAINST THE APOSTLE PAUL'S LEADERSHIP by the unrepentant minority in Corinth was, in effect, rebellion against God himself who had appointed Paul. And Paul, as a close student of Israel's history, as well as from his own apostolic experience, knew that this did not bode well for the rebellious in Corinth.

The famous story of Korah, chronicled in Numbers 16, had long made the point. Three rebellious Levites—Korah, Dathan, and Abiram—plus some 250 well-known leaders rose up against Moses' leadership in an effort to take over the priesthood.

> They assembled themselves together against Moses and against Aaron and said to them, "You have gone too far! For all in the congregation are holy, every one of them, and the LORD is among them. Why then do you exalt yourselves above the assembly of the LORD?" When Moses heard it, he fell on his face, and he said to Korah and all his company, "In the morning the LORD will show who is his, and who is holy, and will bring him near to him. The one whom he chooses he will bring near to him." (Numbers 16:3–5)

Thus Moses prepared a showdown. Korah, Dathan, and Abiram and their entire families including the 250 presented themselves rebelliously carrying their priestly censers burning with incense. Opposite them stood Aaron and his priests with their censers hot with incense. High noon on the Sinai.

Tension gripped every soul. Then the glory of the Lord appeared to all the congregation. And the Lord ordered Moses and Aaron and his priests and the rest of the vast congregation to distance themselves from the rebels. So all moved back from the tents of Korah like a receding wave. With Israel at a safe distance Moses mightily prophesied their imminent destruction—a literal gobbling up by the earth:

> And as soon as he had finished speaking all these words, the ground under them split apart. And the earth opened its mouth and swallowed them up, with their households and all the people who belonged to Korah and all their goods. So they and all that belonged to them went down alive into Sheol, and the earth closed over them, and they perished from the midst of the assembly. And all Israel who were around them fled at their cry, for they said, "Lest the earth swallow us up!" And fire came out from the LORD and consumed the 250 men offering the incense. (vv. 31–35)

All that remained amidst the incinerated desolation were the 250 bronze censers glowing orange in the ashes (now made holy through judgment), which were gathered and hammered out into a covering for the altar and a visual warning to Israel against spiritual rebellion. God had delivered Moses from the rebellious usurpers, vindicating Moses' words to Korah the previous day: "In the morning the LORD will show who is his" (16:5).

Coming back to Corinth, Paul knew that apart from the fireworks a similar vindication could well take place in Corinth if his detractors persisted in rejecting his apostleship. The earth would not likely open up for another dinner, but his enemies would be marginalized and would perish forever at the hand of God. And this Paul wanted to avoid if at all possible. Paul longed to come to the Corinthians with gentleness, not severity.

Now come the final warning and exhortation and prayers in Paul's letter to the Corinthians.

Final Warning (vv. 1–4)

Discipline imminent. Paul had visited Corinth twice. The first time was his extended stay when he planted the church (cf. Acts 18:1–11), and the second was the painful visit during which he was so taken back by the brutal personal attack that he thought it better to stay away for a while (cf. 2:14). Significantly, it was in response to the rejection and abuse of the second visit that Paul issued dire warnings to his offenders if they did not repent.

As Paul begins here, he warns them that there will be nothing arbitrary in his next visit: "This is the third time I am coming to you. Every charge must be established by the evidence of two or three witnesses" (v. 1). The apostle's judgments will be eminently measured and fair—a terrifying thought if taken to heart. Even more, his judgments will be unsparing: "I warned those who sinned before and all the others, and I warn them now while absent, as I did when present on my second visit, that if I come again I will not spare them—since you seek proof that Christ is speaking in me" (vv. 2, 3a).

There is biting irony here. Paul's critics were so far from Christ in their thinking that they rejected Christlike humility and gentleness as evidence that Christ was speaking in Paul. So the irony is that if the only proof that will convince them of the authenticity of his words is power, they may get far more than they bargained for. Ironically, in holding up Paul's alleged weaknesses as reason to reject his authority, they were actually challenging Christ, who had come himself in weakness.

Christ's power. The Corinthians' understanding of Christ's power was confused and outright wrong. They viewed Christ's power through their triumphalist lens as displayed in health and wealth and showy displays of power. Their views of power were Corinthian, not Christian. So Paul gives them the corrective on Christ: "He is not weak in dealing with you, but is powerful among you. For he was crucified in weakness, but lives by the power of God" (vv. 3b, 4a). Paul says that *both* the cross and the resurrection display God's power. Only an all-powerful God could be strong enough to live out the weakness of the cross. Christ's taking on frail human flesh was a testament to his power, as were his arrest and beatings and crucifixion and becoming sin and death. *Christ's weakness demonstrated his power*. And further, his weakness was the platform from which his mighty resurrection was launched. Both Christ's suffering and resurrection demonstrated his power.

Paul's power. Paul's point is that his very own experience of weakness and power reflect that of Christ: "For we also are weak in him, but in dealing with you we will live with him by the power of God" (v. 4b). Paul's ministerial style was that of a humble servant—ostensible weakness. He sought no prominence. He rejected show. He sought only their souls. He spent himself for the Corinthians. However, just as the crucified, weak Jesus gave way to the powerful, resurrected Christ who will come again in judgment, so also will Paul come in Christ's power to judge the Corinthians if they do not repent. Just as his former visit appeared to be one of weakness, his enemies will find his next visit to be marked by power. As to what Paul might have done, we have some idea.

Corinth had earlier witnessed Paul's power to unleash judgment when an unrepentant member was delivered over to Satan "for the destruction of the flesh" (1 Corinthians 5:5)—that is, so Satan would afflict him with a fatal illness that could only be ended by the sinner's repentance and God's gracious restoration.[1] This wasn't the only time Paul engaged in such discipline. In Ephesus he delivered over Hymenaeus and Alexander to a similar fate so they would be taught not to blaspheme (cf. 1 Timothy 1:19, 20). Also, 1 Corinthians explains about those who abused the Lord's Supper: "That is why many of you are weak and ill, and some have died" (11:30). For those so judged, it was as if the ground opened up and swallowed them whole.

Final Exhortation (vv. 5, 6)

Since Paul's painful visit he had given the Corinthians some time, a gracious space, in which to repent. But when he comes for his third visit he will pursue his apostolic mandate to be "to one a fragrance from death to death, to the other a fragrance from life to life" (2:16). To disregard Paul will be to embrace death.

Test yourselves. Paul's enemies judged Paul to have failed their spiritual tests in that he was sub par in everything. His looks, his eloquence, his lifestyle, his experience, his success—all were found lacking.

So now Paul turns the tables on them: "Examine yourselves, to see whether you are in the faith. Test yourselves. Or do you not realize this about yourselves, that Jesus Christ is in you?—unless indeed you fail to meet the test! I hope you will find out that we have not failed the test" (vv. 5, 6). The test is simple: Is Jesus Christ *in* you?

The test is notably subjective. Paul doesn't demand, as he does elsewhere, substantive beliefs—things we must confess (cf. Romans 10:9, 10; 1 Corinthians 15:1–4). He allows that the bar of their own consciences will substantiate or disprove the genuineness of their faith.[2] And because the question is so subjective, it is open to delusion and abuse. Anyone can *say* that Christ is in him or her. Nevertheless, it is intentionally subjective. No one truly knew except the Corinthians themselves. Paul believes they will be honest. His playfully ironic "unless indeed you fail to meet the test" indicates that he is confident in them.

This is a good question for all of us to ponder. Is Christ in you? How do you know? What proof is there of his presence in your life? Of course, along with Paul, I believe there is a core of belief that surrounds true faith. But this test asks about your subjective awareness. So, is Christ in you? The wily old apostle is very clever here as he slips in, "I hope you will find out that we have not failed the test." He knows that if the Corinthians discern that Christ is in them, they must admit that Christ is in him—because he introduced them to Christ! And, therefore, they must embrace his apostleship.

Final Prayer (vv. 7–9)

When others in the church reject you or criticize you, the natural thing is to stop praying for them and devote your prayers to the vindication of yourself. But here Paul prays that his Corinthian enemies will do no wrong: "But we pray to God that you may not do wrong—not that we may appear to have met the test, but that you may do what is right, though we may seem to have failed. For we cannot do anything against the truth, but only for the truth" (vv. 7, 8). Paul's prayer that his detractors "may not do wrong" is not a prayer that they will prove they have passed the test, so that it will be seen that Paul has passed the test and is authentic. Rather, Paul is so selfless that he prays that the Corinthians "may not do wrong" and will "do what is right," even though it may make him appear to have failed.

Some of his enemies were so unsparingly critical that they would maintain with twisted logic that Paul's decision not to display mighty acts of judgment (on the *repentant* Corinthians) proved that he was weak and fraudulent![3] But, of course, the abiding rule for Paul is that he "cannot do anything against the truth, but only for the truth" (v. 8). His apostolic powers can never be displayed to show off, but only to enhance and effect the truth.

Paul closes the commentary on his prayers with an extension of the thought: "For we are glad when we are weak and you are strong. Your restoration is what we pray for" (v. 9). If the Corinthians are "strong" due to their repentance and embrace of Paul's authority, then he will appear "weak" because he will not have to enforce his authority with powerful acts.[4] Paul's heart-desire for his critics in Corinth was their restoration to their former favorable condition even at his apparent expense.[5]

The apostle's heart was so much like that of his Master. When Jesus was crucified, he prayed repeatedly (as the Greek imperfect tense indicates), "Father, forgive them, for they do not know what they are doing" (Luke 23:34). This is the ultimate example of loving intercession, because on the cross the Son of God assaulted Heaven for the souls of his tormentors. Here in respect to Corinth, Paul beseeches Heaven for those who have belittled him and rejected him. But he prays that his critics will do no wrong, but only what is right, and that his detractors will be strong and he will remain weak.

Jesus says to us all, "But I say to you, Love your enemies and pray for those who persecute you, so that you may be sons of your Father who is in heaven" (Matthew 5:44, 45). Such prayers do not make us his sons and daughters, but they indicate that we are living like his sons and daughters—the way he redeemed us to live. Don't give up praying for your critics. Pray that they will do good. Pray that they will be strong, though you are weak.

The thought of the desolation of the rebellion of Korah, the censers glowing like coals amidst the ashes covering the communal grave, gave Paul no pleasure. And more, the smoking wreckage of the Corinthian church at the hand of God's judgment would have broken Paul's heart. So Paul concludes, "For this reason I write these things while I am away from you, that when I come I may not have to be severe in my use of the authority that the Lord has given me for building up and not for tearing down" (v. 10).

Today the warning stands over the church, and especially those who have transmitted the present cultural values into the church, so that church is little more than a Christianized version of modern culture. The warning stands where leadership is built on the cult of personality—where image is everything. The warning looms where worship is show time—where preaching is entertainment—where God's Word is muzzled and the pulpit panders to itching ears. The warning echoes where we are the focus of worship—our feelings, our comfort, our health, our wealth—where super-apostles are preferred over Paul.

Paul's warnings do have relevance. Christ does come and judge his church. See the wrecks of time! Those who honestly test themselves to see if Christ is *in* them will enjoy the wonder of his presence. God does answer the prayers of those who pray that others, even their critics, will not do wrong but rather right.

It was the Corinthians' last chance. And the decision rested with them—as it yet does with us.

30

Apostolic Optimism

2 CORINTHIANS 13:11–14

CORINTH HAD BEEN A TOUGH GO FOR THE APOSTLE PAUL. As we noted at the beginning of this book, the similarities to modern Western culture were so striking that we could well call Paul's epistles "First and Second Californians." Corinth's eighty-year rise from the cold ashes of classical Corinth was that of a first-century boomtown overflowing with ex-slaves (freedmen) and ex-Roman soldiers and entrepreneurs of every ethnic stripe and background, including a substantial Jewish community. Corinth was a sports and entertainment culture.

The good, the bad, and the ugly were there side-by-side: business, sport, tourism, sex, religious pluralism. Nevertheless, Paul and his cohorts had planted a remarkable church in Corinth. And all went quite well until the arrival of those whom Paul called "super-apostles," men who preached a strange amalgam of Christianity and old-covenant strictures and triumphalist theology that imported the values of Corinthian culture right into the church. From the super-apostles' perspective, Paul suffered too much, his ministry lacked luster, his preaching was dull, he had no ecstatic stories to tell, he had no letters of commendation, and he was a poor laborer who worked with his hands. Tragically, the great apostle found himself rejected by many in the very church he had founded!

Thus, in the brilliant and stormy second letter to the Corinthians he defends his apostleship and defines authentic ministry. Chapters 1—7 address both friends and foes in Corinth, laying out for all time the ministry of the new covenant in Christ (2:12—7:1). Then chapters 8—9 explain the implications for repentant Corinthians, while the final chapters (10—13) detail the implications for the unrepentant in the Corinthian church.

The Apostle Paul bares his soul in 2 Corinthians as he does in no other of his writings. The great motif that gets repeated, passionate expression is *strength in weakness*, peaking with Jesus' words in 12:9: "But he said to me, 'My grace is sufficient for you, for my power is made perfect in weakness.'"

From this pinnacle, the warning to the unrepentant becomes more intense. Chapter 13 could well be titled "Last Chance" as the apostle issues final warnings, exhortations, and prayers.

Now in verses 11–14 he surprises us as he closes his letter on a remarkably upbeat and memorable note, concluding with perhaps the most beautiful benediction in the New Testament. The closing remarks of the conventional correspondence of Paul's day were normally terse and disconnected to the contents. But not so with Paul's letters. Paul's closings artfully echo chosen themes and concerns.[1] They are meant to impress and exert lasting influence. Here Paul has carefully structured his final words with a brief series of closing *admonitions* (v. 11), closing *greetings* (vv. 12, 13), and a closing *benediction* (v. 14).

Closing Admonitions (v. 11)

The five brief admonitions listed in verse 11 show a distinct change in tone as Paul introduces them with "Finally, brothers, rejoice." Paul had earlier used the term "brothers" when he opened each of the first two major sections of the letter (cf. 1:8; 8:1). But "brothers" is noticeably absent in the final section (chapters 10—13), in which he assails the unrepentant in the Corinthian church.

Now, however, he addresses everyone in the Corinthian church as "brothers" in hopes that all will be considered brothers (and sisters) due to their repentance.[2] Optimism brightens Paul's final words.

The five brief, mostly one-word imperatives (in the Greek) come rapid-fire and with a singular focus on bringing unity to the Corinthian church.

The command "rejoice" comes first because Paul longed for the Corinthians to be a cause for his own rejoicing. He knew there would be rejoicing in the Corinthian church if the errant members repented. So "rejoice" is a bright imperative full of faith and the expectation that the Corinthians are on the verge of joyous unity.

The second imperative, "Aim for restoration," has the sense of "to put back in place or mend" and therefore is an exhortation to the Corinthians to work at restoring their unity in Christ. Paul lays the responsibility directly on them—"Pull yourselves together"[3]—work at restoration. This would call for forbearance and love, much as Paul would admonish the Ephesian church to "walk in a manner worthy of the calling to which you have been called, with all humility and gentleness, with patience, bearing with one another in love, eager to maintain the unity of the Spirit in the bond of peace"

(Ephesians 4:1b-3). Restoration was foremost in Paul's prayers for the Corinthians (cf. 13:10).

So the Corinthians were first to "rejoice," second to "aim for restoration," and third to "comfort one another." Paul was aware of the depth of the hurt among both those who were in the right and those in the wrong. He himself had needed comfort during this Corinthian fray, and Titus had been the man: "But God, who comforts the downcast, comforted us by the coming of Titus, and not only by his coming but also by the comfort with which he was comforted by you" (7:6, 7). The situation then and now in Corinth demanded mutual tenderness and comfort. Comfort is the currency of concord and unity.

The next command is to "agree with one another." Every church needs this admonition, but no church needed it more than Corinth! The triumphalist, Corinthianized super-apostles took issue with everything Paul stood for. So this command to "agree with one another" was not a call for harmony for the sake of harmony, but for unity in the apostolic truth that Paul has been teaching in this letter. They were to agree with one another on the main things, not on everything. This meant that God's Word must be the standard and the source of unity.

Lastly, that "live in peace" flows out of such agreement is self-explanatory. Nevertheless, living in peace requires thought and determination. Now, stepping back and looking at the whole, we see that the power of Paul's closing admonitions lies in no single command but in the aggregate of these five terse, staccato injunctions about rejoicing, restoring, comforting, agreeing, and living in peace—all present imperatives calling the Corinthians to continuous action day in and day out. If the Corinthians persist, then they have a promise: "and the God of love and peace will be with you" (v. 11b). God imparts his unique inner qualities to his children as they actively do his will.

In truth, therefore, the Christian life and the existence of unity within the church do not come through passivity. We must work at every aspect all the time. Restoration is work, comfort is work, agreement is work, peace is work, and even rejoicing requires thought and effort. Paul called for continuous, specific effort for the church—and everything depended upon their response.

But he was optimistic. That is why he commanded that they rejoice and keep on rejoicing.

Closing Greetings (vv. 12, 13)

Kiss! Paul was so concerned about restoration and unity in Corinth that he became remarkably directive about demonstrating affection: "Greet one another with a holy kiss" (v. 12).

Note carefully that Paul was the very first person in the Greco-Roman world to instruct members of a *mixed social group* to greet one another with a kiss.[4] William Klassen's article "Kiss" in the *Anchor Bible Dictionary* says, "There is general agreement that the 'holy kiss' had its origin in the practice which emerged in the early church among the believers themselves, with the impetus probably coming from the shape of their life with Jesus himself. Nothing analogous to it is to be found among any Greco-Roman societies, nor indeed at Qumran."[5] Further, he notes that ethical teachers were "not noted for urging people to kiss" and that Paul "was certainly the first popular ethical teacher known to instruct members of a mixed social group to greet each other with a kiss." Thus, "The holy kiss is to be seen in a living context of people who are building a new social reality." Klassen concludes, "The admonitions to kiss one another serve to stress the liberty to express without inhibition to all people of whatever background, rank or gender, the ardor of *agape* in any context. The 'holy kiss' is a public declaration of the affirmation of faith: 'In Christ there is neither male nor female, Jew nor Greek, slave nor free' (Gal. 3:28)."[6]

Therefore the "holy kiss" between unrelated men and women for the purpose of receiving others as family was a Christian innovation, unique in the sprawling paganism of the Roman Empire. The descriptive "holy" indicates that it was non-erotic, and probably not to the mouth.[7]

Paul's injunction was brilliant. First, because to call another person "brother" was a breech of Roman protocol, as it was unlawful to call people brothers or sisters who were not of one's family. Thus the everyday language of Christianity asserted that Christians were family in spiritual relationship. Second, the kiss was an expression of affection among family members—a token of deepest relationship and unity.

Here Paul's insistence upon the kiss, including the heretofore dissident factions, was a call to symbolize and celebrate deep spiritual reality—and, we might add, to enhance the spiritual oneness of the Body of Christ in Corinth. In other words, the mutual exchange of the holy kiss could well effect the restoration of dissident brothers. The act of loving could revive loving hearts. Elsewhere, Paul would command, "And above all these put on love, which binds everything together in perfect harmony" (Colossians 3:14). He knew that volitional love builds up. Remember, too, that this command to "greet one another with a holy kiss" was initially read aloud to the church in Corinth. Perhaps it was then, at the conclusion of the reading of this letter, that the holy kiss was used to initiate the longed-for restoration.

As we make the journey from Corinth to our own home town or church, we must own that our language and our actions have so much to do with our concord and unity. *Brothers* and *sisters* is the language of the covenant community, and we ought to use such terms with forthright affection, not derision. And the holy kiss? Well, it survives as a public convention in most European cultures—the obligatory kiss on each cheek. Maybe it's time to bring it back to the church, for we are family.

Paul extends the greetings of his cohorts in Ephesus with "All the saints greet you" (v. 13). The unity he desires to reestablish in Corinth is universal. Christian unity is true for the whole Body of Christ.

Closing Benediction (v. 14)

Now we come to the lovely, lyrical benediction: "The grace of the Lord Jesus Christ and the love of God and the fellowship of the Holy Spirit be with you all" (v. 14). The mere intonation "the grace" sets our hearts to recite the trio of benediction. We could not offer a better wish.

The benediction is, of course, Trinitarian. But Paul is not attempting to teach us the ontological distinctives of the Trinity or to parse the three persons. The triune God is simply the air Paul breathes, as is seen in his other references to the Trinity (cf. Galatians 4:4–6; 1 Corinthians 12:4–6; Ephesians 1:3, 13, 14; 2:18; 3:14–17; 4:4–6).

What surprises us here is the order because where we would expect the Father-Son-Holy Spirit of the later creeds, we have the Son (Jesus Christ) first, then God, and then the Holy Spirit.

This is because Paul's benediction mirrors the experience of all those who have come to Christ. It is ordered in the sequence of salvation. It is the subjective testimony of our hearts.

The grace. First, there is "the grace of the Lord Jesus Christ." It is said that Virgil's greatest impact on Dante was helping him un-forget his own experience of *caritas*, that is, grace. There is no more powerful educating than calling others to their own experience of grace.[8] And this is what "the grace" does. It takes us back to the sheer mercy of God that we experienced in salvation as we were exposed to the fire hose of Christ's relentless grace and goodness. And now we live in the overflow of grace. Truly, there always is "more grace" (cf. James 4:6). The pitcher of his grace remains tipped and tottering over each of us, waiting to pour upon us a fresh shower of love. The grace of our Lord Jesus Christ has made us rich: "For you know the grace of our Lord Jesus Christ, that though he was rich, yet for your sake he became poor, so that you by his poverty might become rich" (8:9).

Paul loved to bless with grace. To the Thessalonians he prayed, "The grace of our Lord Jesus Christ be with you" (1 Thessalonians 5:28). To the Galatians, "The grace of our Lord Jesus Christ be with your spirit, brothers. Amen" (Galatians 6:18). To the Corinthians earlier, "The grace of the Lord Jesus be with you" (1 Corinthians 16:23). To the Romans, "The grace of our Lord Jesus Christ be with you" (Romans 16:20b). To Philemon, "The grace of the Lord Jesus Christ be with your spirit" (Philemon 25). How lovely—"the grace of the Lord Jesus Christ."

The love. Next, as a consequence of knowing "the grace," there came the knowledge of "the love of God," which is seen in the death of his Son. "But God shows his love for us in that while we were still sinners, Christ died for us" (Romans 5:8). "In this is love, not that we have loved God but that he loved us and sent his Son to be the propitiation for our sins" (1 John 4:10). "For God so loved the world, that he gave his only Son, that whoever believes in him should not perish but have eternal life" (John 3:16). This is our assurance—"that neither death nor life, nor angels nor rulers, nor things present nor things to come, nor powers, nor height nor depth, nor anything else in all creation, will be able to separate us from the love of God in Christ Jesus our Lord" (Romans 8:38, 39). Therefore we affirm:

> To write the love of God above,
> Would drain the oceans dry.
> Nor could the scroll contain the whole,
> Though stretched from sky to sky.
>
> F. M. Lehman

What a good word—the love of God!

The fellowship. The ultimate consequence of Christ's grace and God's love is "the fellowship of the Holy Spirit." This is the blessing of the new covenant—"a new covenant, not of the letter but of the Spirit. For the letter kills, but the Spirit gives life" (3:6).

God has poured out his Holy Spirit upon us, and the result is a stunning unity of fellowship. The Apostle John later testified, "that which we have seen and heard we proclaim also to you, so that you too may have fellowship with us; and indeed our fellowship is with the Father and with his Son Jesus Christ" (1 John 1:3). The fellowship of the Holy Spirit includes fellowship with the Father and the Son—Trinitarian fellowship—and then a profound fellowship with others who share in that fellowship. The benedictions fall like refreshing fragrances. The *grace*: "The grace of the Lord Jesus Christ," grace upon grace, exponential mercy and goodness. The *love*: "The love of God," infinite and unending. The *fellowship*: "The fellowship of the Holy Spirit," a fellowship with Heaven itself. What greater things could we wish?

Paul's five concluding admonitions called for continuous rejoicing, continuous restoring, continuous comforting, continuous agreeing, and continuous living in peace. These admonitions, if held to, would help bring concord and unity to the fractured church.

Paul's charge to "Greet one another with a holy kiss" would place public, loving affection at the center of the church. It would affirm amidst the Greco-Roman landscape that they were truly brothers and sisters. And that kiss would volitionally move them toward expanding their God-given unity.

Paul's grand benediction was for them *all*—"The grace of the Lord Jesus Christ and the love of God and the fellowship of the Holy Spirit be with you all." The Trinitarian blessing was for the whole congregation—the good, the bad, and the ugly. It was their great hope. And today it is ours too!

Soli Deo gloria!

Notes

Chapter One: Exalted Identities

1. Scott J. Hafemann, *2 Corinthians*, The NIV Application Commentary (Grand Rapids MI: Zondervan, 2000), p. 23.
2. Timothy B. Savage, *Power Through Weakness*, Society for New Testament Studies Monograph Series 86 (Cambridge, UK: Cambridge University Press, 1996), p. 42.
3. *Ibid.*, p. 35.
4. Hafemann, *2 Corinthians*, p. 24.
5. Savage, *Power Through Weakness*, p. 48.
6. Philip Edgcumbe Hughes, *Paul's Second Epistle to the Corinthians* (Grand Rapids MI: Eerdmans, 1962), p. 2.
7. Hafemann, *2 Corinthians*, p. 45.
8. Paul Barnett, *The Message of 2 Corinthians* (Downers Grove, IL: InterVarsity Press, 1988), p. 26 writes:

   But what did Paul mean? The word *ekklesia* occurred frequently in the Greek Old Testament, the Septuagint, which Paul usually quoted. There it was used of great "gatherings" of the people of God, for example when "all the tribes of Israel stood before the Lord in the assembly *(ekklesia)* of the Lord, and in the audience of our God." In addressing them as "the church of God" Paul meant the Corinthian believers to understand that in their gathering together they were all that the gathered tribes of Israel had been—the church of God, no less. If to us *church* means a religious building or institution and to the Corinthians it simply meant an assembly of any kind, to Paul it meant specifically "an assembly" of God's people in God's presence to hear God's word.
9. Hafemann, *2 Corinthians*, p. 51 provides several cogent paragraphs that argue for the application of 2 Corinthians to today's church.
10. *Ibid.*, p. 47.

Chapter Two: The Comfort of God

1. Dietrich Bonhoeffer, *Letters and Papers from Prison*, ed. Eberhard Bethge (New York: Macmillan, 1953), p. 221.
2. Personal correspondence of Joseph Bayly, June 23, 1980.
3. Scott J. Hafemann, *2 Corinthians*, The NIV Application Commentary (Grand Rapids MI: Zondervan, 2000), pp. 59, 60.
4. Paul Barnett, *The Second Epistle to the Corinthians*, (Grand Rapids MI: Eerdmans, 1997), p. 67, quoting the benediction from E. Schüer, *Jewish People*, 2.456.
5. Victor Paul Furnish, *The Anchor Bible*, *II Corinthians*, translated with Introduction, Notes, and Commentary (Garden City, NY: Doubleday, 1984), p. 109.
6. Hafemann, *2 Corinthians*, p. 60.
7. Paul Barnett, *The Message of 2 Corinthians* (Downers Grove IL: InterVarsity Press, 1988), p. 1.
8. C. K. Barrett, *A Commentary on the Second Epistle to the Corinthians* (New York: Harper & Row, 1973), p. 61.

9. Barnett, *The Second Epistle to the Corinthians*, p. 77 explains:

   The "comfort and salvation" from the first half of the sentence are explained in the second by the phrase "comfort, which produces in you patient endurance," or, more literally, "comfort, which is energized in, that, by, patient endurance (*hypomonē*)," the divine passive pointing to God as the source of that comfort. In this, God's "day of salvation," God brings that salvation by means of the gospel (Rom 1:16) and energizes his servants for that salvation by means of "patient endurance" in the midst of "afflictions." This "patient endurance" is very important in the letter since it is one of the marks by which Paul commends himself as an authentic "minister of God" (6:4) and as an "apostle" of Christ (12:12). Note: this view is delineated by K. W. Clark, "The meaning of ἐνεργέω and χαταργέω in the New Testament," JBL 54 (1935), pp. 93–101.
10. Philip Edgcumbe Hughes, *Paul's Second Epistle to the Corinthians* (Grand Rapids MI: Eerdmans, 1962), p. 15.

Chapter Three: Affliction and Resurrection

1. Scott J. Hafemann, *2 Corinthians*, The NIV Application Commentary (Grand Rapids, MI: Zondervan, 2000), p. 67.
2. Ralph P. Martin, Word Biblical Commentary, Vol. 40, *2 Corinthians* (Nashville: Thomas Nelson, 1986), p. 14, writes: "Such pleonasms point to the intensity of the experience Paul endured and has in his vivid recall."
3. C. K. Barrett, *A Commentary on the Second Epistle to the Corinthians* (New York: Harper & Row, 1973), p. 64.
4. Charles Hodge, *A Commentary on 1 & 2 Corinthians* (Carlisle, PA: Banner of Truth Trust, 1974), p. 386: "the allusion is to a wearied animal that sinks in despair under a burden that is beyond its strength."
5. Paul Barnett, *The Second Epistle to the Corinthians* (Grand Rapids, MI: Eerdmans, 1997), p. 85, note 23:

   Gk. ἐξαπορηῆναι=ἐ+ξ+απόρος—lit., "without a way," or "to be in despair."
6. Margaret E. Thrall, *A Critical and Exegetical Commentary on the Second Epistle to the Corinthians*, Vol. I, I-VII (Edinburgh: T & T Clark, 1994), p. 118.
7. Murray J. Harris, *The Expositor's Bible Commentary,* Vol. 10, *Romans-Galatians*, gen. ed. Frank E. Gaebelein (Grand Rapids, MI: Zondervan, 1976), p. 322.
8. *Ibid.*
9. Rev Alfred Plummer, *A Critical and Exegetical Commentary on the Second Epistle of St Paul to the Corinthians* (Edinburgh: T & T Clark, 1915), p. 18.
10. Quoted in Philip Edgcumbe Hughes, *Paul's Second Epistle to the Corinthians* (Grand Rapids, MI: Eerdmans, 1962), p. 22.
11. Kent and Barbara Hughes, *Liberating Ministry from the Success Syndrome* (Wheaton, IL: Tyndale House, Inc., 1987).
12. Wayne Martindale and Jerry Root, eds., *The Quotable Lewis* (Wheaton, IL: Tyndale House, 1989), p. 187, #414.
13. Philip Edgcumbe Hughes, *Paul's Second Epistle to the Corinthians*, p. 22.
14. Barnett, *The Second Epistle to the Corinthians*, p. 90. See also Hodge, *A Commentary on 1 & 2 Corinthians*, p. 388.
15. Barnett, *The Second Epistle to the Corinthians*, p. 80.

Chapter Four: Integrity and Ministry

1. "The Larger Catechism," *The Westminster Standards* (Philadelphia: Great Commission Publications, n.d.), p. 61.

   Question 151.

   What are those aggravations that make some sins more heinous than others?

1. From the persons offending; if they be of riper age, greater experience of grace, eminent for profession, gifts, place, office, guides to others, and whose example is likely to be followed by others.

2. From the parties offended: if immediately against God, his attributes and worship; against Christ, and his grace; the Holy Spirit, his witness, and workings; against superiors, men of eminency, and such as we stand especially related and engaged unto; against any of the saints, particularly weak brethren, the souls of them, or any other, and the common good of all or many.

3. From the nature and quality of the offence; if it be against the express letter of the law, break many commandments, contain in it many sins; if not only conceived in the heart, but breaks forth in words and actions, scandalize others, and admit of no reparation; if against means, mercies, judgments, light of nature, conviction of conscience, public or private admonitions, censures of the church, civil punishments; and our prayers, purposes, promises, vows, covenants, and engagements to God or men. . . .

4. From circumstances of time and place . . . if in public, or in the presence of others, who are thereby likely to be provoked or defiled.

2. *The Reformed Journal*, October 1990, p. 14, relating an anecdote from F. F. Bruce.
3. Scott J. Hafemann, *2 Corinthians*, The NIV Application Commentary (Grand Rapids, MI: Zondervan, 2000), p. 84, explains:

   Paul's purpose in wanting to visit the Corinthians twice was that they might have (lit.) "a second [expression of] grace." As chapters 8–9 make clear, this twofold experience of grace refers to the Corinthians' being able to have two opportunities to contribute financially to the collection. In 8:1, 4, 6–7, 19, "grace" is used to describe the act of contributing to the collection since, according to 9:6–11, the ability to give to others is a manifestation of God's gracious ability to meet one's own needs. The Corinthians' willingness and ability to give to those who cannot repay is a demonstration that they too have received "grace." For this reason, when Paul planned this unanticipated second visit it was not an act of the "flesh" (i.e., "making plans in a worldly manner") by which he had hoped to benefit personally (v. 17). He did it for the Corinthians, fully aware that to provide them an opportunity to give twice would benefit them twice as much, since "God loves a cheerful giver" (9:7).

4. James M. Scott, *2 Corinthians*, New International Biblical Commentary (Peabody, MA: Hendrickson Publishers, 1998), pp. 38, 39, explains:

   Yet, as L. L. Welborn has now shown, the double affirmation (yes, yes) and the double negation ambiguity of the situation in which Paul finds himself is a result of the Corinthians' suspicions about him. In effect, Paul answers the charge of vacillating in his travel plans by stating that the Corinthians have forced him into establishing the truth of his statements with an oath.

5. Philip Edgcumbe Hughes, *Paul's Second Epistle to the Corinthians* (Grand Rapids, MI: Eerdmans, 1962), pp. 36, 37.
6. Timothy Dudley-Smith, *John Stott, the Making of a Leader* (Downers Grove, IL: InterVarsity, 1999), pp. 298, 299.
7. Harvey K. McArthur, *Understanding the Sermon on the Mount* (New York: Harper, 1960), p. 161, quoting Cornelius A. Lapide, *Commentary on Matthew's Gospel* on 7:28, records this quotation that I have adapted: "A sermon of Basil's was like thunder, because his life was like lightning."
8. Paul Barnett, *The Second Epistle to the Corinthians* (Grand Rapids, MI: Eerdmans, 1997), p. 113.
9. Hafemann, *2 Corinthians*, p. 87.
10. Scott, *2 Corinthians*, p. 45, explains:

   The distress (*thlipsis*) that Paul experienced over the situation at Corinth is different from the life-threatening "hardships" he suffered at the same time in the province of Asia (1:8), although the same Greek word is used of both. Perhaps the term is used in the present context so that the Corinthians will realize that the anguish of soul they caused Paul at that time added internal grief to external affliction. This interpretation of *thlipsis* correlates with 7:5, where Paul uses a related term (*thlibomenoi*) to suggest that the tribulations that he suffered during the period before he heard from Titus included an external and an internal component ("conflicts on the outside, fears within"). We may also compare 11:28, which includes external dangers alongside the daily pressure on the apostle because of his concern for all the churches.

Chapter Five: Forgiveness and Ministry

1. Frederick William Danker, ed., *A Greek-English Lexicon of the New Testament and Other Early Christian Literature* (*BDAG*), 3rd edition (Chicago: University of Chicago Press, 2000), p. 368, explains:

   ἵνα μὴ ἐπιβαρῶ 2 Cor 2:5 seems to have the mng. "in order not to heap up too great a burden of words"=*in order not to say too much* (Heinrici, Schmiedel, Ltzm., H-DWendland), although there are no exx. of it in this mng. Other possibilities are *exaggerate, be too severe with.* On the rhetorical aspects. CClassen, WienerStud 107/108, '94/95, 333.—DELG s.v. βαρύς. M-M.
2. Scott J. Hafemann, *2 Corinthians*, The NIV Application Commentary (Grand Rapids, MI: Zondervan, 2000), p. 95.
3. Colin Kruse, *The Second Epistle of Paul to the Corinthians* (Grand Rapids, MI: Eerdmans, 1987, reprint: 2002), p. 82, who explains:

   The Greek word translated *to reaffirm* (*kyrōsai*) was used in the papyri to denote the confirming of a sale or the ratification of an appointment. The confirmation of love for which Paul calls, then, appears to be some formal act by the congregation, in the same way that the imposition of punishment in the first place appears to have been formal and judicial.
4. Corrie ten Boom, *The Hiding Place* (Grand Rapids, MI: Chosen Books, 1971), p. 215.

Chapter Six: Triumphal Procession in Christ

1. C. S. Lewis, *The Last Battle* (New York: Collier Books, 1956), p. 84.
2. Scott J. Hafemann, *Suffering and Ministry in the Spirit* (Grand Rapids, MI: Eerdmans, 1990), p. 19.
3. James M. Scott, *2 Corinthians*, New International Biblical Commentary (Peabody, MA: Hendrickson Publishers, 1998), p. 61.
4. Hafemann, *Suffering and Ministry in the Spirit*, p. 21, referencing H. S. Vernel's *Triumphus: An Inquiry into the Origin, Development and Meaning of the Roman Triumph* (Leiden: Brill, 1970).
5. *Ibid.*, p. 27 who quotes Appian, *The Mithridatic Wars*, XII. 116, 117.
6. *Ibid.*
7. Scott J. Hafemann, *2 Corinthians*, The NIV Application Commentary (Grand Rapids, MI: Zondervan, 2000), p. 109.
8. *Ibid.*, p. 120.
9. Philip Edgcumbe Hughes, *Paul's Second Epistle to the Corinthians* (Grand Rapids, MI: Eerdmans, 1962), p. 80.
10. Paul Barnett, *The Second Epistle to the Corinthians* (Grand Rapids, MI: Eerdmans, 1997), p. 159.

Chapter Seven: Credentials of Ministry

1. Margaret E. Thrall, *A Critical and Exegetical Commentary on The Second Epistle to the Corinthians*, Vol. I, I-VII (Edinburgh: T & T Clark, 1994), p. 219, explains:

The τινές themselves, it is generally agreed, are the same people as the πολλοί of 2.17, in view of the proximity of the two allusions.

2. Philip Edgcumbe Hughes, *Paul's Second Epistle to the Corinthians* (Grand Rapids, MI: Eerdmans, 1962), p. 87.
3. Victor Paul Furnish, *The Anchor Bible*, *II Corinthians*, translated with Introduction, Notes, and Commentary (Garden City, NY: Doubleday, 1984), p. 194, whose elegant descriptive phrase is: "one's heart, the most interior and secret dimension of one's being."
4. *Theological Dictionary of the New Testament* (*TDNT*), III, ed. Gerhard Kittel and Gerhard Friedrich (Grand Rapids, MI: Eerdmans, 1965), pp. 611–613.
5. Paul Barnett, *The Second Epistle to the Corinthians* (Grand Rapids, MI: Eerdmans, 1997), p. 164, n. 28.
6. Philip Edgcumbe Hughes, *Paul's Second Epistle to the Corinthians,* p. 86.
7. James M. Scott, *2 Corinthians*, New International Biblical Commentary (Peabody, MA: Hendrickson Publishers, 1998), p. 68.
8. Thrall, *A Critical and Exegetical Commentary on The Second Epistle to the Corinthians*, p. 224.
9. Colin Kruse, *The Second Epistle of Paul to the Corinthians* (Grand Rapids, MI: Eerdmans, 1987, reprint: 2002), p. 90.
10. John Calvin, *The Second Epistle of Paul to the Corinthians, and the Epistles to Timothy, Titus and Philemon*, Calvin's New Testament Commentaries, ed., David W. Torrance and Thomas F. Torrance, trans. T. A. Smail (Edinburgh: Oliver and Boyd, 1964, reprint: 1973), p. 39.
11. John Blanchard, *The Truth for Life* (West Sussex, UK: H.E. Walter, 1982), p. 231.

Chapter Eight: Sufficient for Ministry

1. Vance Havner, *Three Score & Ten* (Old Tappan, NJ: Fleming H. Revell, 1973), p. 49.
2. Rev. Alfred Plummer, *A Critical and Exegetical Commentary on the Second Epistle of St Paul to the Corinthians* (Edinburgh: T & T Clark, 1915), p. 84.
3. John Calvin, *The Second Epistle of Paul to the Corinthians, and the Epistles to Timothy, Titus and Philemon*, Calvin's New Testament Commentaries, ed., David W. Torrance and Thomas F. Torrance, trans. T. A. Smail (Edinburgh: Oliver and Boyd, 1964, reprint: 1973), p. 40.
4. Scott J. Hafemann, *2 Corinthians*, The NIV Application Commentary (Grand Rapids, MI: Zondervan, 2000), p. 127.
5. "Man's Weakness—God's Strength," *Missionary Crusader* (December 1964), p. 7.
6. Margaret E. Thrall, *A Critical and Exegetical Commentary on The Second Epistle to the Corinthians*, Vol. I, I-VII (Edinburgh: T & T Clark, 1994), p. 213.
7. Philip Edgcumbe Hughes, *Paul's Second Epistle to the Corinthians* (Grand Rapids, MI: Eerdmans, 1962), p. 93 provides the chain of quotations from Acts and 1 Timothy.
8. Hafemann, *2 Corinthians*, p. 127.
9. Gail MacDonald, *High Call, High Privilege* (Peabody, MA: Hendrickson Publishers, 1998), p. 222.
10. Hafemann, *2 Corinthians*, p. 127.
11. Philip Edgcumbe Hughes, *Paul's Second Epistle to the Corinthians*, pp. 99, 100, who quotes Augustine, *De Spiritus et Littera*, V and XVII.
12. *Ibid.*, p. 99 quoting William Tyndale, *The Obedience of a Christian Man*, in *Doctrinal Treatises* (Parker Society, Cambridge, 1849), pp. 303ff.
13. Hafemann, *2 Corinthians*, p. 133.
14. Timothy Dudley-Smith, *John Stott, the Making of a Leader* (Downers Grove, IL: InterVarsity, 1999), p. 358.
15. *Ibid.*, p. 359.
16. *Ibid.*, p. 360.
17. *Ibid.*, p. 361.

18. *Ibid.*, p. 364.
19. *Ibid.*, p. 365.

Chapter Nine: A More Glorious Ministry

1. Scott J. Hafemann, *2 Corinthians*, The NIV Application Commentary (Grand Rapids, MI: Zondervan, 2000), p. 144.
2. *Ibid.*, p. 148, provides the rationale for this interpretation:

   Paul's final statement in 3:7 is to describe the glory on Moses' face with the passive participle *katargoumenen*, which is usually translated here and elsewhere throughout the passage as "fading away" (cf. 3:7, 11, 13). Paul is thus understood to be saying that Moses veiled himself to keep Israel from discovering that the glory was passing away in order to protect his own authority. When Moses subsequently returned to the tent of meeting, he removed the veil, thereby "recharging" the glory on his face. After again showing his face to the people, Moses would then quickly veil himself to hide the fact that the glory was fading away. Rather than protecting Israel from the judgment of God that would have ensued from encountering God's glory, Moses' veiling himself was an act of duplicity. Rendered in this way, it is obvious why readers have concluded that Paul radically reinterprets Exodus 34:29–35 *against* its original context, for there is no indication in 34:29–35 whatsoever that the glory on Moses' face was fading or that Moses veiled himself to hide something from Israel.

   The evidence, however, does not warrant such a translation and conclusion concerning Paul's argument. A study of *katargeo* throughout Paul's writings reveals a narrow semantic field for its meaning and a uniform context for its use. Its Pauline context is consistently eschatological and its meaning is best translated in accordance with its rare, but unvaried use elsewhere in the ancient world, "to render (something) inoperative, ineffective, powerless," or "to nullify (something) in terms of its effects or impact."

   A footnote in Hafemann's book further amplifies:

   This is my own definition. The verb occurs 27 times in the New Testament, 25 of which are in Paul's writings (the exceptions are Luke 13:7 and Heb. 2:14). In contrast, there are less than 20 occurrences of the verb in all the literature prior to or outside of the New Testament and its circle of influence, including its four uses in 2 Esdras 4:21, 23; 5:5; 6:8. *Katargeo* is a rare word with a specific meaning that Paul introduced into the vocabulary of the early Christians (cf. its approximately 250 uses in the early church fathers, all of which derive from allusions to or quotes from Paul!). For a detailed study of this term, see my *Paul and Moses*, 301–9.
3. *Ibid.*, p. 152.
4. James M. Scott, *2 Corinthians*, New International Biblical Commentary (Peabody, MA: Hendrickson Publishers, 1998), p. 77.
5. Murray J. Harris, *The Expositor's Bible Commentary* Vol. 10, *Romans-Galatians*, gen. ed. Frank E. Gaebelein (Grand Rapids, MI: Zondervan, 1976), p. 339, n. 12: "*Παρρησία* (*parrhesia*) originally meant 'frankness or freedom in speaking' or 'fearless candor' but came to denote 'barefacedness,' 'boldness,' or 'confidence' or 'openness' in action."
6. Hafemann, *2 Corinthians*, p. 157.
7. Scott, *2 Corinthians*, p. 81.
8. Hafemann, *2 Corinthians*, p. 160.
9. A. J. Gossip, *From the Edge of the Crowd* (New York: Charles Scribner's Sons, n.d.), p. 12.

Chapter Ten: Doing Ministry

1. C. H. Spurgeon, *Lectures to My Students* (Grand Rapids, MI: Zondervan, 1954), pp 156, 157.

2. Paul Barnett, *The Second Epistle to the Corinthians* (Grand Rapids, MI: Eerdmans, 1997), p. 212, n. 8.

   Gk. ἐλεήθημεν . . . Paul's past life as a persecutor and his deep appreciation of God's mercy (note the divine passive, "received mercy") are implied by this expression. See also 1 Cor. 7:25; 1 Tim 1:13, 16.
3. *Focal Point*, Vol. 6, No. 3, July-September 1986 (Denver Conservative Baptist Seminary).
4. Philip Edgcumbe Hughes, *Paul's Second Epistle to the Corinthians* (Grand Rapids, MI: Eerdmans, 1962), p. 122, n. 25, explains:

   Ἀπειπάμεθα should be given a genuine aoristic force (like *ηλεήθημεν* in the previous verse). Similarly, Thrall vol. 1, p. 300–303 and Barnett, p. 212.
5. C. K. Barrett, *A Commentary on the Second Epistle to the Corinthians* (New York: Harper & Row, 1973), p. 128.
6. Philip Edgcumbe Hughes, *Paul's Second Epistle to the Corinthians,* p. 123.
7. Barnett, *The Second Epistle to the Corinthians*, p. 213.
8. *BDAG*, 256, "to make false through deception or distortion, *falsify, adulterate*."
9. Halford E. Luccock, *More Preaching Values in the Epistles of Paul*, Vol. 2 (New York: Harper and Brothers, 1961), p. 45.
10. Eta Linneman, *Historical Criticism of the Bible, Methodology or Ideology?* (Grand Rapids, MI: Baker, 1990), pp. 87, 88, who describes her experience of critical ideology as a one-time member of the guild.
11. Gordon D. Fee, *1 and 2 Timothy, Titus* (Peabody, MA: Hendrickson, 1984), p. 255.
12. Philip Edgcumbe Hughes, *Paul's Second Epistle to the Corinthians,* p. 125.
13. *Ibid.*, p. 131.
14. John Piper hymn in *The Worshiping Church*, ed. Donald P. Hustad (Carol Stream, IL: Hope Publishing Company, 1990), #716.

Chapter Eleven: The Power of New-Covenant Ministry

1. Murray J. Harris, *The Expositor's Bible Commentary* Vol. 10, *Romans-Galatians*, gen. ed. Frank E. Gaebelein (Grand Rapids, MI: Zondervan, 1976), p. 342.
2. Timothy B. Savage, *Power Through Weakness*, Society for New Testament Studies Monograph Series 86 (Cambridge, UK: Cambridge University Press, 1996), p. 171. Savage explains:

   But verses 8 and 9 represent more than a mere catalogue of suffering. They comprise a series of antitheses in which Paul seeks to give a remarkable interpretation to his suffering. The two participles in each antithesis are joined by the particle οὐκ (rather than the customary μή) which indicates that Paul is emphatic about this interpretation—"we are hard pressed, but *by no means* crushed."
3. Paul Barnett, *The Second Epistle to the Corinthians* (Grand Rapids, MI: Eerdmans, 1997), p. 233.
4. Halford E. Luccock, *More Preaching Values in the Epistles of Paul*, Vol. 2 (New York: Harper and Brothers, 1961), p. 53.
5. Philip Edgcumbe Hughes, *Paul's Second Epistle to the Corinthians* (Grand Rapids, MI: Eerdmans, 1962), p. 138.
6. Scott J. Hafemann, *2 Corinthians*, The NIV Application Commentary (Grand Rapids, MI: Zondervan, 2000), p. 184. Hafemann says:

   And God's rescuing Paul in the *past* gave him confidence that God could and would rescue him in the *future*, so that his hope enabled Paul to endure in the *present* (cf. 1:8–10). Within this framework, the reference to not being "abandoned" in 4:9 is especially significant. Its background in the LXX indicates that this is a "divine passive," which speaks of being abandoned by God (cf. Gen. 28:15; Deut. 31:6, 8; 1 Chron. 28:20; Ps. 16:10; 37:25, 28; Sir. 2:10). Just as God did not ultimately abandon Jesus in the grave, so too God's resurrection power sustains Paul in his own experiences of "death."

7. C. K. Barrett, *A Commentary on the Second Epistle to the Corinthians* (New York: Harper & Row, 1973), p. 139, 140.
8. Rev Alfred Plummer, *A Critical and Exegetical Commentary on the Second Epistle of St Paul to the Corinthians* (Edinburgh: T & T Clark, 1915), p. 131.

Chapter Twelve: "Futures" and Steadfastness

1. D. A. Carson, *et al*, eds., *New Bible Commentary: 21st Century Edition* (Downers Grove, IL: InterVarsity, 2002), p. 563.
2. Paul Barnett, *The Second Epistle to the Corinthians* (Grand Rapids, MI: Eerdmans, 1997), p. 241.
3. James M. Scott, *2 Corinthians*, New International Biblical Commentary (Peabody, MA: Hendrickson Publishers, 1998), p. 106.
4. Samuel Parker, *Epitaphs and Epigrams: Curious, Quaint, Amusing* (London: n.p., 1869).
5. Scott J. Hafemann, *2 Corinthians*, The NIV Application Commentary (Grand Rapids, MI: Zondervan, 2000), p. 198, who quotes Timothy B. Savage, *Power Through Weakness*, SNTS Monograph Series 86 (Cambridge, UK: Cambridge University Press, 1996), p. 181.
6. William Barclay, *The Letter to the Hebrews* (Philadelphia: Westminster, 1957), pp. 123, 124.
7. Frederick Catherwood, *First Things First* (Downers Grove, IL: InterVarsity, 1979), pp. 10, 11.
8. Scott, *2 Corinthians,* pp. 126, 127, quotes Marvin O. Pate, *Adam Christology*, p. 110; cf. p. 112. See also Paul Barnett, *The Second Epistle to the Corinthians*, p. 246 who cogently summarizes:

   The outer person (*exō anthrōpos*), who belongs to the present age, is wasting away, while the inner person (*esō anthrōpos*), who belongs to the coming age, is being renewed (4:16).
9. The phrase "beyond measure" is twice repeated in the Greek for intensification.
10. C. K. Barrett, *A Commentary on the Second Epistle to the Corinthians* (New York: Harper & Row, 1973), p. 147.
11. Hafemann, *2 Corinthians*, p. 190, who cites Savage, *Power Through Weakness*, p. 183.
12. Philip Edgcumbe Hughes, *Paul's Second Epistle to the Corinthians* (Grand Rapids, MI: Eerdmans, 1962), p. 157.

Chapter Thirteen: More Beyond

1. Scott J. Hafemann, *2 Corinthians*, The NIV Application Commentary (Grand Rapids, MI: Zondervan, 2000), p. 209 explains:

   5:1 is best read as an event (cf. the use of the aorist tense), not as a parallel to the ongoing process of 4:16–18, where the verbs "wasting away," "being renewed," and "achieving" were all in the present, continuous tense. The future orientation of 5:1–5, as well as 5:6–10, is difficult to deny.
2. *Ibid.*, p. 211, n 9.
3. Wayne Grudem, *Systematic Theology* (Grand Rapids, MI: Zondervan, 1994), p. 835.
4. Hafemann, *2 Corinthians*, p. 211, explains:

   In contemplating this future, Paul's longing is not for death per se, but to be transformed into his resurrection body (5:2, 4). There is therefore no explicit reference in this passage to an intermediate state. Ellis has convincingly argued that the "nakedness" in view is an ethical term, referring to the shame of exposure before the judgment of God, not an anthropological term that refers to a state of human existence (the common view), or a material term that refers to the absence of God's glory (Pate's view). Paul's focus is exclusively on the future resurrection at the judgment seat of Christ.

   And again, pp. 212, 213:

Paul longs to "be clothed with" his heavenly dwelling because he can assume that he "will not be found naked" (like Adam after the Fall), that is, that he will not be condemned by God in the final judgment (5:30). Inasmuch as the image of "being clothed" in 5:2–3 refers primarily to the resurrection body . . .

5. Paul Barnett, *The Message of 2 Corinthians* (Downers Grove, IL: InterVarsity Press, 1988), p. 100.
6. C. S. Lewis, *The Problem of Pain* (New York: Macmillan, 1978), pp. 145–147.
7. Murray J. Harris, *The Expositor's Bible Commentary*, Vol. 10, *Romans-Galatians*, gen. ed. Frank E. Gaebelein (Grand Rapids, MI: Zondervan, 1976), p. 348 explains:

   What did Paul understand to be involved in being "at home with the Lord"? To be sure, the Greek preposition *pros* (here meaning "with") in itself simply denotes location. Yet when it describes the interrelation of two persons, it necessarily implies a fellowship both active and reciprocal (cf. *pros* in Mark 6:3: "Are not his sisters here *with* us?). In any case, since the phrase "at home with the Lord" depicts the Christian's eternal destiny (cf. 1 Thess. 4:17; Phil. 1:23), what is thus signified must supersede earthly experience where the believer "knows" the Lord (Phil. 3:10). So being "at home with the Lord" is a higher form of the intimate fellowship with Christ than the believer experiences on earth.

Chapter Fourteen: Paul's Driving Motivations

1. John McCook Roots, *Chou: An Informal Biography of China's Legendary Chou En-Lai* (New York: Doubleday, n.d.), p. 34.
2. See Caleb Rojado, *Christianity Today*, August 15, 1994, p. 24.
3. Scott J. Hafemann, *2 Corinthians*, The NIV Application Commentary (Grand Rapids, MI: Zondervan, 2000), p. 235, n. 1. See also Duane Litfin, *St. Paul's Theology of Proclamation* (Cambridge, UK: Cambridge University Press, 1994), pp. 8, 244–262.
4. *Ibid.*
5. Paul Barnett, *The Second Epistle to the Corinthians* (Grand Rapids, MI: Eerdmans, 1997), p. 281.
6. James Denney, *The Second Epistle to the Corinthians*, ed. W. Robertson Nicoll (New York: A. C. Armstrong and Son, 1903), p. 189.
7. Ned Bernard Stonehouse, ed, *God Transcendent* (Edinburgh: Banner of Truth, n.d.), pp. 144, 145.
8. *BDAG*, p. 971.
9. Stonehouse, ed, *God Transcendent*, p. 151.
10. Roots, *Chou: An Informal Biography of China's Legendary Chou En-Lai*, p. 35.
11. David Aikman, *Jesus in Beijing* (Washington, DC: Regnery, 2003).

Chapter Fifteen: Gospel Regard

1. James M. Scott, *2 Corinthians*, New International Biblical Commentary (Peabody, MA: Hendrickson, 1998), p. 134.
2. James Denney, *The Second Epistle to the Corinthians*, ed. W. Robertson Nicoll (New York: A. C. Armstrong and Son, 1903), p. 198, explains:

   The inferences which are here drawn depend upon what has just been said of Christ's death for all, and the death of all in that death of His. In that death, as inclusive of ours, the old life died, and with it died all its distinctions. All that men were, apart from Christ, all that constituted the "appearance" (πρόσωπον, v. 12) of their life, all that marked them off from each other as such and such outwardly, ceased to have significance the moment Christ's death was understood as Paul here understands it. He dates his inference with ἀπὸ τοῦ νῦν ("henceforth"). This does not mean from the time at which he writes, but from the time at which he saw that One had died for all, and so all died.
3. *Ibid.*, p. 199.

4. Note that the Greek ὥστε ("therefore," which begins v. 16 and v. 17) refers to v. 14, so that Paul now gives a further result of the Christian's participation in the death and resurrection of Christ.
5. Philip Edgcumbe Hughes, *Paul's Second Epistle to the Corinthians* (Grand Rapids, MI: Eerdmans, 1962), p. 202.
6. Note that "passed away" is aorist, indicating a completed once-and-for-all condition, and that "has come" is perfect, indicating an ongoing condition.
7. Philip Edgcumbe Hughes, *Paul's Second Epistle to the Corinthians*, p. 203.

Chapter Sixteen: God's Reconciliation

1. James Denney, *The Second Epistle to the Corinthians*, ed. W. Robertson Nicoll (New York: A. C. Armstrong and Son, 1903), pp. 213, 214.
2. James M. Scott, *2 Corinthians*, New International Biblical Commentary (Peabody, MA: Hendrickson Publishers, 1998), p. 140.
3. Paul Barnett, *The Second Epistle to the Corinthians* (Grand Rapids, MI: Eerdmans, 1997), p. 311.
4. Denney, *The Second Epistle to the Corinthians*, p. 218.
5. Philip Edgcumbe Hughes, *Paul's Second Epistle to the Corinthians* (Grand Rapids, MI: Eerdmans, 1962), pp. 212, 213.
6. Murray J. Harris, *The Expositor's Bible Commentary*, Vol. 10, *Romans-Galatians*, gen. ed. Frank E. Gaebelein (Grand Rapids, MI: Zondervan, 1976), p. 355.
7. Scott J. Hafemann, *2 Corinthians*, The NIV Application Commentary (Grand Rapids, MI: Zondervan, 2000), p. 251. As Hafemann explains:

   > The "righteousness of God" is thus both a legal quality describing his just character and a dynamic concept describing his way of acting in the world. To take on God's righteousness *in Christ* (5:21) is therefore to be declared legally righteous, in accordance with his righteous standards, because of Christ's sacrificial death on our behalf. But it is also to enjoy the new way of life as a "new creation" that Christ's death for us makes possible, on the basis of which we will be declared righteous in the judgment yet to come (5:10, 15). These two aspects of God's righteousness are organically related. God acts righteously because he is righteous. We act righteously because God has made us righteous. As such, his righteousness is expressed in his reconciling work on the basis of Christ's death on the cross.
8. Hugh Evan Hopkins, *Charles Simeon of Cambridge* (Grand Rapids, MI: Eerdmans, n.d.), p. 66.

Chapter Seventeen: Ministry That Commends

1. Scott J. Hafemann, *2 Corinthians*, The NIV Application Commentary (Grand Rapids, MI: Zondervan, 2000), p. 269, explains:

   > Since the catalog in 6:3–10 supports the exhortation in 6:1, the key interpretive decision here is whether Paul's reference to "endurance" in 6:4a is a descriptive heading for all that follows, or whether it is simply another element of the catalog itself. In other words, is "endurance" the general category that is specified in what follows? Or is it simply the first of the various members in the list, all of which together modify "commending ourselves"?
   >
   > In answer to this question, various translations punctuate the text differently. There are three reasons why . . . (1) Paul modified "endurance" with "great," in contrast to the unqualified designations that follow; (2) "endurance" is a singular, abstract virtue, while what follows is a list of plural adversities; and (3) it is difficult to see how hardships in and of themselves could commend Paul if they are not related to the positive virtue of endurance. As a general statement, Paul commends himself as a servant of God by his "great endurance" (cf. 12:12). Specifically, Paul's endurance takes place in the midst of the adversities that follow.

2. Timothy Dudley-Smith, *John Stott, a Global Ministry* (Leicester, England: Inter-Varsity, 2001), p. 433.
3. Philip Edgcumbe Hughes, *Paul's Second Epistle to the Corinthians* (Grand Rapids, MI: Eerdmans, 1962), p. 226, quotes from Clement of Rome, *Ep. ad Cor.*, 5, Bishop Lightfoot's translation.
4. Paul Barnett, *The Second Epistle to the Corinthians* (Grand Rapids, MI: Eerdmans, 1997), p. 330.
5. Rev Alfred Plummer, *A Critical and Exegetical Commentary on the Second Epistle of St Paul to the Corinthians* (Edinburgh: T & T Clark, 1915), p. 199.
6. Philip Edgcumbe Hughes, *Paul's Second Epistle to the Corinthians*, p. 236.
7. Hafemann, *2 Corinthians*, p. 272.
8. *Ibid.*, p. 273.

Chapter Eighteen: Bringing Holiness to Completion

1. Charles Colson, *Kingdoms in Conflict* (New York/Grand Rapids, MI: William Morrow/ Zondervan, 1987), pp. 137, 138.
2. *Ibid.*, p. 138.
3. Scott J. Hafemann, *2 Corinthians*, The NIV Application Commentary (Grand Rapids, MI: Zondervan, 2000), p. 303, quoting Langdon Gilkey, *How the Church Can Minister Without Losing Itself* (New York: Harper & Row, 1964), p. 1.
4. Joseph T. Bayly, *Out of My Mind, The Best of Joe Bayly* (Grand Rapids, MI: Zondervan, 1993), p. 185.
5. James M. Scott, *2 Corinthians*, New International Biblical Commentary (Peabody, MA: Hendrickson Publishers, 1998), pp. 154, 155, explains:

   > The six citations in verses 16d-18b are treated as a single quotation introduced by an introductory formula and concluded by a closing formula, rather than by six separate formulas. The passage has corresponding beginning and ending premises with practical implications in the middle. Hence, the citations form three parts consisting of three lines each. In fact, the citation combination in our passage is so symmetrical that "says the Lord" (*legei kyrios*) in verse 17 bisects the citations into equal halves and thus lies precisely equidistant from the opening and closing formulas. Thus, God's promises of a reciprocal relationship between himself and his people expressed in the first person singular bracket a center section that gives the practical implications of this relationship to God. The bilateral symmetry of the citation combination corresponds to the bilateral relationship between God and his people (vv. 16ef, 18ab). As a result, form and content blend beautifully in these modified citations to communicate Paul's message.

6. G. K. Beale, ed., *The Right Doctrine from the Wrong Texts?* (Grand Rapids, MI: Baker, 1994), p. 235. Note: Pages 217–247 contain a reprint of Beale's article, "The Old Testament Background of Reconciliation in 2 Corinthians 5–7 and Its Bearing on the Literacy Problem of 2 Corinthians 4:14–7:1," *New Testament Studies* 35 (1989): 550–581.
7. Beale, ed., *The Right Doctrine from the Wrong Texts?*, p. 241.
8. Hafemann, *2 Corinthians*, p. 284.
9. Beale, ed., *The Right Doctrine from the Wrong Texts?*, pp. 237, 238.
10. Hafemann, *2 Corinthians*, p. 285.

Chapter Nineteen: Comfort and Joy for a Caring Heart

1. Warren Wiersbe, *Walking with the Giants* (Grand Rapids, MI: Baker, 1979), pp. 263–265, which provides the accounts of Spurgeon, Jowett, and Whyte.
2. *Ibid.*, p. 264.
3. Philip Edgcumbe Hughes, *Paul's Second Epistle to the Corinthians* (Grand Rapids, MI: Eerdmans, 1962), p. 266, n. 3 explains:

The force of ταπεινός here is psychological, = "downcast", "depressed", rather than ethical, = "lowly", "humble".

See also Paul Barnett, *The Second Epistle to the Corinthians* (Grand Rapids, MI: Eerdmans, 1997), p. 369, n. 16:

Gk. ταπεινός, which, although bearing the meaning "humble" elsewhere (e.g., 10:1), is required by the present context to be understood as "depressed," "downcast."

4. Colin Kruse, *The Second Epistle of Paul to the Corinthians* (Grand Rapids, MI: Eerdmans, 1987, reprint: 2002), p. 144, explains:

   The word "fightings" (*machai*), where found elsewhere in the New Testament (2 Tim. 2:23; Tit. 3:9; Jas. 4:1), applies only to quarrels and disputes, so Paul's "fightings" may have been heated disputations with either unbelievers (cf. Acts 17:5–14) or Christian opponents (cf. Phil. 3:2) in Macedonia.

5. Phillips Brooks, *The Influence of Jesus* (London: H.R. Allenson, 1895), p. 191.
6. James Hastings, ed., *The Speaker's Bible*, Vol. 15 (Grand Rapids, MI: Baker, 1971), p. 131, which quotes from Alexander Irvine, *My Lady of the Chimney Corner*, which has been here adapted and modernized.
7. James M. Scott, *2 Corinthians*, New International Biblical Commentary (Peabody, MA: Hendrickson Publishers, 1998), pp. 165, 166 explains:

   God comforted Paul through the instrumentality of Titus's coming. Paul characterizes God here as one who comforts the downcast (*ho parakalōn tous tapeinous).* This alludes to Isaiah 49:13 LXX: "Rejoice, O heavens, and let the earth be glad; let the mountains break forth with joy; for the Lord has had mercy on his people, and has comforted the downcast of his people (*tous tapeinous tou laou autou parekalesen*)." Paul has already alluded to Isaiah 49:9 in the previous context (cf. 2 Cor. 6:2), and this passage is also crucial to Paul's apostolic self-concept (cf. Gal. 1:15–16; Isa. 49:1). Just as in 6:2 Paul views the Corinthians as in danger of forfeiting the eschatological salvation prophesied in Isaiah 49, so also in 7:6 he perceives his own relief over the coming of Titus as an evidence of God's comfort of his people in the endtime.

8. Barnett, *The Second Epistle to the Corinthians*, p. 369, 370.
9. Philip Edgcumbe Hughes, *Paul's Second Epistle to the Corinthians*, pp. 272, 273.
10. William Temple, *Christianity and the Social Order* (London: SCM, 1950), p. 36.
11. James M. Scott, *2 Corinthians,* p. 171 explains:

    The OT formula fear and trembling, which Paul uses also in Philippians 2:12 and 1 Corinthians 2:3 (cf. Eph. 6:5), most often describes the fearful attitude of people before God (cf. Exod. 15:16; Deut. 2:25; 11:25; Jdt. [Judith, in the Apocrypha] 15:2; Isa. 19:16; Ps. 2:11; but see Ps. 55:5; Jdt. 2:28). In that case, the Corinthians received Paul's messenger with the same fear and trembling that is due God himself. This indirectly underscores Paul's apostolic role as an ambassador of Christ.

Chapter Twenty: The Grace of Giving

1. Scott J. Hafemann, *2 Corinthians*, The NIV Application Commentary (Grand Rapids, MI: Zondervan, 2000), p. 331.
2. Rev Alfred Plummer, *A Critical and Exegetical Commentary on the Second Epistle of St Paul to the Corinthians* (Edinburgh: T & T Clark, 1915), p. 234.
3. Walter Baxendale, *Dictionary of Illustrations for Pulpit and Platform* (Chicago: Moody Press, 1949), p. 247.
4. Hafemann, *2 Corinthians*, p. 341.
5. *Ibid.* explains:

   But whereas the equality in the "first Exodus" was established miraculously by God *for the people* because of their hard hearts (cf. Ex. 16:18, 28), now it is being established *by the people themselves* through their *own* Spirit-led sharing. While God supplied Israel's physical needs with manna and quail but did not change their spiritual condition, under the new covenant God is meeting the spiritual needs of the Corinthians in order that *they* might meet the physical needs of others (cf. 2 Cor. 9:8–11). Paul's expectation in 8:11 is thus one more expression of his confidence in the transforming power of the presence of God under the new covenant (cf. 3:3, 6, 18). For this reason, Paul leaves the amount of their giving up to the Corinthians, convinced that, as a new creation in Christ (5:17), the quantity of their giving will match the quality of their changed hearts (5:15).

Chapter Twenty-One: Integrity and Giving

1. Philip Edgcumbe Hughes, *Paul's Second Epistle to the Corinthians* (Grand Rapids, MI: Eerdmans, 1962), pp. 312–316.
2. Ralph P. Martin, *2 Corinthians*, Word Biblical Commentary, Vol. 40 (Nashville: Thomas Nelson, 1986), p. 276.
3. John Calvin, *Calvin's New Testament Commentaries, The Second Epistle of Paul to the Corinthians and the Epistles to Timothy Titus and Philemon*, trans. T. A. Smail (Grand Rapids, MI: Eerdmans, 1964), p. 116.
4. *Ibid.*
5. William Barclay, *The Letters to the Corinthians* (Philadelphia: The Westminster Press, 1956), p. 258.
6. James Denney, *The Second Epistle to the Corinthians*, ed. W. Robertson Nicoll (New York: A. C. Armstrong and Son, 1903), p. 278.
7. Kenneth L. Chafin, *The Communicator's Commentary, 2 Corinthians* (Waco, TX: Word, 1985), p. 263.
8. Colin Kruse, *The Second Epistle of Paul to the Corinthians* (Grand Rapids, MI: Eerdmans, 1987, reprint: 2002), p. 161.
9. Martin, *2 Corinthians*, p. 276.
10. Scott J. Hafemann, *2 Corinthians*, The NIV Application Commentary (Grand Rapids, MI: Zondervan, 2000), p. 362.
11. Denney, *The Second Epistle to the Corinthians*, pp. 278, 279.

Chapter Twenty-Two: Ready, Willing, Generous Giving

1. Frederick Williams Danker, ed., *A Greek-English Lexicon of the New Testament and Other Early Christian Literature* (*BADG*), 3rd edition (Chicago: University of Chicago Press, 2000), p. 842 explains: "In 2 Corinthians 9:5 the context calls for the pregnant meaning, *a gift that is grudgingly granted by avarice*."
2. Scott J. Hafemann, *2 Corinthians*, The NIV Application Commentary (Grand Rapids, MI: Zondervan, 2000), p. 366.
3. Halford E. Luccock, *More Preaching Values in the Epistles of Paul*, Vol. 2 (New York: Harper and Brothers, 1961), p. 95.
4. Hafemann, *2 Corinthians*, pp. 367, 368 explains:

   Paul's exhortation echoes Deuteronomy 15:10, an admonition to lend and give freely to the poor without being reluctant or grieving in one's heart, knowing that the Lord will bless such actions. The original context of this passage concerns the "Sabbath year of remission" in which, in remembrance of their deliverance, Israel was to forgive all debts (cf. 31:10–11). This year of remission every seventh year pointed forward to the fiftieth year (after seven times seven years of remission), the "year of Jubilee," which was to be a symbol of the ultimate redemption of God's people (cf. Lev. 25:8–55, cf. esp. vv. 38, 42, 55).

   Paul's use of Deuteronomy 15:10 is yet another indication that he understands the church, as the continuation of the faithful remnant within Israel, to be the eschatological people of God (cf. Lev. 25:20–22, where keeping the year of remission, like the Sabbath, was a call to exercise faith in God's ongoing provision). Therefore what was given to Israel to do every seventh year is now, under the new covenant, to be the *daily* pattern of those in Christ.

5. Colin Kruse, *The Second Epistle of Paul to the Corinthians* (Grand Rapids, MI: Eerdmans, 1987, reprint: 2002), p. 166.

Chapter Twenty-Three: Call to Church Discipline

1. Donald A. Carson, *From Triumphalism to Maturity, a New Exposition of 2 Corinthians 10–13* (Leicester, UK: Inter-Varsity Press, 1984), p. 44.
2. *Ibid.*, p. 35.
3. James M. Scott, *2 Corinthians*, New International Biblical Commentary (Peabody, MA: Hendrickson Publishers, 1998), p. 194.
4. R. V. G. Tasker, *The Second Epistle of Paul to the Corinthians* (London: The Tyndale Press, 1964), p. 173.
5. Victor Paul Furnish, *The Anchor Bible, II Corinthians*, translated with Introduction, Notes, and Commentary (Garden City, NY: Doubleday, 1984), p. 459.
6. Tasker, *The Second Epistle of Paul to the Corinthians*, p. 174.
7. *Ibid.*
8. Carson, *From Triumphalism to Maturity*, p. 47.
9. Furnish, *The Anchor Bible, II Corinthians*, p. 458, who cites Hughes, pp. 353, 354, n. 10.
10. Carson, *From Triumphalism to Maturity*, p. 50.

Chapter Twenty-Four: Boasting in the Lord

1. Rev Alfred Plummer, *A Critical and Exegetical Commentary on the Second Epistle of St Paul to the Corinthians* (Edinburgh: T & T Clark, 1915), p. 280.
2. Donald A. Carson, *From Triumphalism to Maturity, a New Exposition of 2 Corinthians 10–13* (Leicester, England: Inter-Varsity Press, 1984), p. 64, who quotes Harris:

   > Paul "argues that the right to make a subjective claim based on personal conviction cannot fairly be granted to his opponents and yet denied him" (Harris).
3. Scott J. Hafemann, *2 Corinthians*, The NIV Application Commentary (Grand Rapids, MI: Zondervan, 2000), pp. 398, 399.
4. Plummer, *A Critical and Exegetical Commentary on the Second Epistle of St Paul to the Corinthians*, p. 283.
5. Victor Paul Furnish, *The Anchor Bible, II Corinthians*, translated with Introduction, Notes, and Commentary (Garden City, NY: Doubleday, 1984), p. 468, writes:

   > In the present instance *weak (asthenēs)* stands in direct contrast to *impressive* (*ischyros*, literally "strong"), so that the criticism would seem to be that the apostle cuts a sorry figure in person. Cf. Epictetus' emphasis on the importance of the physical appearance of the true Cynic, III.xxii.86–89, and Lucian, *The Lover of Lies* 34 (discussed by Betz 1972:53–54) and *The Dream* 13 (cited by Hock 1980:99 n. 95); also Dio Chrysostom VIII, 2 (cited by Mussies 1972:178).
6. Carson, *From Triumphalism to Maturity*, p. 63.
7. Plummer, *A Critical and Exegetical Commentary on the Second Epistle of St Paul to the Corinthians*, p. 284. Note: my comment is a paraphrase of Plummer.
8. Carson, *From Triumphalism to Maturity*, p. 73.
9. *Ibid.*, p. 77.
10. Hafemann, *2 Corinthians*, p. 405.

Chapter Twenty-Five: Apologia for Boasting

1. *The Wesleyan Advocate*, quoting *The Banner*.
2. Murray J. Harris, *The Expositor's Bible Commentary*, Vol. 10, *Romans-Galatians*, gen. ed. Frank E. Gaebelein (Grand Rapids, MI: Zondervan, 1976), p. 385.
3. Donald A. Carson, *From Triumphalism to Maturity, a New Exposition of 2 Corinthians 10–13* (Leicester, England: Inter-Varsity Press, 1984), p. 86.
4. *Ibid.*

5. Scott J. Hafemann, *2 Corinthians*, The NIV Application Commentary (Grand Rapids, MI: Zondervan, 2000), p. 429.
6. Carson, *From Triumphalism to Maturity*, pp. 91, 92.
7. James M. Scott, *2 Corinthians*, New International Biblical Commentary (Peabody, MA: Hendrickson Publishers, 1998), p. 208.
8. Rev Alfred Plummer, *A Critical and Exegetical Commentary on the Second Epistle of St Paul to the Corinthians* (Edinburgh: T & T Clark, 1915), p. 284.
9. Scott, *2 Corinthians*, p. 210.
10. *Ibid.*
11. Javoslav Pelikan, *Bach Among the Theologians* (Philadelphia: Fortress, 1986), p. 89.
12. Carson, *From Triumphalism to Maturity*, p. 100.
13. C. S. Lewis, *The Screwtape Letters* (London: Geoffrey Bles: The Centenary Press, 1942), p. 65.
14. *Christianity Today*, October 5, 1998, Vol. 42, No. 11, p. 88, quoting from Ronald Knox, *Let Dons Delight*.
15. Carson, *From Triumphalism to Maturity*, p. 103, where he helpfully and more fully expounds these ideas.
16. *Ibid.*

Chapter Twenty-Six: Paul's Boasting

1. Donald A. Carson, *From Triumphalism to Maturity, a New Exposition of 2 Corinthians 10–13* (Leicester, England: Inter-Varsity Press, 1984), p. 113.
2. James M. Scott, *2 Corinthians*, New International Biblical Commentary (Peabody, MA: Hendrickson Publishers, 1998), p. 214.
3. Carson, *From Triumphalism to Maturity*, p. 116.
4. *Ibid.*, p. 117.
5. Ben Witherington III, *Conflict and Community in Corinth: A Social Rhetorical Commentary on 1 and 2 Corinthians* (Grand Rapids, MI: Eerdmans, 1995), pp. 450–452.

   > One of the social functions of both the imperial *res gestae* and Paul's catalog is public assertion of rightful authority over a group of people in view of the accomplishments and the things undergone on their behalf. The difference is that Paul boasts in his weaknesses and his apparent defeats, while Augustus does the reverse. Paul and Augustus are similar in their attempts to show the great sacrifices they have made for their people. Since the *res gestae* was posted in various places in the provinces in temples to Augustus, and in view of the status of Corinth as a Roman colony, the Corinthians were probably familiar with the *res gestae* and would have recognized Paul's parody of the public standards by which leaders were normally judged to be great and legitimate.

6. Paul Barnett, *The Second Epistle to the Corinthians* (Grand Rapids, MI: Eerdmans, 1997), p. 545.
7. *Ibid.*, p. 546.
8. Scott, *2 Corinthians*, p. 219.
9. Barnett, *The Second Epistle to the Corinthians*, p. 548.
10. Rev Alfred Plummer, *A Critical and Exegetical Commentary on the Second Epistle of St Paul to the Corinthians* (Edinburgh: T & T Clark, 1915), p. 329.
11. Scott J. Hafemann, *2 Corinthians*, The NIV Application Commentary (Grand Rapids, MI: Zondervan, 2000), p. 441.
12. Scott, *2 Corinthians*, p. 220.
13. Carson, *From Triumphalism to Maturity*, p. 128.

Chapter Twenty-Seven: Paul's Greatest Boast

1. James M. Scott, *2 Corinthians*, New International Biblical Commentary (Peabody, MA: Hendrickson Publishers, 1998), p. 223 argues convincingly that the Greek is an objective genitive "of the Lord" and not as the NIV has it, "from the Lord."
2. Scott J. Hafemann, *2 Corinthians*, The NIV Application Commentary (Grand Rapids, MI: Zondervan, 2000), p. 458. See also Paul Barnett, *The Second Epistle to the Corinthians* (Grand Rapids, MI: Eerdmans, 1997), p. 561.
3. Hafemann, *2 Corinthians*, p. 457, n. 4 explains:

   The idea of a threefold heaven (i.e., the atmosphere; the place of the stars; and the abode of God) is apparently built on 1 Kings 8:27; 2 Chron. 2:6; 6:18; Neh. 9:6; Ps. 148:4.
4. Philip Edgcumbe Hughes, *Paul's Second Epistle to the Corinthians* (Grand Rapids, MI: Eerdmans, 1962), p. 436 explains:

   We do not hesitate to assert that the Paradise of which Christ spoke to the penitent thief is identical with that of our text and of Rev. 2:7. If our Lord descended to hades, it was to liberate the souls of the just who had been awaiting His triumph and thence to lead them to the heavenly Paradise won for them through His conquest on the Cross. It was there that the penitent thief was *with Him* on the day of his death. It was thither that Paul was transported in this rapture which he experienced. It is there that, after death, the souls of believers are *with Christ* even now (Phil. 1:23), rejoicing in His presence.
5. *Ibid.*, p. 438.
6. *Ibid.*
7. John Calvin, *Calvin's New Testament Commentaries, The Second Epistle of Paul to the Corinthians and the Epistles to Timothy, Titus and Philemon*, trans. T. A. Smail (Grand Rapids, MI: Eerdmans, 1964), p. 157.
8. Donald A. Carson, *From Triumphalism to Maturity, a New Exposition of 2 Corinthians 10–13* (Leicester, England: Inter-Varsity Press, 1984), p. 144.
9. Philip Edgcumbe Hughes, *Paul's Second Epistle to the Corinthians*, p. 446.
10. Scott, *2 Corinthians*, p. 226 explains:

    In this section Paul makes a startling admission, one that would have been potentially damaging to him in the hands of his opponents. The apostle admits that God himself is ultimately responsible for his physical weakness! Just as God was responsible for his heavenly ascent (note the divine passives in vv. 2 and 4), so also God was responsible for his receiving a "thorn in the flesh" (note the divine passive in v. 7).
11. Hafemann, *2 Corinthians*, p. 464 explains:

    That Paul prayed "three times" may simply be a conventional way to emphasize that the prayer was repeated (cf. Ps. 55:17, where the psalmist utters his complaint three times a day). In this case, Paul is simply saying that he prayed repeatedly about the matter. The problem with this reading is that Paul stopped praying after the third time. The reference to "three times" is therefore better taken as signaling an event that is now over and done with, having gone through its beginning, middle, and end. Read in this way, Paul's threefold prayer parallels Jesus' threefold prayer in the Garden of Gethsemane, which also culminated in confidence that the prayer had been answered, even though the cup of suffering remained (Mark 14:32–41).
12. Philip Edgcumbe Hughes, *Paul's Second Epistle to the Corinthians*, p. 441 writes:

    Thus the Lord's answers to prayer are never negative, except in a superficial and proximate sense; for essentially and in the ultimate issue they are fully positive, and directed to the eternal blessing of His people.
13. *Ibid.*, p. 441.
14. Barnett, *The Second Epistle to the Corinthians*, p. 572.
15. *Ibid.*, p. 574.
16. *Ibid.*, p. 575.
17. Ethel Mae Baldwin and D. V. Benson, *Henrietta Mears and How She Did It* (Ventura, CA: Regal Books, 1966), p. 39.

Chapter Twenty-Eight: Authenticating Apostleship

1. Paul Barnett, *The Second Epistle to the Corinthians* (Grand Rapids, MI: Eerdmans, 1997), p. 581. See n. 18, which reads:

   As, e.g., in Exod 7:3; cf. 1:9, 10; 3:20; 8:23; 10:1, 2; 15:11; Num 14:21; Deut 4:34; 6:22; 7:19; 26:8; 29:3; Josh 3:5; 24:17; Ps 135:9; Neh 9:10; Jer 32:21. See further D.A. Carson, "Signs and Wonders," 89–118.
2. *Ibid.*
3. John Calvin, *Calvin's New Testament Commentaries, The Second Epistle of Paul to the Corinthians and the Epistles to Timothy, Titus and Philemon*, trans. T. A. Smail (Grand Rapids, MI: Eerdmans, 1964), p. 164.
4. Barnett, *The Second Epistle to the Corinthians*, p. 586.
5. R. V. G. Tasker, *The Second Epistle of Paul to the Corinthians, An Introduction and Commentary* (London: The Tyndale Press, 1964), p. 183.
6. Barnett, *The Second Epistle to the Corinthians*, p. 592.
7. Phillips Brooks, *The Influence of Jesus* (London: H.R. Allenson, 1895), p. 191.

Chapter Twenty-Nine: Final Warnings and Exhortations

1. Donald A. Carson, *From Triumphalism to Maturity, a New Exposition of 2 Corinthians 10–13* (Leicester, England: Inter-Varsity Press, 1984), p. 173.
2. Philip Edgcumbe Hughes, *Paul's Second Epistle to the Corinthians* (Grand Rapids, MI: Eerdmans, 1962), p. 481.
3. Paul Barnett, *The Second Epistle to the Corinthians* (Grand Rapids, MI: Eerdmans, 1997), p. 610, explains:

   If the Corinthians hear and obey their letter as they respond to Paul's prayer for them (summed up as "not do evil/but do good"), then his apostolic purpose will have been thoroughly fulfilled. There will be no need for him to do something physical or visible in relation to the various unresolved errors of the Corinthians noted above (v. 6). The "proof" of his apostleship will already have been achieved by this letter in advance of his arrival; he will have been "approved." Those who demand "proof" (see on 13:3) may feel that the absence of such "proof" when he comes is evidence of Paul's "disproof."
4. Philip Edgcumbe Hughes, *Paul's Second Epistle to the Corinthians*, p. 483.
5. Frederick Williams Danker, ed., *A Greek-English Lexicon of the New Testament and Other Early Christian Literature* (BADG), 3rd edition (Chicago: University of Chicago Press, 2000), p. 526.

Chapter Thirty: Apostolic Optimism

1. Scott J. Hafemann, *2 Corinthians*, The NIV Application Commentary (Grand Rapids, MI: Zondervan, 2000), pp. 495, 496.
2. *Ibid.*, p. 497.
3. C. K. Barrett, *A Commentary on the Second Epistle to the Corinthians* (New York: Harper & Row, 1973), p. 342.
4. James M. Scott, *2 Corinthians*, New International Biblical Commentary (Peabody, MA: Hendrickson Publishers, 1998), p. 263.
5. David Noel Freedman, ed., *The Anchor Bible Dictionary*, Vol. 4 (New York: Doubleday, 1991), p. 91.
6. *Ibid.*, p. 92.
7. Paul Barnett, *The Second Epistle to the Corinthians* (Grand Rapids, MI: Eerdmans, 1997), p. 617.
8. Leland Ryken, ed., *The Christian Imagination: The Practice of Faith in Literature and Writing* (Colorado Springs: Waterbrook Press, 2002), pp. 74, 75, writes:

And one need not even search that far. Virgil's greatest impact on Dante was helping him to un-forget his own original encounter with love, the "Beatrice experience" that introduced him to *caritas*. There is no more powerful "educating" than calling the attention of others to their own experience of grace, of *communion*.

Scripture Index

General Index

Index of Sermon Illustrations